Sites
of
Antiquity

Sites
of
Antiquity

FROM ANCIENT EGYPT TO THE FALL OF ROME

50 Sites that Explain the Classical World

by Charles Freeman

SOMERSET BOOKS

Sites of Antiquity: from Ancient Egypt to the Fall of Rome
50 Sites that Explain the Classical World
First edition

Conceived, created and designed by Blue Guides Limited,
a Somerset Books Company
Winchester House, Deane Gate Avenue, Taunton, Somerset TA1 2UH
www.blueguides.com
'Blue Guide' is a registered trademark

Text © Charles Freeman 2009

Editor: Annabel Barber

Photo research, editing and pre-press: Hadley Kincade

Page design and layout: Anikó Kuzmich, Blue Guides

Maps by Dimap Bt
Colour diagrams and site plans by Imre Bába
Line drawings by Gabriella Juhász and Michael Mansell RIBA

With thanks to Delia Pemberton, who supplied the glossary text on the gods of
ancient Egypt.

ISBN 978–1–905131–31–0

A CIP catalogue record of this book is available from the British Library.

Distributed in the United States of America by
WW Norton and Company, Inc.
500 Fifth Avenue, New York, NY 10110

All other acknowledgements, photo credits and copyright information are given
on pp. 246–48, which form part of this copyright page.

Printed in Hungary by Dürer Nyomda Kft.

Contents

THE 50 SITES

Atlantic

Ocean

Hadrian's Wall

BRITAIN

Rhine

GAUL

Trier

Danube

Rhône

Pont du Gard

Nîmes

ITALY

Ravenna

Split

IBERIA

Corsica

Rome   Tivoli

Ostia

Pompeii

Paestum

Adriatic Sea

Sardinia

Tyrrhenian

Sea

Dodona

GR

Mediterranea

Segesta

Selinunte   *Sicily*

Agrigento   Piazza Armerina

Ionian

Sea

Olympia

AFRICA

Leptis Magna

Aral
Sea

Caspian Sea

Pontus Euxinus
(Black Sea)

Danube

Constantinople ●

Hittites

Parthians

Pergamon ●

EECE   ASIA MINOR   ASSYRIA   PERSIA

Delphi ●

Athens ●   Ephesus ●   Sasanians

Mycenae ●

Delos ●   ● Aphrodisias   *Euphrates*   *Tigris*

Epidaurus ●   Priene ●

n   SYRIA   MESOPOTAMIA

S e a   *Cyprus*   ✗   ● Palmyra

Knossos ●   Qadesh
                        1274 BC

Crete   Persian Gulf

Jerusalem ●

Petra ●

Giza ●

Saqqara ●   ● St Catherine's

Dahshur ●

EGYPT

Tel el-Amarna ●   *Red*

Dendera ●   *Sea*

Valley of the Kings ●● Karnak   0   100   200   300 miles

Western Thebes   Luxor

Edfu ●   0   250   500 km

NUBIA   ● Philae

Abu Simbel ●

Nile

The ancient
EGYPTIAN
world

'About Egypt I shall have a great deal more to relate
because of the fact that more monuments which beggar
description are to be found there than anywhere else in
the world ...'

Herodotus, *The Histories*, 5th century BC

Historical overview

The uniqueness of ancient Egypt came partly from its unusual setting. Rainfall was virtually unknown so the fertility of the land depended entirely on the river. As the snows melted in the mountains of Ethiopia each year, the silt was swept down the Nile valley, whose narrow strip was made three or four times more fertile than land watered by rain alone. Yet beyond the valley was desert, and the contrast between the dark richness of the valley soil and the redness of the barren sand beyond haunted the Egyptian imagination. Any land above the floodline was bone dry and this is why we have so many preserved goods, including a mass of papyrus documents that would have mouldered away in any wetter climate.

Egypt was relatively isolated from the other cultures of the eastern Mediterranean and Near East. There was little contact with the Mediterranean before Alexander the Great founded the port of Alexandria in 332. Until the rise of the Assyrian empire in the 8th century BC, there was no state strong enough in the Near East to challenge Egypt. This meant that a vigorous Egyptian ruler could achieve and sustain control over an environment rich in resources. The wealth that resulted was poured into vast building projects and exquisite craftsmanship.

Above: The annual flooding of the Nile valley makes for a dramatic contrast between fertile land and the desert beyond. Far back in history there had been rain in Egypt, but its frequency decreased and the early settlers were driven closer and closer to the Nile. By 4000 BC agriculture had developed, and as yields grew, settlements were formed along the river. The First Cataract, pictured above, was the last point where the flow of the Nile northwards was broken, by boulders in the stream.

Previous page: Head of Akhenaten, the heretical pharaoh (*see p. 34*).

THE FIRST DYNASTIES

In about 280 BC Manetho, an Egyptian priest, went through the records of 3,000 years of Egyptian history and drew up a list of the pharaohs. He arranged them into 31 dynasties which—though archaeological evidence does not always confirm the list—still provides the framework within which scholars work. It was during the first three dynasties that the most important features of Egyptian kingship were developed. They included tight control of all officials, an efficient bureaucracy and the gathering of surplus goods from the peasants who worked the land between the floods.

The earliest pharaohs were buried at Abydos but then a new burial ground was developed at Saqqara, near to Memphis. It was here, about 2650, that king Djoser of the Third Dynasty broke through convention to build a stepped pyramid over his burial chamber. The Pyramid Age had begun.

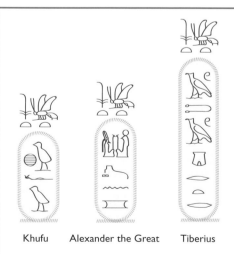

Khufu   Alexander the Great   Tiberius

THE CONTINUITY OF HIEROGLYPHICS

When the lands of the Nile delta and those bordering the river running south were first united into one kingdom in about 3100 BC, Narmer, the ruler who brought unification, was shown in reliefs with a threatening mace in his right hand. Nearly 3,000 years later, Alexander the Great, who prised Egypt out of the Persian empire, is shown in much the same way. So are the Roman emperors when Egypt became a province of the empire in 30 BC. The continuity of ancient Egyptian civilisation is extraordinary and the ways it represented itself and its rulers were sustained unchanged over many centuries. Opposite are three sets of hieroglyphs, one for Khufu (26th century BC), one for Alexander the Great (4th century BC) and one for the Roman emperor Tiberius (1st century AD). Hieroglyphs were a formal script used mainly for carving sacred texts on stone. Most were pictograms representing an object, a syllable in a word or even an abstract concept. A papyrus roll stands for writing. The names of rulers were enclosed in cartouches, above which appeared the symbols of Upper Egypt (a sedge plant) and Lower Egypt (a bee).

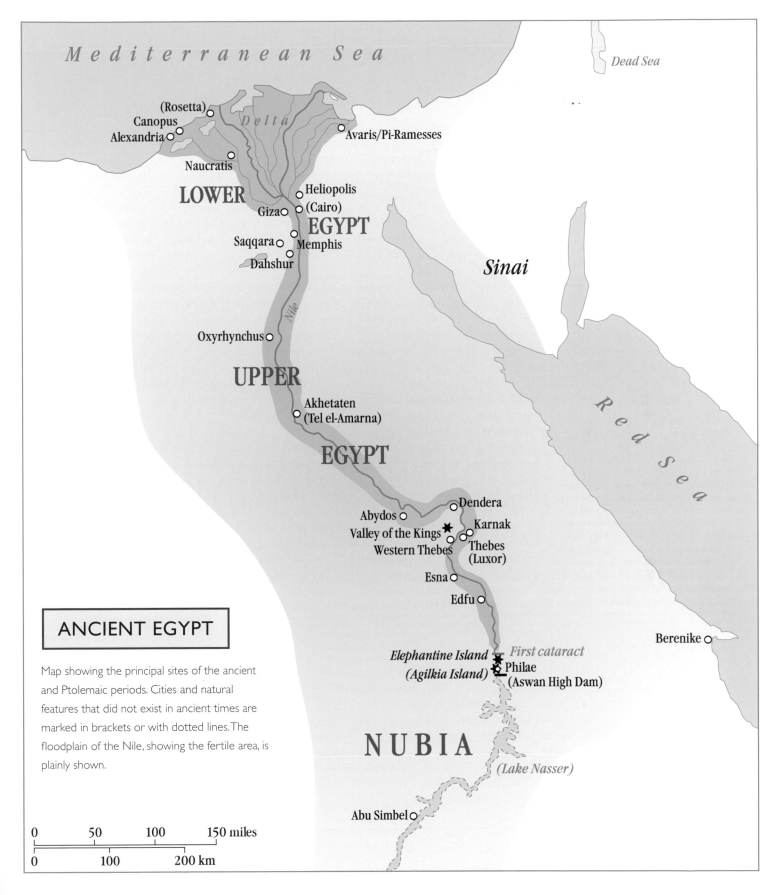

Mediterranean Sea

Dead Sea

(Rosetta)
Canopus
Alexandria
Naucratis

Delta

Avaris/Pi-Ramesses

LOWER

Heliopolis
Giza
(Cairo)

EGYPT

Saqqara
Memphis
Dahshur

Sinai

Nile

Oxyrhynchus

UPPER

Akhetaten
(Tel el-Amarna)

EGYPT

Red Sea

Dendera
Abydos
Valley of the Kings
Western Thebes

Karnak
Thebes
(Luxor)

Esna
Edfu

Berenike

ANCIENT EGYPT

Map showing the principal sites of the ancient
and Ptolemaic periods. Cities and natural
features that did not exist in ancient times are
marked in brackets or with dotted lines. The
floodplain of the Nile, showing the fertile area, is
plainly shown.

Elephantine Island
(Agilkia Island)

First cataract

Philae
(Aswan High Dam)

NUBIA

(Lake Nasser)

Abu Simbel

| 0 | 50 | 100 | 150 miles |

| 0 | 100 | 200 km |

The seated scribe might appear to be of low status but his occupation was a crucial and respected one to which any well-educated boy might aspire.

WRITING IN ANCIENT EGYPT

The earliest Egyptian writing seems to have been in the form of pictures inscribed on pottery. With time, the early pictograms developed into hieroglyphics, which survived as a form of writing language until the 6th century AD. After that they were forgotten, and it was not until the French scholar Champollion deciphered the script in the 19th century that the world of ancient Egypt could be explored in its own words. By the Middle Kingdom the most prestigious of occupations was that of scribe. It involved not only mastering the complexities of hieroglyphics but also presenting them as an art form. In the texts the scribes often denigrate other occupations (they were certainly a snobbish elite) but there is a cultured emphasis on the importance of literature in its own right. Thanks to their labours, we have a mass of texts, much of it fiction and poetry, including the so-called 'Wisdom Literature', which reflects on the meaning of life or offers guidance for the perplexed. There is also some rudimentary science. The Kahun Medical Papyrus deals with the ailments of women and includes contraceptive advice (a mixture of crocodile excrement and sour milk will do the trick) and a pregnancy test involving mixing urine and barley and seeing whether the seed will germinate. Another text contains the records of a doctor allocated to a building team and is full of advice on dealing with the crushed bones and dislocated limbs that must have been an everyday hazard with stone workers.

Above: Painted limestone figure of a scribe from Saqqara (Old Kingdom).

Below right: One of the four gold coffin-shaped containers placed in the Canopic chest found in the tomb of Tutankhamun. The coffins contained the dead pharaoh's vital organs.

THE PYRAMID AGE

The pyramid-building kings of the Fourth Dynasty ruled during the period known as the Old Kingdom (3rd millennium BC), an era when the whole energy of Egyptian society was directed towards the afterlife of the pharaoh. The pace could not be kept up for ever, and by the time of the Fifth Dynasty this highly centralised state was beginning to disintegrate. Slowly the local administrators on whom the regime depended became more independent. Instead of each being directly appointed by the pharaoh, many posts became hereditary and so out of the direct control of the ruler.

The weakened state faced new challenges at the end of the Sixth Dynasty, about 2181 BC. There may well have been a crisis in the climate: the annual floods seem to falter, leading to unrest among the peasantry. The quality of building falls, and there are accounts of raids from across the desert. Traditionally the next hundred years have been seen as a period of upheaval and social unrest. It is known as the First Intermediate Period and there are texts in which the wealthy complain that their world has been turned upside down.

ROYAL ICONOGRAPHY

An elaborate iconography of kingship was used to express the power of the pharaoh. A common head covering was the *nemes*, a piece of striped cloth pulled tightly across the forehead and tied at the back. Two strands fell down at the front over the shoulders. In the centre on the brow, two important royal symbols, the cobra (*uraeus*) and vulture, both symbols of gods, were displayed.

In everyday Egyptian life facial hair was not a mark of status, but the gods were assumed to have beards and so a pharaoh was often shown with a false plaited beard protruding from his chin. In depictions after death the beard is often shown with a slight curling up at the end (as can be seen in the mask of Tutankhamun). Even the female pharaoh Hatshepsut is depicted with this important mark of divinity (*see illustration overleaf*).

Pharaohs are often shown with a crook and a flail crossed across the chest. A crook symbolised the act of government, fulfilling much the same role as a sceptre (it survives in Christianity as the bishop's crozier, a metamorphosis of the shepherd's crook). The flail may have been in origin a fly-whisk, which is still part of the royal regalia in a number of African and Oriental countries today.

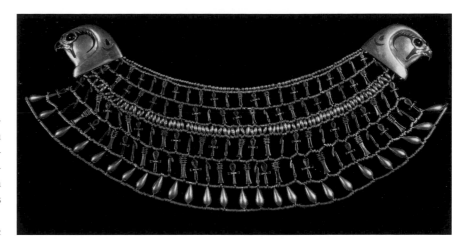

THE MIDDLE KINGDOM

The first effective king of the Eleventh Dynasty was Mentuhotep II. His home was Thebes, far up the Nile, and in about 2055 he launched a programme of conquest northwards. His power also extended southwards into Nubia, beyond the First Cataract, where the river's flow was broken up by boulders in the stream. Here his successors built forts and began to exploit the gold mines.

Mentuhotep chose to be buried near his capital, at the modern Deir el-Bahri (*see p. 29*). He had seen the pyramids, of course, and he copied some of their features such as the valley temple and the causeway leading to the burial complex. His tomb at the end of the causeway, marked by a series of spacious terraces, is a much less forbidding structure, however, and it marks a different mood. The Middle Kingdom which follows, from about 1985 BC, is one in which the relationship between king and people was more balanced. Certainly the power of the pharaohs remained absolute but the proclaimed ideology was *ma'at*, harmony. All things had to be kept in balance and administration and justice had to be conducted with moderation. On a divine level, the gods were brought together as if in a family. Amun was the god of Thebes, and so of the Eleventh Dynasty. Ra, the sun god, was the powerful god of the north. Now the two emerged as Amun-Ra, a supreme deity.

The Middle Kingdom was also an era of craftsmanship. Stoneworking is on a more human scale, so that the statues of the pharaohs are not merely propaganda images but show the personal characteristics of each ruler. The finest jewellery also dates from this time.

THE NEW KINGDOM

About 1770 the power of the Middle Kingdom rulers began to wane. Control over Nubia weakened while in the northeast a mass of immigrants from Syria and Palestine flooded in. The Egyptians sensed that they were losing control and dubbed the invaders the Hyksos, the 'chiefs of foreign lands'. Manetho's dynasties become especially confused at this point. This time of breakdown is known as the Second Intermediate Period.

The fragmentation was healed c. 1550 BC by Ahmose, the ruler of Thebes, recorded by Manetho as the first pharaoh of the Eighteenth Dynasty. He must have been a remarkable man. He struck north, reconquering the Delta and the city of Avaris, from where he continued eastwards and then north into Asia to enforce a new border. Not content with this victory he then marched south into Nubia to re-establish Egyptian control there. The New Kingdom which he established was to last some 500 years.

The New Kingdom rulers prided themselves on their status as warrior kings. Thutmose I (1504–1492), for instance, reached the Euphrates with his troops. There are graphic accounts too of his slaughter of the Nubians, followed by tight control of their trade routes so that the riches of Africa, especially gold, could be brought northwards. This was the age when the cradle of the dynasty, Thebes, and its protecting god, Amun, were glorified with the massive temple complex at Karnak (*see p. 26*). When Thutmose died, his was the first of 62 tombs in what is now known as the Valley of the Kings.

Perhaps the most interesting of the early New Kingdom rulers is a queen, Hatshepsut, the daughter of Thutmose. She married her half-brother, Thutmose II, and when he died in 1479 she became co-regent with Thutmose III, his son by a concubine. She was supported by an immensely talented official, Senenmut, who designed an imposing tomb for her at Deir el-Bahri next to that of Mentuhotep (gossip at the time said that Senenmut was her lover). Despite her successes Hatshepsut vanishes from the record in about 1458 BC. It appears that Thutmose III, now adult, grasped

The Middle Kingdom was remarkable for its elegant and beautifully-crafted jewellery. This is a *wesekh*, a wide collar, which was believed to have protective power. Typically Middle Kingdom jewellery would have a gold framework into which semi-precious stones were fitted or added. The two falcon heads are used to fix the *wesekh* in place.

CHRONOLOGY OF ANCIENT EGYPT

- EARLY DYNASTIC PERIOD
(1st–2nd dynasties) 2890–2686

- OLD KINGDOM
(3rd–6th dynasties) 2686–2181

- FIRST INTERMEDIATE PERIOD
(7th–10th dynasties; 11th in Thebes) 2181–2055

- MIDDLE KINGDOM
(11th–14th dynasties) 2055–1650

- SECOND INTERMEDIATE PERIOD
(15th–17th dynasties) 1650–1550

- NEW KINGDOM
(18th–20th dynasties) 1550–1069

- THIRD INTERMEDIATE PERIOD
(21st–24th dynasties) 1069–747

- LATE PERIOD
(25th–30th dynasties) 747–332

- MACEDONIAN PERIOD
332–305

- PTOLEMAIC PERIOD
305–31

- ROMAN EMPIRE
31 BC– AD 395

Above: Watercolour of Queen Hatshepsut by Howard Carter, who discovered her tomb in 1903 (and that of Tutankhamun in 1922). Hatshepsut fascinates for the skills that she used to survive as 'pharaoh' in a world in which the rulers were always male. She exploited her position effectively, adapting all the traditional male symbols of the pharaohs to portray herself as supreme ruler. In some respect, however, the way in which she is usually shown with a beard may show how difficult it was for the stonemasons to portray a female ruler. Such ambiguities were eventually dealt with by erasing her from most monuments.

Facing page: Hatshepsut's reign was peaceful and one of its most famous exploits was an expedition to the mysterious land of Punt, celebrated in detail with a relief in her mortuary temple at Deir el-Bahri. Punt has never been identified but it was probably on the African coastline of the Red Sea. Incense, ebony, electrum and cattle were brought back into Egypt. The detail here shows two porters. The relief may have had the overall propaganda purpose of extolling the peacefulness of the queen's reign but it also shows how the Egyptians saw another culture and appeared to barter with them. In other parts of the relief the ruler of Punt is portrayed in an exotic costume and the houses are shown as conical reed-built huts. So different did Punt appear to be that it was talked of as a fantasy land—an Eldorado—and it appeared as such in folk tales.

back control, and in a campaign to obliterate any memory of a female pharaoh Hatshepsut's name was erased from the monuments. Thutmose was, however, successful in his own right. Although he launched new raids into Syria, he valued Syrian culture. It is possible that all three of his wives were Syrian, and the reliefs on his temples depict plants and flowers he brought back (*see illustration on p. 26*). He was known too for his love of ancient literature.

One of his successors, Amenhotep III (1390–1352 BC), conducted a vast building programme in Thebes that consolidated the power of the temples. The high priest of Amun was a major state official with far-reaching supervisory powers. This now became a problem. The temples threatened to become alternative centres of power and Amenhotep's relationship with the grandees of Thebes deteriorated. His son Akhenaten severed the relationship altogether, instituting the worship not of Amun but of the sun in its physical form, Aten.

Akhenaten founded a new capital, the modern Tel el-Amarna (*see p. 34*), but his revolution was not a success. He failed to uproot traditional religious beliefs and his son, Tutankhaten, signalled a return to the old religion of Amun by renaming himself Tutankhamun. Yet he was dead by the age of 19 and it was by sheer chance that this pharaoh, who was otherwise of little historical importance, should have survived intact inside his tomb until discovered by Howard Carter in 1922.

The most influential pharaoh of the Nineteenth Dynasty was Ramesses II (c. 1279–1213 BC). He was faced by the growing power of the Hittites, a tenacious people whose power extended right to the borders of Egypt. Ramesses held them off at the famous battle of Qadesh (*see p. 43*) but despite his glorification of the campaign as a victory, Ramesses knew he was lucky to have survived and he sensibly made an alliance with his adversaries. He then devoted himself to a programme of new building, which included the temples at Abu Simbel.

It was a last gasp. The Twentieth Dynasty oversaw the slow decline of Egypt, beset by major upheavals in the Near East, the mysterious raids of the Sea Peoples in the Mediterranean, and incursions from Libya as the Sahara became drier and ancient settlements were displaced. The gold mines at Nubia, which had provided Egypt with metal for so long, were exhausted by 1060. The most vivid evidence of the collapse of royal authority is seen in the texts decrying the looting of ancient tombs, even those of royalty. This was a state which had lost its vigour.

EGYPT MEETS GREECE AND ROME

After 1060 there were moments when a single pharaoh briefly revived the state but at other times there were as many as ten rulers vying for power at once. Nubians, Assyrians and Persians all fought for portions of Egyptian soil. Greek settlers and traders also established themselves, notably at Naucratis, a trading post in the western Delta. Yet no one could have predicted the dramatic collapse of the Persian empire in the 330s BC at the hands of Alexander the Great. Alexander spent little time in Egypt, but his founding of the port of Alexandria brought the country fully into the trading network of the Mediterranean. On Alexander's death, Egypt was seized by one of his generals, Ptolemy. His dynasty ruled until the last of the line, Cleopatra VII, was defeated by the Roman general Octavian at Actium in 31 BC and Egypt was absorbed into the Roman empire.

The Greeks and the Romans preserved many aspects of Egyptian culture. While Alexandria and other new settlements along the Nile were fully Greek, there had to be some accommodation with the native population if the wealth of the valley was to be channelled upwards to the rulers. Thus it was that the Ptolemies built 'new' temples at Edfu, Dendera and Philae (*see p. 46*). The Romans were always concerned that Egypt and its wealth might provide a launching point for rebellion, so they too were careful to recognise Egyptian culture. The turning point came in the 390s AD when the Christian emperor Theodosius ordered the suppression of all pagan cults. Although a few temples remained open for another hundred years, one of the great civilisations of the world began to disappear under the sand.

The Pyramids of Saqqara and Dahshur

The ancestors of the Egyptian pyramids are the tombs known as mastabas, flat rectangular or trapezoidal platforms which were modelled in the shape of a palace. There was always a false door through which the *ka* or spirit of the pharaoh could move back and forth. The burial chamber itself was underground, with the embalmed body enclosed alongside the grave goods in a wood-lined cavity.

There is no clear reason why this model should not have continued, but in about 2650 BC a revolutionary development took place. The royal architect of King Djoser, Imhotep (*see opposite*), decided to place one mastaba on top of another until there were six in total. While many earlier tombs had been in mud-brick, this was all in stone. The resulting 'stepped pyramid', at Saqqara, was almost 200 ft high and could be seen as far away as the king's own capital at Memphis. It still stands as the world's first-known large stone building. Some texts suggest that the steps were seen as providing a stairway up which the pharaoh could ascend to the heavens.

The Stepped Pyramid was part of a larger burial complex. Beside the tomb chamber of Djoser there were a further eleven chambers for the members of his family. The pyramid was set within a much larger enclosure with buildings that included a mortuary chapel, where offerings would be left for the dead pharaoh, and smaller chapels representing the provinces of Egypt. Some of the architectural innovations, the recessed walls and the fluted columns in the hall of pillars (probably a representation of bound reeds), were to become consistent themes in Egyptian art.

The illustrations on these pages show the evolution of the Egyptian pyramid in the 3rd millennium BC. First came the simple mastaba tomb (diagram opposite), then a series of mastabas was placed one above the other making the Stepped Pyramid at Saqqara (photograph opposite top). At Dahshur a pyramid with a smooth slope was built by King Sneferu, but the slope had a double pitch, and the structure is known as the Bent Pyramid (pictured right). Sneferu's second pyramid, the one within which his body was laid to rest, is the so-called Red Pyramid (pictured far right).

A stepped pyramid could be transformed into a full pyramid by covering the steps with a flat sloping surface. However, a successor of Djoser, Sneferu, decided to build a pyramid which was planned as such from the beginning. In fact he built two, at Dahshur, close to Saqqara: the famous 'Bent' Pyramid and then another, which sloped at a constant angle. It is in the second that Sneferu was buried, and his decision to build a true pyramid probably reflects his adoption of the cult of the sun god Ra (a pyramid could be seen as the representation of the rays of the sun coming downwards).

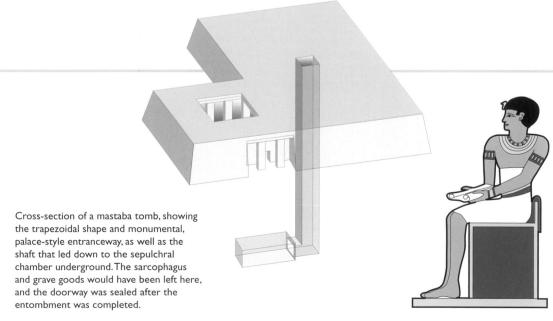

Cross-section of a mastaba tomb, showing the trapezoidal shape and monumental, palace-style entranceway, as well as the shaft that led down to the sepulchral chamber underground. The sarcophagus and grave goods would have been left here, and the doorway was sealed after the entombment was completed.

Imhotep is credited with placing six mastabas on top of each other to create the Stepped Pyramid of Djoser at Saqqara. Even the invention of building in dressed stone was attributed to him. With each generation his reputation as a man of great wisdom grew and he became linked to the art of writing and medicine. Eventually, in the 1st millennium BC, he became worshipped as a god, the son not of a mortal but of the craftsman god Ptah. He is always shown with a papyrus roll, the symbol of the wise man.

The Pyramids of Giza

Royal tombs of the Old Kingdom 3rd millennium BC

The pyramid of Sneferu at Dahshur (*see previous chapter*) was the first of the true Egyptian pyramids. It was Sneferu's son Khufu (or Cheops, in the Greek form of his name) who chose to move the building of his own pyramid to the more stable limestone plateau of Giza. His is the largest of three mammoth constructions, the two others belonging to succeeding rulers of the same dynasty, Khafra (Chephren in Greek) and Menkaura (Mycerinus).

THE MORTUARY COMPLEX

A pyramid itself **(1)** was only part of a much larger complex. Once the king had been embalmed, his funerary boat would have brought the body to the valley temple **(2)** at the edge of the flooded Nile. Here there would have been a ritual welcome by the priests before the body was transported up the causeway **(3)** towards the pyramid. It would then rest at the mortuary temple **(4)**, before being taken inside the pyramid. The embalmed organs and the other grave goods would have been placed with the sarcophagus before the whole was sealed.

Khufu's court officials were buried alongside the pyramid in mastaba tombs **(5)**. Only the survival of the king's spirit could be assured, but those that rose with him could share in his afterlife. It must have been an excellent way of ensuring loyalty. The tombs were arranged as if they were in a town, with streets between them. The more senior the official, the closer he was allowed to be to the pyramid itself. The pharaoh was responsible for providing the sarcophagus, as the cost of quarrying, transporting and shaping the stone would have been beyond the means of most. Status is reflected in the distinction between the prestige granite sarcophagi and the more easily carved and available limestone ones.

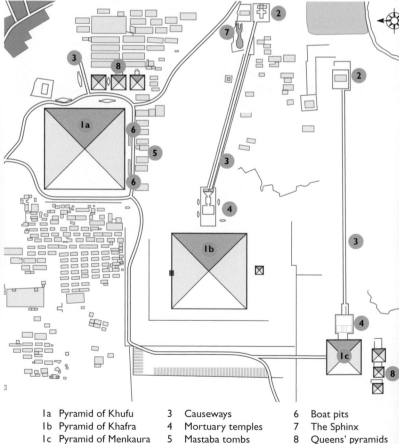

1a	Pyramid of Khufu	3	Causeways	6	Boat pits
1b	Pyramid of Khafra	4	Mortuary temples	7	The Sphinx
1c	Pyramid of Menkaura	5	Mastaba tombs	8	Queens' pyramids
2	Valley temples				

Khufu's pyramid, often known as the 'Great Pyramid', required 2,500,000 limestone blocks. Their average weight was 2.5 tons. The limestone could be obtained from mines in the vicinity but the more prestigious granite, which lined the burial chamber and the lower courses of some pyramids, had to be brought from Aswan, some hundreds of miles upstream. Unlike the other pyramids, the Great Pyramid had three chambers, one well below the surface, the other two within the structure itself (*see cross-section below*). The decision to house Khufu's body in a stone sarcophagus, the first time that this is recorded, appears to have created a crisis—it simply could not be fitted down into the subterranean chamber. So a new space had to be constructed in the middle of the pyramid. When Khafra built his pyramid the lesson had been learned and the subterranean chamber was built so that the granite sarcophagus could be lowered into it.

THE GREAT PYRAMID

In the Great Pyramid the large corbelled 'King's Chamber' presented major structural challenges. Its roof had to be designed so that the weight of stone above it was distributed to avoid crushing it. The long ascending passage (the 'Grand Gallery') had to be sealed with granite after the body had been placed within it but this required stones of the right size to be fixed into place and the workmen had to be able to get out afterwards. The granite must have been 'stored' during construction so that it was close to where it needed to be when the passages were closed off.

In 1872, narrow shafts were discovered running up from the King's Chamber (there were another two shafts running from the so-called Queen's Chamber below). They had been blocked and the first attempt (in 1993) to send up a robot camera to find where they led ended when one door in the shaft simply led to another. An old theory that they were air vents for the workers has been discarded but the orientation of one towards the constellation of Orion, which was associated with Osiris, god of death and rebirth, and the other to the ancient pole star gives some support for the theory that the king's spirit might have ascended along them towards his new home in the stars.

A King's Chamber
B Grand Gallery
C Queen's Chamber
D Subterranean chamber
E Shafts from Queen's Chamber
F Shafts from King's Chamber
G Position of the constellation Orion

THE BOAT PITS

Some of the more fascinating finds in the immediate vicinity of the Great Pyramid are a number of boat pits. Two, on the southern side of the pyramid, have proved especially important. Both were closed off by large limestone blocks, and when these were removed from one of them, the boat was found inside (*see illustration*). The second pit has not yet been excavated but the inside can now be seen through an inserted video link. The name of Khufu's successor Djedefra was found in the first pit and it is likely that he ordered the dismantling of both boats and their storage after the death of Khufu. They may have been the very boats used to convey Khufu's body on its last journey, but it is also possible that they were intended for his use in the afterlife when he accompanied his father Ra on his orbit round the earth. The tradition was that one boat would be used during the day and the other during the night, hence the two which were found.

Reconstructed river boat made of cedarwood and acacia, complete with oars, from a boat pit near the Great Pyramid of Khufu. It was a meticulous process to reassemble the 1,224 pieces into a single craft, some 142 ft long. It is now on display close to the pyramid.

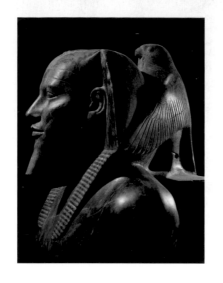

'I protect the chapel of thy tomb, I guard thy gate, I ward off the intruding stranger, I hurl thy foes to the ground. I drive away the wicked one from the chapel of thy tomb, I destroy thine adversaries in their hiding place.' (Text from the pedestal of an Egyptian sphinx c. 600 BC.)
The Sphinx at Giza (pictured opposite) guards the central of the three pyramids, that of Khafra. The photograph clearly shows how most of the outer limestone cladding of the pyramid has gone (it was commonly robbed for other buildings or burned down for lime). The Sphinx wears the *nemes* head covering (*see p. 12*) and the cobra figure or *uraeus* on the brow is still partly preserved.

Above: Detail from a diorite-gneiss statue of Khafra with the sky god Horus behind him. Khafra is thought to be the pharaoh represented in the head of the Sphinx.

BUILDING A PYRAMID

The site of a proposed pyramid had to be carefully chosen so that the weight of the building could be supported on the underlying rock. It also had to be close enough to the flood level for stone to be brought up by water. In the case of the Great Pyramid the base was laid out by levelling the outer areas and leaving a mound of rock in the middle. So careful was the work that there is less than half an inch discrepancy between the highest and lowest parts of the platform.

The building process must have involved ramps. Though no traces remain at Giza, at other pyramid sites a number of different kinds of ramp are known, some heading up one side, others zig-zagging. The commonest form seems to have been a wide ramp perpendicular to the pyramid, which would have been lengthened as the pyramid rose so that the gradient remained constant.

Cutting the stone was a major problem. Granite, the prestige material, is very hard and the copper tools that the Egyptians used would have worn so fast that only the pharaoh would have had the resources to employ the mass of workers needed. Experiments have shown that the Egyptians probably introduced quartz crystals to provide friction between the tools and the stone.

One estimate of the workforce required to complete the Great Pyramid is that 25,000 men would have been able to build it in 20 years. Perhaps 4,000 of these would have been frontline workers, masons and quarriers, housed permanently on site with their families. The burial grounds by the workers' sites show a large proportion of women and children. While the fields were flooded, another 20,000 men could be drafted in for less skilled work, mixing the mortar or building up the ramps. The administration of these groups was meticulous. The smallest unit under a single leader was 20 men, but these gangs could be increased to make units of up to 2,000. There was a lot of camaraderie. One unit on the Menkaura pyramid nicknamed themselves 'the Drunkards of Menkaura'.

Studies of the workers' DNA suggest that they were native Egyptians drawn from all over the country. They were never slaves. Perhaps many were drafted in against their will, but the sheer size of the project must have inspired others to leave home for the experience. Whatever the reality of days of back-breaking lifting and pulling, everyone would have brought home tales to tell. At the same time, the workers would have learned skills which might have given them a new livelihood when they returned home. Even so, some pharaohs seem to have managed their workforce better than others. Sneferu went down in Egyptian mythology as a good king; his son Khufu as a tyrant, and his reputation lingered for centuries. Herodotus claims he even prostituted his own daughter to help pay for the work.

THE SPHINX

There was an Egyptian belief that the gates of the underworld were guarded by a lion. This seems to have been the inspiration for the famous Sphinx at Giza, a recumbent lion with a human head, probably that of Khafra, whose tomb it appears to guard. It is placed close to the causeway which ascends to his pyramid. The word sphinx is probably a corruption by Greek speakers of the Egyptian *shese-ankh*, 'living image'.

Two hundred feet long and 65 ft high and carved from a natural outcrop of rock, the Sphinx is the largest known stone statue from the ancient world. Weathered with time and with the limestone flaking off, the fact that it is recognisable at all is the result of it having been buried in sand for much of its history. There is even a record of the future Thutmose IV (c. 1400 BC) coming across it on a hunting expedition and learning in a dream that if he uncovered it he would be pharaoh.

The sphinx was a potent symbol of protection in Egypt and it was common to line the processional routes leading to temples with avenues of sphinxes, either with human or rams' heads (*see p. 27*). The sphinx also became a cultural export. Areas of Egyptian trade or influence, including Minoan Crete and the Near East, adopted it—in the Near East the sphinx even sprouts wings. In the Greek world the sphinx becomes female and is found on shields as a protective symbol. One of the finest examples is the winged sphinx offered to the shrine of Delphi by the people of Naxos about 570 BC. Sphinxes are also found in Etruscan and Roman art, and the emperor Augustus, who added Egypt to the Roman empire, adopted a sphinx as his personal symbol.

THE PYRAMID TEXTS

These texts have been found inscribed on the walls of later Old Kingdom pyramids but such was the natural conservatism of the Egyptians that it is believed many refer back to the beliefs of the earlier pharaohs. The act of carving was believed to release the power of the words themselves. In the example included here much is made of Horus, the protective falcon-god of the pharaohs. It is texts such as the one below which provide evidence that the pharaoh was expected to be reborn among the stars.

The reed floats of the sky are set down for Horus,
    that he may cross on them to the horizon, to Horakhty,
The reed floats of the sky are set down for the pharaoh,
    that he may cross on them to the horizon, to Horakhty…
[These verses are repeated]
    The Nurse Canal is opened, the Winding Water is flooded,
    the Fields of Reeds are filled with water,
So that the pharaoh is ferried over thereon
    to that eastern side of the sky
    to the place where the gods fashion him,
    where he is born again, new and young.

Utterance 264. Tr. R.O. Faulkner

The falcon-headed god Horus was worshipped as a sky god, Horus-on-the-Horizon or Horakhty. The Egyptians often merged gods, and as the sun god Ra became more prominent, he was amalgamated with Horakhty to make Ra-Horakhty, the supreme deity before the rise of Amun-Ra. He is shown here second from the left, wearing a sun disc. As protector of the pharaohs, Ra-Horakhty was believed to wait on the horizon to greet the dead king and ensure that he would be reborn. His wife Hathor, seated behind him, was known in a funerary context as the 'Lady of the West'. She protected the setting sun during the night and it was hoped that she would offer similar protections to the dead.

DEATH, BURIAL, AFTERLIFE

The Egyptians believed that death was a temporary interruption of life and that there were means of ensuring that life could continue on an eternal plane. After his death, the *ka*, or spirit of the pharaoh ascended to his father and was often shown alongside Ra on the sun boat which travelled under the world each night so that Ra would be in place to rise the next morning in the east. Yet the pharaoh would only reappear in the next world if certain conditions were fulfilled. The deceased had to have shown piety towards the gods, and his heart was weighed at a judgment to test its worthiness. During the Old Kingdom a new god of the dead, Osiris, emerged to judge the deceased. An ethical life on earth was rewarded with an afterlife of ease and plenty. In addition to this, the correct burial rituals had to be followed. The body had to be embalmed, the name of the deceased had to be recorded in the tomb, and provisions for the afterlife had to be left with the body.

Obviously the richer the individual, the more elaborate the tomb goods, and an unrobbed tomb such as that of Tutankhamun shows the astonishing range and quality of what could be provided. Some items had purely ritual purposes, such as images of the pharaoh himself and of deities in gilded wood. A wooden frame was found in Tutankhamun's tomb into which Nile silt had been placed, sown with corn. The corn would have germinated as a symbol of resurrection. There were ritual couches, one of which had been allocated for the transfer of the pharaoh's body to heaven.

Yet most grave goods were designed to serve the deceased in his future life. His workforce was represented by *shabtis*, small wooden figures, sometimes equipped with tools. Tutankhamun had 413 of these, one for each day of the year, with extras to supervise them. There was virtually every aid to living that one could dream of: jewellery, cosmetics, clothing, sandals, lamps and torches, head-rests, chairs, boxes and stools. Different kinds of bread (as well as a model granary), grain and cakes were provided, as well as meat from ducks, sheep and cows. There was a bunch of garlic, honey and spices, fruit and almonds. There were many vessels with wine in them, and some had dockets that named the vintage, the vine-yard and even the winemaker. Sophisticated living indeed. Entertainment was provided by musical instruments, including trumpets and sistra (rattles), and by board games. There were swords, daggers and shields, fine chariots, and, of course, models of boats, no less than 35 of them, some for ceremonial purposes, such as following the course of the sun under the earth. Others were everyday river craft.

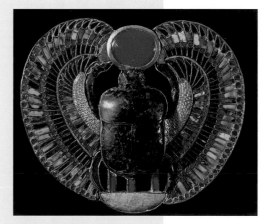

Above: The weighing of the heart of the deceased against a feather was the ritual which gave access to the afterlife and here it is carefully portrayed. The ceremony is presided over by Osiris, who sits in judgement under a canopy with his sister-wife Isis and sister Nephthys behind him. The deceased is led forward by jackal-headed Anubis, the god associated with embalming, who also oversees the weighing of the heart. Thoth, the god of wisdom and calculation, here shown in human form with an ibis head, faces the scales and checks the outcome. If it is unfavourable, the crocodile-headed Ammut will gobble up the heart. This depiction of the rituals comes from a Book of the Dead in the collection of the British Museum, here Spell 125, which traditionally shows the judgement. The Book was normally deposited in the coffin and acted as a 'good luck' offering to help the deceased through the judgement rituals.

Left: The scarab was sacred to the ancient Egyptians. It was believed to renew itself without a female and was linked to the idea of spontaneous regeneration and so to the return of the sun each day. The pushing of a ball of dung by the scarab was seen as identical to the movement of the sun across the sky. A scarab was often placed on the heart of the deceased (this example comes from the coffin of Tutankhamun) to boost the chances of the heart being judged as pure.

Eastern Thebes: Luxor

Thebes was the name the Greeks gave to the ancient city of Waset. It was in an excellent position, able to benefit from resources brought northwards from Nubia but also at the end of eastern trading routes from across the desert. It was far enough from the traditional centres of royal power in the north, such as Memphis, to develop its own status as a provincial capital. It was in the Eleventh Dynasty (Middle Kingdom), in about 2050 BC under Mentuhotep, that the city first rose to national prominence. Even though Mentuhotep decided to move his own capital north, he returned here to be buried, on the west bank of the Nile across from Thebes.

It was under Ahmose, the founding pharaoh of the New Kingdom, that Thebes became capital of the whole of Egypt and its presiding god, Amun, became the supreme deity. On the east bank of the Nile, two important temples to Amun developed at Luxor and Karnak, suburbs of Thebes. They were linked to each other by a processional route of sphinxes along which the images of the gods passed during the Festival of Opet (*see box on p. 28*).

Temple complex of a supreme god 2nd millennium BC

LUXOR

The core of the temple at Luxor is the work of Amenhotep III (1390–1352), and close to the inner shrine he included a record of his divine birth, which followed the union of his mother with the great god Amun. The open peristyle court with papyrus-bundle columns (*see diagram right*) is a famous sight. A hundred years after Amenhotep, Ramesses II incorporated the shrine of Amun into a great peristyle court of his own, and so created a succession of courtyards, gateways and halls which lengthened the temple complex to nearly 850 ft. Inside his court, statues of Ramesses stand alongside reliefs showing him with the favoured gods. The temple was entered through a gateway (pylon), also built by Ramesses, on which the pharaoh trumpeted his victory at Qadesh (*see p. 43*).

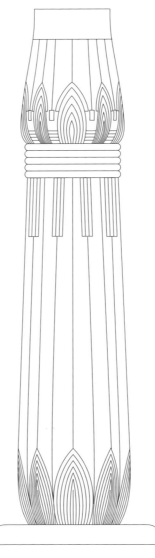

Left: Papyrus flourished in Lower Egypt, especially in the marshes of the Delta. It had many practical uses. Papyrus sheets for writing on have been found from the earliest dynasties. They were wetted, beaten together and then dried and could be made into long rolls. Papyrus had many symbolic uses, too. As it was believed to have grown from the earliest mound of creation it was reproduced in the columns of the hypostyle halls that symbolised that moment of creation. It may be that the fluted columns of Greek temples derived from Egyptian models of bound papyrus stalks. The diagram shows a typical papyrus-bundle column, such as occur in Amenhotep's peristyle court at Luxor.

Facing page: Seated statue of Ramesses II in front of the first gateway of the temple at Luxor. Behind him stretches a peristyle court of open papyrus-topped columns.

Eastern Thebes: Karnak

'This forsaken city so haunted our imagination that at the sight of these scattered ruins the army came to a halt of its own volition and spontaneously began to applaud.'

Dominique Vivant Denon on the arrival of Napoleon's army at Karnak in 1799

The processional route from Luxor leads to Karnak, 'The Most Select of Places', home to the most imposing temple complex in ancient Egypt. There are actually three enclosures here. The smallest is that of Montu **(A)**, an ancient god of war and probably the original protecting god of Thebes. His temple is yet another building project of Amenhotep III as is the Temple of Mut, the consort of Amun, at the southern end of Karnak. Both were restored with gateways added by the Ptolemies.

The most imposing of the temples is the Great Temple to Amun himself **(B)**, built, rebuilt and enlarged over 2,000 years of Egyptian history. The sanctuary is the work of Thutmose III (1479–1425), one of the most culturally sophisticated of the pharaohs. Behind it Thutmose built his own Festival Temple **(C)** and it is here that his love of exotic plants and animals is shown in the reliefs on the walls.

The most famous building is the vast, awe-inspiring Hypostyle Hall **(D)** (*illustrated opposite*), normally credited to Ramesses II (1279–1213) although there are reliefs showing his predecessor Seti I. There are no less than 134 columns, with those in the centre higher than those alongside them. The outside of the Hall provided a fine opportunity for both kings to show off their victories in Syria and Palestine in reliefs.

Sanctuaries of the gods of Thebes 2nd millennium BC

Above: Thutmose III was one of the most cultured of the Egyptian pharaohs and in the sanctuary of his temple to Amun at Karnak he shows his love of plants and wildlife, many of the likenesses taken from examples he had seen while on campaign in the Near East.

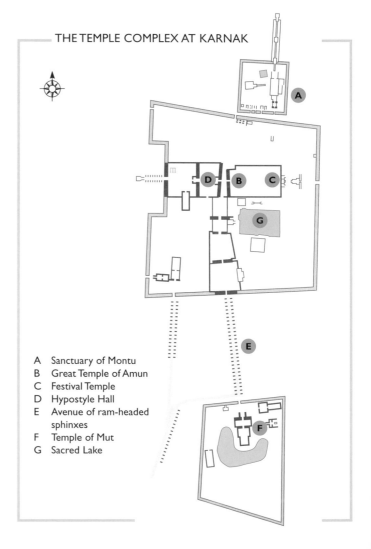

THE TEMPLE COMPLEX AT KARNAK

A Sanctuary of Montu
B Great Temple of Amun
C Festival Temple
D Hypostyle Hall
E Avenue of ram-headed
    sphinxes
F Temple of Mut
G Sacred Lake

The original alignment of the Great Temple was from east to west with the final addition of a gateway by the river as late as the 4th century BC. Yet there is also an extension of gateways and court-yards southwards to the enclosure wall, which then opens out onto an avenue of ram-headed sphinxes **(E)** leading to the Temple of Mut **(F)**. In the angle between this extension and the sanctuary proper is a Sacred Lake **(G)**. These lakes were reservoirs which provided water for the purification rituals, but might also house sacred animals such as crocodiles or geese.

Above: The ram had been worshipped in Egypt from the earliest times, notably because of its fertility. Khnum, the god creator of mankind (illustrated), was a ram god and during the New Kingdom his cult was absorbed into that of Amun. Hence the processional ways of ram-headed sphinxes leading up to a temple of Amun.

Left: The Hypostyle Hall of the Great Temple of Karnak. 'How often has it been written, and how often must it be repeated, that the Great Hall at Karnack is the noblest work of art ever designed and executed by human hands? One writer tells us that it covers four times the area occupied by the Cathedral of Notre Dame. Another measures it against St Peter's. All admit their inability to describe it; yet all attempt the description … There is, in truth, no building in the wide world to compare with it. The Pyramids are more stupendous. The Parthenon is more beautiful. Yet in nobility of conception, in vastness of detail, in majestic beauty of the highest order, the Hall of Pillars exceeds them every one. This doorway, these columns, are the wonders of the world. How was that lintel-stone raised? How were those capitals lifted? Entering among those mighty pillars, says a recent observer, "you feel that you have shrunk to the dimensions and feebleness of a fly." But I think you feel more than that. You are stupefied by the thought of the mighty men who made them. You say to yourself: "There were indeed giants in those days".'
Amelia Edwards, *A Thousand Miles up the Nile*, London 1877

Amun, the principal god of Thebes, and patron of the Theban rulers of the Middle and New Kingdoms, is usually shown as a man with a plumed headdress, though sometimes he is depicted with the head of a ram, his sacred animal. His consort was Mut and their son was Khons, the moon god (shown here), depicted as a youth with a sidelock, wearing a crescent on his head bearing a full lunar disc.

AN EGYPTIAN TEMPLE

The Egyptian temple—like the Greek temple after it—was predominantly the complex which grew up around the shrine where the image of the god was housed. It is not easy to know how early temples were constructed as once a site had been sanctified it tended to be built on again and again. Thus most temples which survive are those of the later periods of Egyptian history, the New Kingdom and the Greek-speaking Ptolemaic kingdom.

The way through to the shrine was marked by a vast gateway, the pylon. The typical pylon consisted of two massive, broad-based tapering towers joined by a bridge (*see illustration on p. 46*). As this was the only part of the temple which the mass of population would see, it was vital to use the towers for propaganda. Often the pharaoh would flaunt his status as the one who had constructed the temple and displayed his piety. His victories would be proclaimed in reliefs. In the larger complexes, such as the temple of Amun at Karnak, new processional routes could be added with pylons of their own, so that the original gateway would become hidden from the public.

Inside a pylon there would be an open courtyard leading into a hypostyle (from the Greek 'resting on pillars') hall. Traditionally the central columns were higher than those in the rows behind so that there would be, as it were, a nave and aisles. These dark spaces, originally lit only from windows above, led towards the shrine. It was here that the pharaoh, or more usually the priest who was his representative, purified himself for his entry to the sanctuary. The floors would become higher and the ceilings lower as one passed inwards, because each temple was a symbolic recreation of the primeval mound, the first fertile land that had risen from the water at the moment of creation (which was, of course, a recurring event in Egyptian life as the floods retreated each year). The columns were usually graced with symbols of papyrus plants, again in recognition of emerging fertility. The texts and reliefs within the halls, seen only by the priests, focused on the pharaoh as the intermediary between man and god, making offerings or carrying out rituals.

The status of a temple was shown by the resources it was granted. The pharaoh might provide precious stone and metals or award a share of the loot from his conquests to a favoured temple. Some temples were given their own gold mines and land. This was all used to maintain the buildings and feed the large temple staff. In the mortuary temple that he built in western Thebes, Ramesses II constructed vast granaries as part of the complex and it has been estimated that these could have fed 3,400 families for a year. The priests, then, were not just the supervisors of rituals but important administrators in their own right. Some temples had their own trading ships. However, the temples were never completely independent. Their wealth could be taxed by the pharaoh and diverted to other projects. In the cash-strapped Twentieth Dynasty, temples were taxed to help with the building of royal tombs in the Valley of the Kings.

RELIGIOUS FESTIVALS

The typical Egyptian religious festival centred on a procession of the cult image from one temple to another. At Thebes the most famous was the Festival of Opet, held over a period of two to four weeks each year during the period when the valley was flooded. The images of the god Amun, his consort the vulture goddess Mut and their son, the moon god Khons, were loaded onto sacred boats (barques) which would be carried along a processional route lined with sphinxes, or in later times sent by water, between Karnak and Luxor. Along the route there would be singing and dancing and the distribution of food gathered for the occasion. One account records the handing out of 11,341 loaves, 85 cakes and 385 jars of beer. This was the only occasion on which the population actually came close to one of the major gods, and questions could be addressed on any issue bothering the enquirer. As the sacred barque tipped this way or that as it was carried forward, an answer could be read from its movements.

Yet the most important feature of the Opet festival was the presence of the pharaoh himself. If not in residence in Thebes he would make a stately progress down the Nile to participate in the procession. The climax would come when he entered the sacred precinct of the temple of Luxor and disappeared into the shrine. Here, in some mysterious moment of union, Amun would merge the pharaoh with his *ka* and so transform him into a divinity. It was a confirmation of his right to rule.

Western Thebes and the Valley of the Kings

Hatshepsut's temple at Deir el-Bahri
on the west bank of the Nile was the
finest of her buildings. It was set out on a
series of terraces and the reliefs portray
the achievements of her reign. She was
never buried there—it was perhaps too
conspicuous when she knew of the
opposition to her rule. It is possible that
the columns of this temple provided the
model that Greek craftsmen copied when
they created the Doric order for their
own temples.

WESTERN THEBES

The first major temple to be built on the West Bank, at Deir el-Bahri, was that of Mentuhotep, the great pharaoh of the Middle Kingdom. He used the hills as a backdrop against which to place a series of terraces graced with palm trees and statues. A causeway ran up to them. Mentuhotep was confident enough to be buried in the complex itself, in a tomb cut 500 ft into the rock. A temple to Amun, the great god of Thebes whose cult originated here, was also built on the West Bank (at Medinet Habu) by the New Kingdom ruler Thutmose III and his co-regent Hatshepsut. For centuries afterwards, the priests of Amun had their administrative headquarters there.

During the New Kingdom the most important activity along the West Bank was the construction of the mortuary temples of the pharaohs. Here they were offered cult worship, even if, from the reign of Thutmose I onwards, they themselves were buried well behind in the secluded Valley of the Kings. Hatshepsut (d. 1458 BC) built her mortuary temple alongside that of Mentuhotep, but she was loth to be buried there (and with some justification when we know how her successors dealt with her memory; *see pp. 13–14*), instead building two tombs for herself hidden well behind her temple complex.

Ramesses II (reigned 1279–1213) built his own vast mortuary temple, the Ramesseum, south of Deir el-Bahri on the edge of the floodplain. Now that the kings themselves were buried in the Valley of the Kings, the mortuary temple became something different, a temple to Amun in which the god's union with the specific pharaoh was celebrated. So the inner shrine contained an image of Amun while the reliefs on the walls of the temple honoured the pharaoh's relationship with him. Within the enclosure of the Ramesseum was a small palace with a Window of Appearance that overlooked the inner courtyard. Here, during festivals, a visiting pharaoh would pass out rewards to favoured officials. The Ramesseum is remarkable for its granaries and for evidence that a scribes' school was established there. Fifty years later Ramesses III copied the Ramesseum of his namesake but used the opportunity to incorporate the ancient temple to Amun at Medinet Habu within it.

Signature of the 19th-century Italian explorer Giovanni Battista Belzoni, an adventurer, former circus performer and antiquities enthusiast who left his mark in every tomb he discovered.

THE VALLEY OF THE KINGS

The Valley of the Kings is in fact two valleys, the East Valley, where most of the tombs have been found, and the West Valley, where there are only two royal tombs. It may have been the New Kingdom ruler Thutmose I (reigned 1493–1482 BC) who built the first royal tomb. The most richly decorated was the tomb of Seti I (early 13th century BC). The tomb of Tutankhamun (1333–1324) is one of the most modest of the royal tombs but the only one to be found intact with its treasures, and constitutes one of the richest archaeological discoveries ever made (*see illustration overleaf*). All the tombs were cut deep into the rock, and their different shapes and depths can partly be explained by the need to construct the passageways and chambers in stable rock. Many tombs have exploratory pits or passages which were begun and then abandoned.

The tomb of Seti I is usually seen as the finest of the New Kingdom tombs of the Valley of the Kings. It was discovered in 1817 by the Italian Giovanni Belzoni (*see illustration left*), who was responsible for much shifting of monuments out of Egypt. The tomb was soon on the itinerary of every traveller.

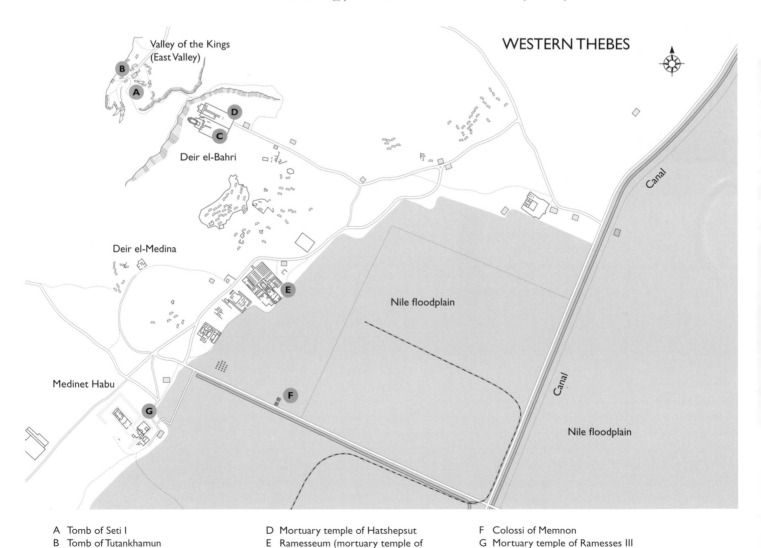

A Tomb of Seti I
B Tomb of Tutankhamun
C Temple and tomb of Mentuhotep

D Mortuary temple of Hatshepsut
E Ramesseum (mortuary temple of Ramesses II)

F Colossi of Memnon
G Mortuary temple of Ramesses III

Right: Among the most celebrated of the monuments on the West Bank are the Colossi of Memnon, two vast seated statues of Amenhotep III. They originally formed part of his mortuary temple, but it was so extensively looted that they now stand alone. In 27 BC an earthquake damaged the northern statue and each morning, as the sun warmed it, it produced an odd whistling sound. The Greeks named it Memnon after a Greek hero who sung to his mother, the dawn, each morning. It became a major tourist attraction for the Romans and the names of visitors were scratched on the feet. In AD 130 the emperor Hadrian visited. On the first morning nothing happened but on the second the statue behaved as hoped for and the imperial party was reassured that he had the favour of the gods. Unfortunately a later emperor, Septimius Severus, carried out a restoration programme on the head of the statue and it never whistled again.

Above: Detail from the tomb of Seti I: the sun god Ra in his sacred barque with attendants. Ra here takes on the attributes of the creator god Khnum (the ram's head), as Khnum was believed to guide the boat. He is identified as Ra by the sun disc between his horns and is protected by a serpent which coils around him. John Lloyd Stephens, in *Incidents of Travel in Egypt, Arabia Petraea and the Holy Land*, published in New York in 1837, describes his visit to the inside of the tomb of Seti I: 'All over the corridors and chambers the walls are adorned with sculptures and paintings in intaglio and relief, representing gods, goddesses, and the hero of the tomb in the most prominent events of his life, priests, religious processions and sacrifices, boats and agricultural scenes, and the most familiar paintings of everyday life, in colours as fresh as if they were painted not more than a month ago; and the large saloon, lighted up with the blaze of our torches, seemed more fitting for a banqueting hall for song and dance than a burial-place for the dead. All travellers concur in pronouncing the sudden transition from the dreary desert without to those magnificent tombs as operating like a scene of enchantment.'

THE MUMMY

Herodotus, writing in the 5th century BC when ancient mummification rituals were still being practised, reports as follows:

'In the best treatment, first of all they draw out the brains through the nostrils with an iron hook. When they have removed what they can this way, they flush out the remainder with drugs. Next they make an incision [with an obsidian blade] in the flank, through which they extract all the internal organs. They then clean out the body cavity, rinsing it with palm wine and pounded spices, all except frankincense, and stitch it up again. And when they have done this they cover the corpse with natron for seventy days, but for no longer, and so mummify it. After the seventy days are up, they wash the corpse and wrap it from head to toe in bandages of the finest linen anointed with gum… Finally they hand over the body to the relatives, who place it in a wooden coffin the shape of a man before shutting it up in a burial chamber, propped upright against a wall.'

Above: 'The impression is overwhelming. It is a sight I have never dreamed of seeing: the ante-chamber of a Pharaoh's tomb still filled with magnificent equipment … still standing as it was placed there when the tomb was last closed in antiquity.' These are the words of the Egyptologist James Henry Breasted as he gazed on the tangle of chariot parts and the three gold ritual couches which filled the entrance room to the tomb of Tutankhamun, and which are shown in this photograph, taken on the opening of the tomb by Howard Carter in 1922.

Right: Once the internal organs were removed and preserved they were placed in four jars, known as Canopic jars from the town of Canopus, where similar vessels with human-head stoppers had been found. Four so-called Sons of Horus each took responsibility for one part of the remains. The jars were placed in the tomb alongside the mummified body, which had itself been placed in a wooden coffin.

THE WORKERS' VILLAGE AT DEIR EL-MEDINA

When the pharaohs decided to move their tombs to the Valley of the Kings, they needed a permanent work-force to construct them. It seems to have been Thutmose I who first set up a workmen's village at Deir el-Medina in about 1500 BC. Excavations have uncovered a vast amount of information about the daily life of its inhabitants. Papyrus texts as well as fragments of writing on pottery sherds have survived and so have added to the details of the excavation. Even the library of a scribe, one Kenher-khepshef, has been found. He was clearly a man of learning, showing an interest in earlier Egyptian literature. There are also texts detailing the rituals followed in the village's own temple, of which Kenher-khepshef may have been a priest.

As the pharaohs wished their tombs to lie undisturbed, secrecy was vital. Deir el-Medina was a closed community of some 120 craftsmen with their families and a supporting staff, including laundresses, millers and messengers: probably a community of 1,200 people in all. It had its own police force. At night the village was shut off, by day the craftsmen were in the valley working. Temples provided their grain, donkeys carried water up from the valley. The members of the community even married among themselves, although children were able to leave the village when they were older. Many, however, chose to learn the skills of their fathers as painters, plasterers or sculptors and to remain in the village.

The workmen were given one free day in every ten, although this seems to have been increased to two in later years. Within the village the workers were free to decorate their own homes and keep their own tools. They fol-

Above left and above: The village of Deir el-Medina has proved one of the richest sources of information on the life of the ordinary Egyptian artisan, even down to the paints he used for decoration, here from one of the tombs.

lowed their masters in constructing tombs for themselves in a well-ordered cemetery on an adjoining hill-side. The houses were quite spacious, with four rooms for a typical family size of perhaps five. There were usually two living rooms, one with a cellar beneath where the family valuables were stored. A back room was used for sleeping, although often the roof seems to have been used and there was a kitchen area at the back. The most prominent of the household gods was Bes, the dwarf god, traditionally the protector of families. Worshipped alongside him was Taweret, the goddess of pregnancy, and Hathor, the daughter of Ra, who was associated with motherhood and female sexuality.

Tel el-Amarna: 'The Horizon of Aten'

Facing page: The distinctive face of Akhenaten.

Right: Akhenaten with his family worshipping the sun. This limestone palette comes from Amarna and it shows the radically different iconography that Akhenaten used in his art. One of the strangest innovations was the way he displayed himself and his family. Their necks are lengthened, their jaws are made heavier and their bellies and hips are swollen. The king wears a crown but his family (six daughters) are shown with elongated skulls. Scholars still debate whether they were really deformed in this way or whether Akhenaten was trying to show a royal family that was distinct from those of his subjects.

Below: Akhenaten's personal god, the sun (Aten), is the only god in the Egyptian pantheon ever to be represented as neither human nor animal. In one of its 'hands' it holds the ankh, symbol of life.

Amarna was born out of a political and religious crisis. The pharaoh Amenhotep III had been a major benefactor of the temples of Thebes and the mortuary temple he built for himself on the West Bank was one of the largest ever known. Yet his reign was a long one, 37 or 38 years (1390–1352 BC), and he appears to have become increasingly enfeebled with age. An examination of his mummified corpse suggests that he was in almost constant pain in his final years. It may have been for this reason that the temples, already centres of economic and spiritual influence, became so powerful that they threatened to undermine the position of the king. Yet though there might have been power struggles, no one would have expected the revolution that followed his death. His son succeeded as Amenhotep IV and he began his reign by visiting Thebes and gaining the traditional support of the god Amun for his rule. The temples he built there, however, were open directly to the sun and it was clear he had set his mind on a new path. This amounted to no less than replacing the traditional religion with a single unrelenting worship of the physical sun, Aten. The rejection of Amun, which involved defacing his name and image, meant that all the other complex cults and rituals which had become associated with Amun and which linked him to other deities were destroyed.

Amenhotep IV renamed himself Akhenaten: 'pious servant of Aten'. Everything was now focused on Aten, and the image of the god as a disc with rays coming downwards, with a hand at the end of each, became the religious symbol of the new regime. Akhenaten and his family, including his powerful queen Nefertiti, became the intermediaries between Aten and humanity.

No accounts of Akhenaten's personality survive. There were no conventions which allowed an individual to be described other than through his actions. Any personal motives went unrecorded. Akhenaten clearly believed himself to be the supreme human power in the land but it is impossible to say what spiritual or political forces drove him. Five years after his accession, he chose to break entirely with the settlements of the past and construct a new city where he and Aten would be honoured. It would be known as Akhetaten, 'The Horizon of Aten', but is usually referred to today by its modern name, Amarna.

Amarna was abandoned after Akhenaten's death (c. 1336), yet even though much of the stone was removed by later pharaohs for their own building projects, it has been possible to excavate large parts of the site. Among the most celebrated of the finds has been the limestone bust of Queen Nefertiti that made its way to Berlin. Nefertiti produced six daughters for Akhenaten but no son. Her title always remained 'great royal wife' but a second wife appeared on the scene, Kiya, who was given her own title, 'greatly beloved wife of the king'. She almost certainly was the mother of Akhenaten's only son, later known as Tutankhamun. Kiya mysteriously disappears about halfway through Akhenaten's reign and his daughters by Nefertiti reassert their status as his heirs.

Was this a palace plot by Nefertiti in revenge for her ousting as favoured wife? In the final years of his reign Akhenaten made Nefertiti co-regent. She had won the struggle to keep at the core of events.

Above: Two children of Akhenaten are depicted here. Meritaten, assumed to be his eldest daughter by Nefertiti, is shown with a misshapen head. There has been intense speculation over whether she suffered a genetic abnormality or not. Tutankhamun, here shown in a sculptured image from his tomb, was Akhenaten's son by a second wife, Kiya.

Right: This sculpture of Akhenaten kissing his daughter is an extraordinarily unconventional piece of Egyptian art, in a style and pose which vanishes completely after Akhenaten's reign.

THE SITE

For his new capital Akhenaten chose a site which lay roughly midway between Memphis and Thebes. There was desert on the eastern side of the river and a cleft in the rocks through which the sun could be seen rising. On the western side of the Nile, the land was already being cultivated and this was incorporated into the new site to provide its food. The total area of the site between boundary markers was 10 by 8 miles. The completeness of the break with the past was further symbolised by Akhenaten's decision to make tombs for himself and his family in the eastern hills. They were surrounded by those of his courtiers, but as the city was only occupied for a short period, perhaps some 17 years, only that of Akhenaten was finished. It copied the pattern of tombs in the Valley of the Kings, consisting of a passage through to inner chambers, but when one of Akhenaten's children died a special chamber was created for her. The reliefs of the family mourning over her dead body are especially poignant.

Above: The site backed by cliffs in which Akhenaten planned royal tombs similar to those in the Valley of the Kings.

Below: Fanciful image of Akhenaten and his queen distributing gifts from the Window of Appearance in the King's House.

THE OATH OF AKHENATEN, FOUND AT AMARNA

'My oath of truth, which it is my desire to pronounce, and of which I will not say "It is false" for ever and ever. Akhetaten extends from the southern tablet as far as the northern tablet, measured between tablet and tablet in the eastern mountain, likewise from the southwest tablet to the northwest tablet in the western mountain of Akhetaten. The area between these four tablets is Akhetaten itself: it belongs to Aten my father: mountains, deserts, meadows, islands, high ground and low ground, water, villages, men, animals and all things which my father Aten shall bring into existence eternally and forever. I shall not neglect this oath which I have made to the Aten my father eternally and forever.' (*Tr. Barry Kemp*)

THE PALACES

At the northern end of the site, on the river, was a well-protected palace, with barracks and granaries set against the cliffs. It was probably self-sufficient. Southwards along the river ran the Royal Road, which led to the Central City, as it is known. Akhenaten had abolished all the traditional religious festivals, and the image of his god was high in the sky, but he tried to create new processions centred on his passage from his palace along the Royal Road. They may have been a daily occurrence and are vividly portrayed in reliefs. In the centre of the city was another palace, the Great Palace, a ceremonial arena with an enormous central courtyard surrounded by statues of Akhenaten. A more intimate building, the King's House, had a Window of Appearance from where the pharaoh would offer rewards, often of gold, to favoured officials or make formal announcements of promotions. The building had all the functions of a court in the sense of being the place where Akhenaten met his officials and conducted business with them. One of the most fascinating discoveries here has been the 'Bureau for the Correspondence of the Pharaoh' where the famous Amarna Letters were preserved (*see overleaf*).

It was inevitable that there would be an impressive temple to Aten, and it was built on the eastern side of the Royal Road, close to the Great Palace. The vast enclosure runs back 800 yards from the road. The buildings were begun in brick, as if to mark them out before they were replaced in stone, but very little of the project was completed. Enough remains

to show that the normal pattern by which entry through a pylon would lead to a courtyard and then a columned hall was reversed so that the visitor would pass through a hall and then into the open courtyards. At the far end of the temple is an area described as 'The Aten is Found'. There is none of the darkness and lowered ceilings and heightened floors of traditional temples (*see p. 28*). Here everything had to be directly open to the sun. Through these courtyards were offering tables and it seems that these were loaded *en masse* during the rituals of presentation to the gods. A smaller temple to the south of the King's House is on the same model as the Great Palace but more like a private royal chapel. It may even have been designed as Akhenaten's mortuary temple as it is orientated towards his tomb in the cliffs.

One of the tablets found at Amarna, a record of the relationships between Akhenaten and his neighbours to the north. They have been called the founding documents of international diplomacy.

THE AMARNA LETTERS

One of the most extraordinary finds from Amarna is a series of clay tablets on which is inscribed the correspondence between Amenhotep III, his son Akhenaten, and the princes of Syria between 1360 and 1335. These so-called Amarna Letters are the earliest evidence of international diplomacy. They are inscribed in Akkadian cuneiform, the *lingua franca* of the ancient Near East.

Many of the correspondents had been subdued by earlier pharaohs of the New Kingdom and were careful to keep contact with their overlords. We see how the state of Mitanni, once an enemy of Egypt, has become an ally but is fearful of the rising power of the Hittites, who in their turn are threatened by the emergence of the Assyrians. One of the most fascinating letters from Ashur-uballit of Assyria is a tentative introduction of himself to Akhenaten, sent with the gifts of a chariot, two horses and a stone of lapis lazuli, in the hope that the pharaoh will recognise his status. Akhenaten appears to have been a skilful diplomat. The small vassal states of Canaan were continually engaged in low-level combat. Akhenaten condoned retaliation of those attacked but warned off any ruler who appeared to be becoming too powerful.

There is also evidence from reliefs at Amarna that Akhenaten held a great festival of royal princes or their representatives there. A letter from a more confident Ashur-uballit complains that his ambassador was left to stand for hours in the sun while the pharaoh remained under a canopy!

THE RESIDENTIAL QUARTER

The mass of the population of Amarna, which may have reached 30,000 to 40,000, lived in two suburbs. They were not well planned and houses jostled up against each other, though the larger houses of officials are impressive. They had their own enclosures, with room inside for a garden and workshops for craftsmen, granaries, and sheds for animals. The largest had a shrine in an ornamental setting. Statues of the pharaoh seem to have been common, as if to confirm the householder's allegiance. The haphazard nature of the building suggests that the poorer households were economically dependent on the richer, so one can talk of self-sustained villages with many households growing grain or raising cattle for the well-to-do.

A prominent feature of the town is the number of wells, far more than is known is other Egyptian cities of the New Kingdom, and it may be that Akhenaten saw this as a symbol of civilisation (in other cities water was brought in from the Nile in containers). Tomb reliefs suggest that leading officials would commute into the King's House in their chariots. They also seem to have had their own estates on the west bank. Even so, there is no sign of enormous opulence, and the distance between ruler and even the most senior of his subjects remained immense.

AFTER AKHENATEN: THE DEMISE OF AMARNA

Akhenaten had hoped that his dynasty would survive, and palaces were built for his eldest daughter, Meritaten, and for Smenkhkara, a shadowy figure, perhaps a son, or even Nefertiti herself in a new guise, who took on the role of Meritaten's consort. They did not survive long after Akhenaten's death and soon the young Tutankhaten succeeded. His mother may have been Kiya, another wife of Akhenaten. There must have been rivalry between her and Nefertiti, for in the twelfth year of Akhenaten's reign Kiya disappears from the records and Akhenaten's daughters by Nefertiti are given greater prominence.

On Smenkhkara's death the supporters of Tutankhaten may have seized their chance to reassert themselves. Tutankhaten abandoned his allegiance to Aten, renamed himself Tutankhamun and left the city to return to Thebes. The text on the so-called Restoration Stele from Tutankhamun's reign deplores the way the traditional gods have abandoned their support of Egypt. The failure of a recent military expedition to Syria is cited as one result of the apostasy.

One of the mysteries of Akhenaten's reign is where his body was buried. It is assumed that at first it was at Amarna itself, and there is a royal tomb there, but it is believed that his son Tutankhamun moved the body to the Valley of the Kings. There it may have been placed in the tomb of his mother, Queen Tiye, a tomb which had later been used for Tutankhamun's mother Kiya. Both bodies had gone when the tomb was excavated, but there was another coffin with a body inside from which all names had been erased. This gold collar carries one of the erased names. DNA tests suggest that the body was of a close relative of Tutankhamun but the age of the man at death, perhaps 20–25, seems far too young for it to be Akhenaten. The mystery continues, though sadly the original poor excavation and publication of the tomb's excavation (in 1907) have destroyed much of the evidence which might have resolved it.

Amarna, after this, had lost its purpose. Akhenaten's revolution had been personal to himself. While his officials showed loyalty to him and were prepared to have his statue in their homes, there is no knowing whether this represented a genuine conversion to the new religion or just a show of loyalty to a status quo. Excavations in the village of the workmen, for example, reveal that they remained committed to the household gods of tradition. The daily processions of the pharaoh from his 'home' palace to his 'business' palace along the Royal Road do not appear to have fostered allegiance to his god. It is interesting that Akhenaten made no attempt to create new festivals around the solar calendar, the equinoxes, for instance. What seems clear above all is that the simplicity of the cult failed to meet the ancient Egyptian desire for mystery. It passed away quickly and no one seems to have resisted the destruction of its symbols. While in Amarna, success in the afterlife appears to have depended on loyalty to Akhenaten, who is depicted on reliefs; now tombs revel in the restoration of the owner's relationship with the gods, and Osiris becomes an even more powerful god of the afterlife.

Abu Simbel

Temples as a display of royal power
13th century BC

Ramesses II was the last of the great Egyptian pharaohs, reigning for 67 years (1279–1213), and this following a period of co-regency with his father, Seti I. It was just over a thousand years since there had been so long a reign, that of King Pepy II, which saw the faltering end of the Old Kingdom.

Ramesses' fame came from his achievements in war—as they were proclaimed by himself—and from his massive building programme. He was also a man of impressive virility. His father had presented him with a harem when he had become co-regent, and he had no less than seven 'great wives', foremost among whom were Nefertari and Isetnefret. Forty daughters and 45 sons of Ramesses are listed in the records or shown in processions on temple walls. One of the most recent discoveries in the Valley of the Kings is a vast tomb for them, with over a hundred chambers for their bodies. Ramesses' twelve eldest sons all predeceased him.

Ramesses wished to have his name known throughout Egypt and his royal cartouche is found planted on buildings in almost every major town. In the north there is his capital, Pi-Ramesses, on the road up to the border with the Hittite empire but connected to a subsidiary of the Nile. It became a major trading centre as well as a defensive outpost in case of a Hittite resurgence after the stalemate battle of Qadesh (*see overleaf*). Then there was a temple to Osiris at Abydos, which is usually rated as the most beautiful that Ramesses ever

built. This was early in his reign and was probably begun when he was still co-regent with his father. The great building projects of Thebes, including Ramesses' mortuary temple, the Ramesseum, and the temples of Abu Simbel, are later. The enormity of these projects took their toll on Ramesses' resources, and standards fall off during the course of his reign. Reliefs carved early in the reign, for example, stand out from the stone. This was an expensive and time consuming process and was ultimately abandoned in favour of reliefs incised into the stone.

Below: The great temple of Abu Simbel as it appeared to the Italian adventurer Giovanni Belzoni in 1817, with the Queen's Temple below it, facing the river.

Facing page: The same two temples today.

'Having, as I supposed, seen all the antiquities of Abu Simbel, I was about to ascend the sandy side of the mountain by the same way I had descended; when having luckily turned more to the southward, I fell in with what is yet visible of four immense colossal statues cut out of the rock, at a distance of about two hundred yards from the temple; they stand in a deep recess, excavated in the mountain; but it is greatly to be regretted, that they are now almost entirely buried beneath the sands, which are blown down here in torrents.

The entire head, and part of the chest and arms of one of the statues are above the surface; of the one next to it scarcely any part is visible, the head being broken off, and the body covered with sand to above the shoulders; of the other two, the bonnets only appear. It is difficult to determine whether these statues are in a sitting or standing posture; their backs adhere to a portion of rock, which projects from the main body, and which may represent a part of a chair, or may be merely a column for support. They do not front the river, like the Queen's Temple, but are turned with their faces due north, towards the more fertile climes of Egypt, so that the line on which they stand forms an angle with the course of the river.'

Excerpt from *Travels in Nubia* by Johann Ludwig Burckhardt, 1813

The two temples at Abu Simbel were built far into Nubia, some 180 miles south of the First Cataract, traditionally the boundary between Egypt and the south. They were essentially a massive display of royal power over a subject territory. Both temples were ready for dedication in the 24th year of Ramesses' reign, with the day of the inauguration itself dated to February 1255 BC.

The collapse of Egyptian power in Nubia after the Twentieth Dynasty meant that the temples were abandoned, and slowly the sand began to blow up around the monuments. By the 6th century BC the sand had reached as high as the knees of the statues and when a group of Greek mercenaries passed that way it was there that they carved their names.

THE GREAT TEMPLE

The larger of the two temples was dedicated to Ramesses himself, and is one of the most famous and iconic sights of the ancient world. Four colossal seated statues of the pharaoh flank the entrance. At their feet bound Nubians emphasise the reality of their plight in the face of the power of Egypt and it is probable that gangs of Nubians were drafted into the building work to make the point. Standing alongside the statues of Ramesses are images of Ramesses' mother, his wife Nefertari, and his elder daughters. Above the door of the

Above: This relief from inside the Great Temple shows Ramesses II in the symbolic role of a hero warrior smiting and trampling on his enemies.

temple is a relief of Ra-Horakhty (*see p. 22*) with Ramesses offering obeisance in the guise of the goddess Ma'at, harmony. This remained visible even when the temples were later covered in sand and provided the incentive for the intrepid circus strongman-turned-archaeologist Giovanni Belzoni to scrape away enough sand to reach the top of the doorway in 1817 and enter the chamber for the first time in hundreds of years. Above the façade a frieze of baboons wait with upstretched arms to greet the rising sun.

As one enters the central doorway there is a vast columned hall which leads on into the inner sanctuary. The reliefs inside show Ramesses' victories and the destruction of his enemies, Nubians, Libyans and Syrians. On the north wall Ramesses cannot resist showing off his 'victory' at Qadesh, the battle against the Hittites he was lucky to survive (*see box opposite*).

Right: Relief of a Nubian captive from the Great Temple, symbolising the traditional Egyptian attitude to the peoples of the south, reinforced at Abu Simbel by the temples' position on the border between Egypt and Nubia.

THE DEITIES OF THE GREAT TEMPLE

Ramesses was a traditionalist. He knew his dynasty had only come into being because his grandfather Ramesses I had been handed power by the general Horemheb, who seized the throne after Tutankhamun's death. It was vital to confirm his legitimacy by honouring gods that had a nationwide role. Seated statues of Amun-Ra, Ptah and Ra-Horakhty line the back of the innermost shrine of his temple at Abu Simbel, with Ramesses himself in a deified form alongside them (*illustrated opposite*).

Amun-Ra was the manifestation of Ra in association with Amun, the most important god of Thebes. No Egyptian pharaoh after Akhenaten could avoid honouring Amun as the supreme deity. Once he had become sole ruler of Egypt, Ramesses II had enacted the ritual of the divine birth of the pharaoh through union with Amun. Ptah was a god of Memphis. From early times he was associated with craftsmanship, a role which seems to have developed into that of a creator god. Here he came into rivalry with Ra, the god of Heliopolis, and in the Old Kingdom the priests of Ra managed to keep him in the background. The priests of Memphis struck back by elevating Ptah as a god from whom all creation emanated, even Ra himself. He was often seen as the deification of the primeval mound which rose from the waters at the beginning of creation.

Horus the falcon-headed god was the symbol of successful kingship, a protective god of legitimate rulers from the Old Kingdom onwards. Legends told of his bitter rivalry with his uncle Seth, the god of chaos and confusion, and of his eventual triumph over him. As a god whose physical form hovered in the sky—Horakhty, 'Horus-on-the-Horizon'—it was natural that he should be absorbed by the sun god Ra, whose native town was Heliopolis (close to the modern Cairo).

Inside the temple hall a deified Ramesses is associated with Osiris, the god of the dead, and thus with eternal existence. Osiris, one of the most ancient of Egyptian gods, had long been associated with fertility and the resurrection of the dead to their new life in the underworld. Here Ramesses is shown in the traditional pose of Osiris, arms crossed with a sceptre in one hand and a flail in the other.

The deities of the Great Temple illuminated by the sun. The inner sanctuary still contains the block on which the sacred barque which bore the deities in procession rested between festivals, and there are four seated figures against the north wall, Ramesses and the three dedicatory gods, Amun-Ra, Ptah and Ra-Horakhty. Twice a year, on February 22nd and October 22nd, the sun's rays penetrate the inner chamber itself.

THE BATTLE OF QADESH

One of the most important reliefs within the Great Temple at Abu Simbel shows the Battle of Qadesh, the great confrontation between Ramesses and the Hittites in 1274 BC (*for the location of Qadesh, see map on p. 7*). Ramesses had campaigned into Syria early in his reign and had defeated allies of the Hittites, now firmly established as a successful empire. At Qadesh he was taken completely by surprise when a large Hittite army emerged from behind the city as the Egyptians passed on narrow roads.

The Hittites waited until the first division of the Egyptian army had passed, then as the third division was crossing a ford, attacked the second. Ramesses appeared to be trapped. As the propaganda accounts have it, 'His Majesty rose like his father Montu [the Theban god of war]; he seized his weapons of war; he girded his coat of mail.' He found himself almost surrounded by 2,500 Hittite chariots. In desperation, he called on Amun and Amun replied: 'Forward, I am with you, I, your father, my hand is with you, I prevail over a hundred thousand men, I am lord of victory, lover of valour'. Ramesses galvanised his shocked troops and managed to retreat with his army intact.

This was the 'victory' that Ramesses trumpeted to his subjects back home on his temple reliefs. They are found at Abydos and on no fewer than five temple façades in Luxor, again on the pylons before the Ramesseum in western Thebes, and here at Abu Simbel. It was without doubt the great moment in the king's life and it was perhaps his realisation that he had so nearly lost the battle that made his 'victory' such a mark of honour to him.

Ramesses made further raids into Syria but the most remarkable legacy of the campaigns was a state-to-state treaty with the Hittites made in the 18th year of his reign. It is the earliest such truce known in history.

THE SECOND TEMPLE

The second, smaller, temple at Abu Simbel is dedicated to one of Ramesses' chief queens, Nefertari. Ramesses, Nefertari and their daughter Meritamnu are recorded as sailing from the Delta upriver to the site of the temples for their inauguration in 1255 BC, but the inscription describing the inauguration does not mention Nefertari, nor do any later records. It can only be assumed that she died. Certainly we know that Ramesses' celebrated peace treaty after the Battle of Qadesh (*see previous page*) was cemented by marriage alliances, and that after Nefertari's death he married the daughter of the Hittite king.

The temple dedicated to Nefertari and Hathor is unique in Egyptian iconography in its portrayal of the queen, here in the centre, equal in size to the pharaoh Ramesses himself.

When she was alive, however, Nefertari had been Ramesses' favourite consort. The façade of her temple (often known as the Queen's Temple) has a statue of her on each side of the entrance, flanked by statues of Ramesses, and with their children between them. This public display on a temple façade of a pharaoh and his consort is unique in Egyptian iconography (although domestic unity had been a major feature of Akhenaten's depiction of his family; *see p. 36*). Inside, once again, there are reliefs of Ramesses slaying his enemies.

In this temple, Nefertari is honoured alongside Hathor, goddess of female sexuality and motherhood. Hathor was one of the most pervasive of the Egyptian gods. She could be shown as a lioness, aggressively protective of her young; as a cow, even in the pose of suckling a young pharaoh in this guise; or as a goddess of the underworld who would extend to the dead her traditional role of protectress of the sun during the night. Here at Abu Simbel she appears on a relief as a woman with a wig, horns and a sun disc on her head (*as shown in the drawing on p. 33*). In the sanctuary, she is carved out of the rock as a cow.

Edfu

Ptolemaic Egypt

The last dynasty of Egypt, the 31st, belonged to the Persians, who conquered the country and incorporated it into their empire. Their rule collapsed when Alexander the Great entered Egypt in 332 BC. The Persians had never been popular rulers, but the Greeks were well known to the Egyptians as traders, so the transition to Macedonian rule was not difficult. Alexander founded a port city, Alexandria, and then crossed the desert to the ancient oracle site of Amun at Siwa. The oracle dutifully announced that he was indeed the son of Amun, and Greek rule was thereby legitimised. After Alexander's death in 323, Ptolemy, one of his generals, seized Egypt for himself, officially proclaiming himself king in 305 BC. The ruling house he founded, the Ptolemies, remained rulers of Egypt until the suicide of Cleopatra VII (the famous Cleopatra of *Antony and Cleopatra*) in 30 BC, when Egypt was absorbed into the Roman empire.

Alexandria became the capital of Ptolemaic and Roman Egypt but it was always isolated from traditional Egyptian life. Egyptians were not even allowed to enter the city unless they had a specific duty to perform. The city was explicitly a Greek foundation with links to the rest of the Mediterranean and the Ptolemies' other possessions in Asia Minor. It was a city of extravagant royal display—but the Ptolemies also sponsored learning. The library made Alexandria the centre of science and mathematics in the Graeco-Roman world. Its lighthouse was one of the famous Seven Wonders.

In order to maintain control of Egypt's wealth the Ptolemies evolved a highly efficient system of tax collecting. One census of 258 BC demanded information of each city's water supplies, the quality of land and how it was cultivated and how much of it was owned by temples. Ptolemaic Egypt sounds an oppressive, bureaucratic state but there are also pharaonic proclamations which stress the importance of justice for the poor. Petitions from aggrieved peasants survive, and these surely would not have been made if trouble-makers were only ever simply crushed. The archaeological evidence suggests that a great deal of local economic activity flourished. At village level Greeks married Egyptians and their offspring often became bilingual intermediaries within the administration. Even so, there were periods of unrest when there were conflicts between rival branches of the ruling family and when substantial parts of the country fell outside the Ptolemies' control. There is little doubt that the Greeks, many of them living in semi-independent cities along the Nile, were a dominant and favoured elite.

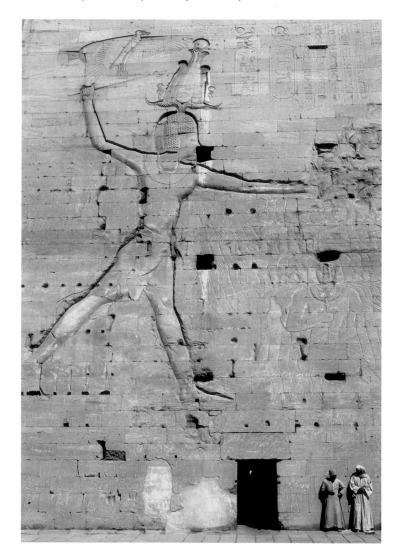

Detail from the Temple of Horus at Edfu. The Greek Ptolemaic pharaoh Ptolemy VIII (170–116 BC) is shown in a traditional pharaonic pose defeating his enemies.

Above left: Horus the falcon god, son of Osiris, who avenged his father's murder and emerged as protector deity of the pharaohs. Osiris (right), god of the dead, is usually shown as a mummiform king, holding the crook and flail, symbols of royal authority. While the living pharaoh was seen as the incarnation of Horus, so the dead pharaoh was identified with Osiris. Osiris was also a fertility god, and his skin is often shown green, a symbol of renewed growth and, by association, a token of resurrection.

THE TEMPLE OF HORUS AT EDFU

The Ptolemies knew that they had to respect religious tradition if they were to secure and preserve their authority among the local population. The temples were such a prominent and ancient feature of provincial life that they would act as centres of resistance if they were not supported. The first major building project of the Ptolemies outside Alexandria was the Temple of Horus at what is now Edfu in Upper Egypt. Edfu was important for the fertility of the broad stretch of land around it, while a road built by Ptolemy II ran across the eastern desert to the port of Berenike on the Red Sea. The trade which came through the town included war elephants and gold and also stone from the desert mines. The Ptolemies garrisoned the city and supplied it with fortifications, so they must have considered it strategically important.

The cult focus of the ancient Temple of Horus, which the Ptolemies reconstructed on a grand scale, was the legend of Horus conquering Seth. This goes back into the 3rd millennium BC and tells how the evil Seth murdered his brother Osiris and how Horus, as the son of Osiris, sought revenge. Seth took out Horus' eye and Horus castrated Seth (the destruction of male fertility was always a symbol of absolute and enduring victory). Horus eventually emerged as the winner, and as the protecting god of the pharaohs, but Seth lingered on as a god of storms and bad weather. The Ptolemies adopted the victory of Horus as their own to emphasise the legitimacy of their dynasty.

Edfu was abandoned in the 390s after the anti-pagan legislation of the Roman emperor Theodosius I, and many of its reliefs were defaced by Christian zealots. When the French archaeologist Auguste Mariette began excavating the site in 1860 he found the temple so deeply embedded in sand that houses had been built on top of the pylons. This is one reason why it remains the best preserved of all Egyptian temples.

Right: The Temple of Horus at Edfu. Reliefs of the god Horus appear on either side of the entrance, and at the outer edge of the pylons the pharaoh is shown in the act of crushing his enemies. The temple roof is perfectly intact and the original windows are in place, which allows modern visitors to see the sophisticated way in which the Egyptians used light to mark the transition from one part of the inner temple to another.

Dendera

Traditional festivals, in which gods visited one temple from another, continued under the Ptolemies, and each year the image of the goddess Hathor was brought by water from her temple at Dendera, north of Thebes, in the 'Festival of the Joyous Union'. Dendera was one of the Nile cities that benefited from its contacts with the trade routes of the eastern desert. Its earliest temples dated back to the Old Kingdom but Ptolemy II began a new temple to Hathor here in 125 BC, and building continued well into the Roman period.

Hathor was the goddess of motherhood and female sexuality. She was honoured at Dendera as the wife of Horus, and the relationship was formally celebrated by the annual visit upstream to Edfu. One of the symbols associated with Hathor is the musical rattling instrument known as the sistrum. It was used in her festivities, always by women, unless the pharaoh himself was present, in which case he led the music. A gilded relief of a sistrum (defaced in the Christian era) was on the south wall of the temple and there are also sistra depicted on the top of the columns of the inner halls.

Dendera was also unusual in being orientated so that the façade of the temple faced north. The traditional orientation of an Egyptian temple was from east to west, and so perpendicular to the Nile. Yet at Dendera the course of the Nile changed and itself ran from east to west. The builders decided to keep the traditional perpendicular orientation rather than place the temple alongside the river.

Sanctuary of Hathor, goddess of motherhood
Flourished 2nd–1st centuries BC

THE BIRTH HOUSES

One of the most important features of the temple at Dendera are the two birth houses. These commemorated the birth of Ihy, son of Horus and Hathor, who is always portrayed as a naked child. The earliest birth house at Dendera, on the western side of the entrance to the temple, was built by Nectanebo in the 4th century, when Egypt was ruled by the Persians, but these birth houses were used by Ptolemies for their own celebrations of the birth of the child-king, which they associated with their own divine birth as legitimate rulers.

Hathor is here shown suckling her son Ihy while the pharaoh, wearing the traditional red crown of Lower Egypt, makes her an offering of a sacred barque. Relief from the Roman birth house at Dendera.

The Romans built a second birth house at Dendera in front of the temple. The tradition of building a sacred lake within the temple enclosure continued under the Ptolemies and at Dendera there is a sanatorium nearby where visitors could stay before they were purified in the lake's waters. There are echoes too of the Greek healing shrines such as Epidaurus (*see p. 80*) in that the goddess was said to visit those sleeping there overnight and pass on advice on their illnesses.

THE TEMPLE OF ISIS

The Romans also built a temple to Isis within the sacred enclosure. When Osiris was cruelly murdered and dismembered by his evil brother Seth (*see p. 46*) his limbs were embalmed and reassembled by his wife Isis, who breathed life into them simultaneously, conceiving their son Horus. Inside the temple of Hathor, a relief shows Isis hovering over the mummified Osiris. The temple to Isis shows that there must have been some confusion over orientation. The outer rooms face east as would be expected in a traditional temple but the inner ones face north and are thus aligned with the temple of Hathor.

Above: Dendera. The remains of the Roman gate, above the encroaching sand.

This painting of the Zodiac at Dendera (1826) was taken from a drawing made by French engineers during Napoleon's expedition to Egypt while the original was still *in situ*. The woman and the hieroglyphics framing her are a later addition.

THE ZODIAC AT DENDERA

Inside the thick walls of the Temple of Hathor there are staircases which lead to the roof. There is a small kiosk here where each year ceremonies took place through which Hathor was united with the sun god. There were also two shrines to Osiris. On the ceiling of one of them is the famous Dendera Zodiac.

The earliest modern description and illustration of the Dendera Zodiac are to be found in Denon's popular account of his visit to Egypt as part of Napoleon's scientific study team between 1798 and 1801. The publication of a drawing of the Zodiac did it no favours. It was soon removed with hacksaws and spirited off to France, where it reappeared in the Royal Library after the restoration of Louis XVIII. In 1964 it was transferred from there to the Louvre. The French donated a copy to Dendera, which can be seen *in situ* today.

At the time of Napoleon's expedition, hieroglyphics had still not been deciphered and there was a major controversy over the dating of the Dendera Zodiac. Some dated it as far back as far as the Old Kingdom. When Champollion (*see overleaf, Rosetta Stone*) had mastered hieroglyphics, he spotted the names of Roman emperors among the reliefs and he placed it in the Roman era. Here he was too late. A precise analysis of the Zodiac suggests that it is consistent with a star pattern on 28th December 47 BC, when Cleopatra was still queen of Egypt. The Roman names are later additions.

The signs of the Zodiac originated in Mesopotamia and were not known in Egypt until the Ptolemaic period. The earliest example dates from 246–180 BC at Esna in Upper Egypt. Here and at Dendera the signs of the Zodiac are inserted among Egyptian celestial bodies. As the Zodiac became more popular in Egypt in Roman times, it was carved on the ceilings of tombs or inside the lids of sarcophagi. A common form was for the signs to be arranged in a circle around an Egyptian goddess such as Isis.

The Island of Philae

The island of Philae was completely submerged by the creation of Lake Nasser. In 1980 UNESCO transferred all its structures to the island of Agilkia, where they were built in exact conformity with the original site. Philae stood at the southern border of Ptolemaic Egypt, and the temple that was built here was probably designed to be a proclamation of Ptolemaic power to the southern tribes. Philae was astonishingly fertile as the island was made entirely of silt, and its sanctity was enhanced by linking it to the primeval mound that rose from the waters at the beginning of creation. The central temple was dedicated to Isis in her role as mother of Horus, and it became a famous centre of pilgrimage. It is relatively small compared to other temples of the Ptolemies. In the front courtyard there is a birth house, commemorating the birth of Horus, son of Isis and Osiris, known here as Harpocrates, 'Horus-as-a-Child'. There is another temple to Horus on the island where he is honoured as Harendotes, 'Horus in the role of the avenger' (of Osiris' murder by Seth; *see p. 46*). The best known monument on the island, the so-called Kiosk of Trajan, was originally designed as a resting place for the barque of Isis when the image of the goddess was carried outside her temple. These resting places were important stages on the routes of the festival processions, and memories of this may linger in the name 'Pharaoh's Bed' linked to the building.

Also on the island is a temple to Imhotep, honoured as the brilliant mind behind Djoser's stepped pyramid (*see p. 17*). Close to Philae, at Elephantine, the town which marked the beginning of the First Cataract and thus a break in navigation, a stele has been found which details a seven-year famine at the time of Djoser, caused by the failure of the floods. Imhotep, the stele records, had discovered that the god Khnum was responsible for the floods in this area and he was honoured in that his temple at Elephantine was accorded all the tithes from a long stretch of the river upstream from that point.

Pilgrimage centre, sacred to Isis 3rd century BC–Roman period

Left top: Harpocrates, the manifestation of Horus as a child, shown with his finger to his mouth (all children were represented like this) and with the plait of hair known as the sidelock of youth.

Left: Watercolour by David Roberts dated to 1846–50 showing what is traditionally known as the Kiosk of Trajan (Roman emperor AD 98–117), although it may date from a hundred years earlier than this. The Kiosk achieved extraordinary popularity with tourists in the 19th century. Amelia Edwards records in 1870: 'We skirt the steep banks and pass close under the beautiful little roofless temple commonly known as Pharaoh's Bed—the temple which has been so often painted, so often photographed that every stone of it, and the platform on which it stands, and the tufted palms that cluster round about it, have been since childhood as familiar to our mind's eye as the Sphinx or the pyramids.'

As part of his restructuring of the Roman empire in the 290s AD, the emperor Diocletian withdrew the boundary to Philae, and the gate which he built on the northern end of the island still stands. The last recorded hieroglyphic (of 24th August AD 394) was inscribed at Philae, and the closure of the temple in 536 during the reign of Justinian marks the end of traditional Egyptian religious worship.

Facing page: Relief of the goddess Isis from her temple at Philae.

THE ROSETTA STONE

'Since King Ptolemy, the ever-living, beloved of Ptah, the god Manifest and Beneficent, born of King Ptolemy and Queen Arsinoë, the father-loving gods, has conferred many benefits on the temples and those who dwell in them and on all the subjects in his kingdom, being a god born of a god and goddess—just like Horus, son of Isis and Osiris, who avenged his father Osiris…' (Tr. M.M. Austin)

The text on the Rosetta Stone refers to a decree issued at Memphis on 27th March 196 BC, the anniversary of the coronation of Ptolemy V by the priests there. The king is described using the traditional terminology of the pharaohs and is honoured for his support of the temples. Behind the scenes, however, there had been revolts against the Ptolemies in Thebes, and the native Egyptians had proclaimed their own kings. Ptolemy V had come to Memphis to reassert his legitimacy and punish the rebels, and the decree recognises the restoration of the tax concessions that the priests of Memphis had traditionally enjoyed.

Of course, the real importance of the Rosetta Stone comes later. It was discovered by the French at Rosetta in the western Delta in 1799 and handed over to the British on the surrender of Napoleon's troops in Egypt. It remains in the British Museum. The decree is in three scripts, Egyptian hieroglyphics, Egyptian demotic (the script increasingly used for non-religious texts, including administration and law) and Greek. Its potential as a means of deciphering hieroglyphs was recognised immediately: it was the French scholar Jean-François Champollion who grasped how the system worked. He started with the royal cartouches, which allowed him to relate the Greek 'Ptolemy' and 'Cleopatra' to their corresponding hieroglyphs. He understood how individual hieroglyphs had both phonetic and pictorial meanings and worked from there. Soon he had deciphered Ramesses and Thutmose from other cartouches on Egyptian monuments and knew the hieroglyphic symbols of an increasing number of sounds. By 1830 Champollion was able to publish the first Egyptian grammar. After fourteen hundred years of silence, the world of ancient Egypt spoke again.

OXYRHYNCHUS

Oxyrhynchus was a Greek town in Egypt some 112 miles south of Cairo, which grew in importance under the Romans. Its Greek name derives from the 'sharp-nosed' elephant-snout fish which was sacred in the region. The town became famous when the rubbish mounds around the city were being excavated by two Oxford archaeologists between 1897 and 1907 and an enormous cache of papyrus documents was uncovered. They date from between the 1st century BC and the 6th century AD and have added immensely to our knowledge of what provincial Greeks read during the period.

There are over a thousand fragments of Homer, an indication that he was honoured as a 'classic' author hundreds of years after his works were first written down. The 5th-century BC playwright Euripides was another favourite. In other words, educated Greek readers in Egypt were at home with their own literary tradition. Within a generation a sophisticated writer such as the 2nd-century AD philosopher and historian Plutarch was also being read in Oxyrhynchus. Many gaps in our knowledge have been filled and modern editions of the historian Herodotus depend on copies of his works found on the site. It is also interesting to see how Classical texts become scarcer as Christianity gains sway. By the time of Justinian (6th century AD) there are virtually no works by Classical authors.

Another trend that can be charted from the texts is the rise of the codex, or book of bound pages (the 'book' as we know it), at the expense of the traditional papyrus roll. The codex is first found in the 1st century AD when about 1.5 percent of texts are in this form. By AD 300 the proportion is 50 percent, rising to 90 percent by AD 500. Included among the texts are private letters and administrative and legal documents, providing vital evidence for our understanding of Roman Egypt.

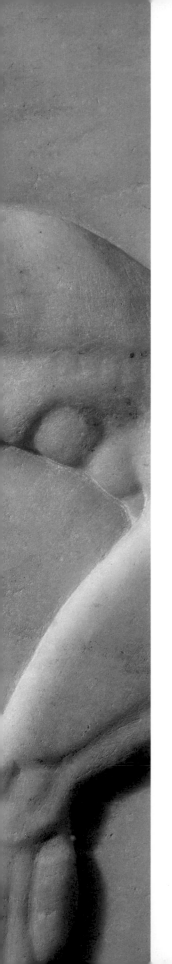

The ancient GREEK world

'No single training
Will look after all of us.
All skills are steep, but bring this prize
And boldly roar aloud
That by divine will this man has been born
Strong of hand, lithe of limb,
With valour in his eyes …'

Pindar's victory ode to Epharmostos, winner of the
wrestling at Olympia in 466 BC (*Tr. Maurice Bowra*)

THE ANCIENT GREEK WORLD

Adriatic Sea

Tiber

Cumae ○ ○ Neapolis (Naples)

Poseidonia/Paestum ○

Tyrrhenian

Sea

Sybaris ○

MAGNA GRAECIA

Croton ○

Ionian

Sea

Segesta ○

Selinous
(Selinunte) ○

Carthage ○

MAGNA

Sicily

Akragas ○
(Agrigento)

Gela ○

○ (Giardini Naxos)

○ Syracuse

MACEDONIA

EPIRUS   Mt Olympus ▲

Dodona ○   **THESSALY**

Pindus

Thermopylae ✕

Mt Parnassus ▲
Delphi ○   **BOEC**
Chaironeia ✕
Leuctra ✕
Plataea

Corinth ○
Elis ○   Nemea ○
Olympia ○   Mycenae ○
Epidaurus ○

PELOPONNESE

Pylos ○   ○ Sparta

M   e   d   i   t   e   r   r   a

0	50	100	150 miles
0	100	200 km	

Danube

Pontus Euxinus
(Black Sea)

PONTUS

THRACE

Bosphorus

Byzantium

Sea of Marmara

Dardanelles Troy

PHRYGIA

ASIA MINOR

Halys

Aegean

Pergamon

Lesbos Mytilene

LYDIA

TIA
Thebes
Eleusis
Marathon
Athens
Salamis

Sea

Samos

Meander

CARIA

Delos

Miletus

Halicarnassus

Paros

Naxos

Kos

Siphnos

Cnidos

Milos

Uluburun
wreck site

Rhodes

Cyprus

PHOENICIA

Malia
Knossos

Phaistos *Crete*

n   e   a   n   S   e   a

Nile

EGYPT

Historical overview

MINOANS AND MYCENAEANS

The rocky landmass of the Greek peninsula and the islands of the Aegean Sea were to produce one of the greatest civilisations the world has ever seen. The earliest important Aegean culture was that of the Minoans on the island of Crete. Named after their legendary founder, King Minos, they exploited the island's fertile valleys so successfully that they had surplus produce to trade abroad—in the eastern Mediterranean and Egypt—for the metals and other raw materials they lacked. As their rulers grew wealthy, palace-like complexes emerged on several sites, notably Knossos near the northern coast. These served as powerful administrative and ritual centres, and though destroyed in c. 1700 BC, probably by an earthquake, they soon re-emerged in even greater splendour. Minoan civilisation flourished until further destructions took place about 1450. Incomers from the Greek mainland, the Mycenaeans, now became the rulers of Crete.

The Mycenaeans emerged from the rugged landscape of mainland Greece about 1600. Like the Minoans, they must have exploited the limited fertility of their land effectively enough to build up a surplus of goods, though they did also mine metals at Lavrion near Athens. The strongholds of the Mycenaean chieftains were on low hills, and their palaces and ceremonial centres were concentrated there. They reached the peak of their power in the 14th century BC, when they absorbed Crete and traded west to Italy and east to Egypt and the coastline of Asia. Mycenaean civilisation collapsed between 1200 and 1100 BC as the complex trading relationships of the eastern Mediterranean fragmented.

Revival was slow, but by the 8th century the Greek world was developing a distinctive culture based on small city-states which shared important religious centres such as Olympia and Delphi. The most prosperous Greek city of the 7th century was Corinth. The city controlled the Isthmus, the narrow piece of land between the Peloponnese and mainland Greece, over which ships could be dragged so as to avoid the tricky passage around the coast to the western Mediterranean. This was an age when the Greeks became major colonisers, settling the fertile lands of Sicily and southern Italy and even founding Marseilles (the Greek Massilia) in about 600 BC. Corinth is credited with the first stone temples and the invention of the trireme, with its three banks of oars (*see p. 97*), later adopted by the Athenians as their war machine.

see p. 97

Right: The Minoan civilisation was known for its beautifully frescoed palaces, network of elegant country houses and advanced towns. The frescoes, in particular, provide an idealised picture of a life of exuberant fertility and carefree enjoyment. This fresco of a blue monkey was found in a house close to the palace of Knossos, Crete.

Facing page: One of the cupbearers from the famous Procession Fresco at the palace of Knossos, recreated from fragments by Arthur Evans and his team in the early 20th century.

Below: There was always a martial element to Mycenaean civilisation and it is not surprising that the epics of Homer draw on the exploits of their warriors. This detail from the so-called Warrior Vase (c. 1200 BC), found at Mycenae, is a very rare example for its date of human figures being represented on pottery instead of in wall frescoes, where they are common.

Previous page (p. 52): Marble relief of athletes wrestling (c. 510 BC) from Attica, Greece.

THE ARCHAIC AGE AND THE PERSIAN WARS

It was in the 6th century BC, the Archaic Age, that Athens emerged as a leading city. The Athenians had a large plain of agricultural land, a growing trade in oil, and an effective ruling family who began to glorify the Acropolis with temples. Finely-painted Athenian pottery flooded the markets. This was also the age of the first philosophers, notably in the city of Miletus on the coast of Asia Minor, and of developments in sculpture. By 510, the Athenians had begun to transfer power to a citizen assembly. Here was the birth of a totally new concept in politics: democracy.

Sparta, in the central Peloponnese, offered a contrast. Their subject population, the helots, were the only Greeks who were slaves. Spartan control was maintained by ruthlessly focusing on military training and the Spartan armies proved a formidable fighting force.

Then came the defining moment in Greek history. The Persian empire had successfully conquered the ancient civilisations of the Near East. It now set out to absorb the Aegean world. The first expedition of 490 ended in failure after the stunning victory of the Athenian forces at Marathon. The second, ten years later, presented a greater challenge. A vast army and navy led by Xerxes made its way across the northern shores of the Aegean down into mainland Greece. It was held briefly at the pass of Thermopylae by a courageous band of 300 Spartans. However, by the autumn, Athens had been sacked and it seemed that the Persians would triumph. Only a brilliant counter-attack by the Athenian navy at Salamis and then a defeat of the remaining Persian armies at Plataea by a combined Greek army dominated by the Spartans, blunted the attack and the Persians were forced to withdraw.

After the Persians, the main challenge to the hegemony of Athens came from the town of Sparta. The Spartans' obsession with military training has fascinated many right up to modern times. This painting by Edgar Degas (National Gallery, London) shows naked Spartan youths exercising together with Spartan girls, also naked except for their famous slit skirts, which so scandalised the Athenians.

The narrative of these wars is to be found in the *Histories* of Herodotus, written later in the century. The Greek *historia* means enquiry, and Herodotus analysed the opposing sides in detail, arguing that, in essence, it was the Greek love of freedom that had triumphed over Persian despotism. Here was another Greek contribution to Western civilisation: the writing of history. The definition of Greek cultural superiority as a contrast to its barbarian neighbours is a key feature of the Classical Age which now dawned.

THE CLASSICAL AGE AND THE PELOPONNESIAN WAR

Athens thrived after her victory over the Persians. She was now the dominant city-state of the Aegean, and her success ushered in the Classical Age, traditionally dated from the Battle of Salamis in 480 to the death of Alexander the Great in 323 BC. Athens ruthlessly set about transforming the league of Greek city-states into an empire. In Athens itself, although the citizen assembly took full power (*see p. 92*), strong leaders could still maintain their influence, and it was Pericles, re-elected year on year as one of the city's generals, who inspired the transformation of the Acropolis into a showpiece of architectural glory centred on the Parthenon. On the slopes of the Acropolis, the Theatre of Dionysus saw the birth of drama. This was also the great age of sculpture. The stiff standing figures of the Archaic Age relax and become transformed into the aesthetically pure and beautifully modelled statues of the 5th century by Pheidias and Polyclitus, who were followed in the 4th century by Praxiteles and Lysippus (*see illustrations opposite*).

But all was not at peace, for there was the question of Sparta. Sparta had won glory in the defeats of Persia but could never reconcile itself to the growing power of Athens. Some kind of conflict was inevitable: and in 431 it came, in the form of the so-called Peloponnesian War, which dragged on for 27 years, ending

with Athenian surrender in 404 BC. The war was written up in another fine history, by Thucydides, who had no illusions about the horrors that war brings, not least in the unscrupulousness of those who use power and violence ruthlessly for their advantage. More scientific than Herodotus, his narratives remain compelling.

The Spartans, however, had never learned the arts of diplomacy, and although they spared Athens from destruction, their clumsy political manoeuvrings left them isolated. In 371, the unthinkable happened. The Spartan army was destroyed by a force from another Greek city, Thebes, at the Battle of Leuctra in Boeotia. The Thebans failed in their turn to exploit their victory and the Greek world entered a period of anarchy, with no one power able to dominate others. The confusion was sensed by a canny and determined ruler from a kingdom at the northern edge of the Greek world: Philip of Macedon. Philip kept an army in place all year round, he bound his generals to him by grants of booty and he was adept at sieges. He moved steadily into Greece. In vain one of Athens' greatest orators, Demosthenes, warned of the threat in a series of speeches, his famous 'Philippics'. In 338, the combined army of Thebes and Athens was routed by Philip at the Battle of Chaironeia. Philip was assassinated in 336 but his death did not spell the end for Macedonia. For Philip had a son who was to conquer more territory than his father can ever have dreamed of. That son was Alexander the Great, and his extraordinary conquest of Persia was a turning point in the history not only of Greece but of the entire Classical world.

KEY DATES IN ANCIENT GREEK HISTORY

2000–1450 BC: Minoan civilisation on Crete

1600–1100 BC: Palaces and shaft graves at Mycenae

c. 1180 BC: Fall of Troy

8th century BC: The age of Homer

776: The first Olympic games

490 BC: First Persian War; Battle of Marathon

480 BC: Second Persian War: victory for the Persians at Thermopylae and for the Greeks at Salamis. The age of the Athenian empire begins

447 BC: Pericles begins the Parthenon

431–404 BC: Peloponnesian War

405 BC: Athens surrenders to Sparta, ending the Peloponnesian War

386 BC: Plato's Academy founded

371 BC: Spartan army defeated by a force of Thebans. Greece descends into internal chaos which leaves the country vulnerable

338 BC: Greeks defeated by Philip of Macedon, father of Alexander the Great

Large Greek sculptures in stone appear in the 7th century BC through the inspiration of Egypt. The first efforts are rigid, slavishly copying models of Egyptian figures, but gradually the sculptors relate their bodies more to real bodies. The youth carrying a calf to sacrifice (left centre), found on the Acropolis in Athens, is dated to about 560 BC and is still rather formal, typical of the *kouroi*, the stiff votive statues of the Archaic Age. A hundred years later, the *Riace Warrior* (top left), one of two superb examples of bronze sculpture found in a shipwreck off southern Italy, and possibly from an Athenian victory monument in Delphi, is heroic but realistic. The *Spear Bearer* by Polyclitus, here in a marble copy of the bronze original of c. 440 BC (above left), attempts to show that a body does, in reality, conform to ideal proportions. This was the supreme achievement of Classical sculpture.

Transitions in pottery are equally marked. In the 7th and 6th centuries BC, exuberant pottery from Corinth, which draws on Oriental motifs, dominates the market (left bottom). In the mid-6th century, Athens seizes the initiative, exploiting its excellent local clay to provide the superb black-figure ware (black figures on a clay-coloured ground; above). In an artistic revolution of the 520s, colours are reversed and red figures, rendered with much more expression, appear on a black ground. The example here (above top), showing Europa's abduction by the bull, is attributed to the Berlin Painter, one of the most talented of all the Attic vase painters.

Knossos

Right top: A view of the reconstructed portico of the northern entrance to the palace at Knossos with the hypostyle (pillared) hall just inside it. These reconstructions by Arthur Evans (mainly of the 1920s) have been highly controversial: are they accurate, do they illuminate the palace for visitors or should the ruins have been left as they were excavated? One observant visitor noted the similarity of the coloured pillars to the Art Deco of the 1920s.

Right: The Minoan 'palaces' served as important centres for storage and the redistribution of resources, grain and oil in particular. Some have even argued that this was the primary function of the complex. As many as 1,100 *pithoi,* giant storage vases, have been found in Knossos.

Below: The early Kamares ware is particularly lively in its decoration, as seen here in a jug of 1800 BC from another Minoan palace site, Phaistos. The teapot-like spout is a particularly Minoan feature.

Knossos was always the pre-eminent settlement in Minoan Crete, occupied long before the palace for which it is famous was built there. The site was set on a low hill in a fertile area where there was also access to wood and stone. It was protected from attack from the sea but close enough to it (some four miles inland) to benefit from maritime trade. Occupation of the site goes back to c. 7000 BC, making it the earliest permanent settlement known in the Aegean. The first settlers appear to have been migrants drawn to the area for its fertility.

The first 'palaces' emerge in about 1950 BC, not only at Knossos but at other sites such as Phaistos, on the south coast, and Malia to the east of Knossos. They are so different from any Minoan structures known before that it is possible that the model was borrowed from one of the Near Eastern civilisations with which the Minoans were in contact. Why the palaces emerged at the same time but retained their own spheres of influence remains unclear.

Knossos as it survives today is the creation of Arthur Evans, an English archaeologist who became fascinated with the site after he had seen the attractive stone seals which had come to light there. His excavations began in 1900, and it was he who coined the word Minoan for the civilisation he uncovered, and he who termed the buildings 'palaces'. His interpretation of the functions of each room at Knossos and his vivid reconstruction of parts of it have been influential to this day, though there is possibly little truth in them.

The 'palaces', in fact, served many purposes and they all had certain features in common. There was always a Central Court at the core of the structure, for example, and this was orientated on a north–south axis. The surviving rooms of the first Knossos palace show that grain and other produce was stored here, partly in pits in the floors of a western 'court' or in the famous giant *pithoi.* Ceramics were also among the stores, while cloth was probably woven inside the palace. Whoever ruled here was accumulating goods, presumably for redistribution. Written accounts, first in what is known as Cretan hieroglyphic and later in Linear A (*see p. 68*), list what is stored. Other rooms in the palace appear to have had a ritual function. Some of the ceramics (known as Kamares ware, after the cave near Phaistos where the type was first identified) are particularly fine. They were used as ritual vessels for ceremonies in the palace.

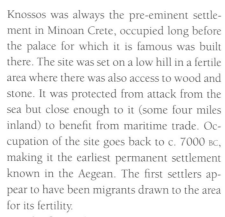

When talking about Crete, archaeologists refer to an Old Palace period and a New Palace period. This is because in about 1700 BC the first palaces were brought down, probably by one or more earthquakes. The Minoans survived the catastrophe, and over the next hundred years the palaces were rebuilt in an even more splendid form. It is from this New (or Second) Palace period that most of the remains of Knossos date. It was a time of great prosperity and apparent security. In the countryside, elegant 'country houses' are linked to the palaces and towns which surround them.

In the middle of the 15th century BC a new catastrophe struck Crete. The palaces and country houses were destroyed but Knossos was left intact. The event has perplexed historians. Did the rulers of Knossos, already the most important site on

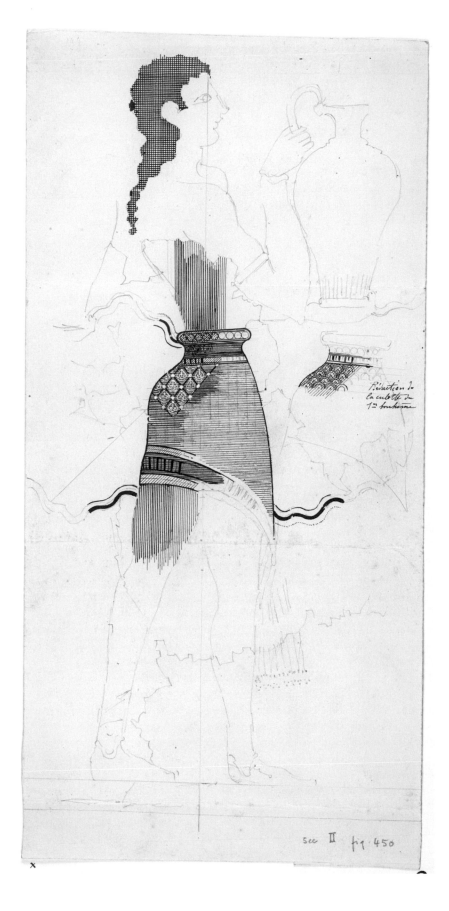

Réduction de
la culotte de
1ᵉ touriesne

see **II** fig 450

Controversially, Sir Arthur Evans decided to restore part of the palace of Knossos. He realised from the surviving fragments how stunning it must have been visually, with its façades, columns and staircases and the colourful and lively decoration on the walls. Knossos was a centre of fresco painting, and under Evans's inspiration restorations and recreations spread through the palace. This ink sketch, executed by Emile Gilliéron, an artist and restorer employed by Evans, shows clearly how many traces of paint remained and how much was conjecture.

Typically a decorated Minoan room would exploit the space of the walls without clear boundaries. Friezes and processions are common. Convention required men to be painted in reddish brown and women in white (it was the same in ancient Egypt) but all are shown as young adults. Compared to the detailed and largely accurate wall paintings in Egyptian tombs, imagination was allowed a great deal of play, but this was a light-hearted and idealised world. The images have certainly provided a softened image of Cretan society. At the shrine of Anemospilia, near Knossos on the slopes of Mount Juktas, remains suggest that a youth might have been sacrificed to ward off, unsuccessfully, an earthquake, evidence which provides an altogether more sobering picture.

Detail of the famous frieze of dolphins and fish in the room that Arthur Evans dubbed the Queen's Megaron, in the palace at Knossos.

the island, ruthlessly conquer rival palaces? Was there a series of earthquakes which may have shattered the relationships between the sites and led to a systems breakdown? And how do the Mycenaeans (*see p. 64*), whose culture appears on the island shortly afterwards, fit in? Had they been called in as allies of a Cretan ruler, or did they independently take advantage of the collapse? Knossos survived for another 75–100 years, as part of Mycenaean civilisation, but much of the rest of the Minoan world never recovered.

THE NEW PALACE AT KNOSSOS

The new palace at Knossos occupies a site some 440 ft square and was approached through the town from the west by a Royal Road. Public rituals may have been celebrated in an open 'Theatral Area', and a western court perhaps served as some kind of entrance hall. This western façade was designed to impress. The impact of the dressed stone, the painted columns and the formal staircases must have been immense. The complicated way into the palace from the west, through a corridor lined with a processional frieze, would have added to the awe of the visitor.

The palace remained a major centre for storage and manufacture, but on the western side of the Central Court were hidden ritual rooms. Arthur Evans, whose interpretation of the site still defines the names of the rooms, called the most secluded the 'Throne Room', but there is no evidence that a ruler presided here. The elegant 'throne' may instead have been the seat of a priest. A basin found here is more suggestive of rituals of purification. There was a shrine on the west side of the Central Court and rooms for the storing of ritual vessels behind it. There is some evidence from frescoes that the ceremonies spilled out from the palace so that they could be seen by assembled crowds.

An imposing staircase, one of the finest achievements of Minoan architecture, leads down from the Central Court to a lower storey to the east, with rooms that were believed by Evans to be the domestic quarters of the ruling family. Evans designated a 'Hall of the Double Axes' for the king and a 'Megaron', or royal hall, for the queen. Whether a king presided here or not, these are the most sophisticated rooms in the palace. They are even arranged so that they can be opened up fully in the summer heat or subdivided into smaller apartments to be heated in winter. Light is filtered in through light wells in the ceiling.

BULLS & CRETE

Legends of Minos, king of Knossos, run far back in Greek history. One account starts with Europa, who is carried off by Zeus disguised as a bull to Crete where she gives birth to three sons, one of them Minos, the other two gods of the afterlife. Homer's *Iliad* tells how Zeus granted Minos rule over Crete, and the story becomes elaborated in other traditions too. As a sign of his favour, Zeus sends Minos a great bull from the sea. He is required to sacrifice it but, reluctant to lose such a fine beast, he hides it in his herd and substitutes a weaker animal. Zeus is furious and he fills Minos' wife Pasiphaë with lust for the bull. The offspring of their union is the Minotaur, a man with a bull's head. So shameful is this hybrid animal that Minos conceals it deep inside his palace, in a labyrinth designed by the master craftsman Daedalus. Every seven years a tribute of seven youths and seven maidens is demanded of the Athenians for the Minotaur to devour.

Theseus, prince of Athens, is determined to thwart Minos. He travels with the victims and arrives at Knossos. Ariadne, the daughter of

Ariadne has been promised that Theseus will take her home to Athens as his bride, but he abandons her on the island of Naxos. She passes a curse on him. Theseus has told his father, Aegeus, that he will hoist a white sail on his ship if he returns from Crete victorious, but the curse causes him to forget and Aegeus, seeing the original black sail on the returning vessel, throws himself off the cliff.

This may all be legend, but Homer writes of Crete as a rich island with 90 cities of which Knossos is supreme, while the historian Thucydides, writing in the 5th century BC, names Minos as the organiser of the first known navy, through which he controlled much of the Aegean, settling colonies and driving out the pirates. This echoes what is known of the Minoan empire. Athens may well have been a subject city of the Minoans at this very early stage in its history.

Arthur Evans, the first major excavator of Knossos, had been caught up in the legends of Minos ever since he had read them in Charles Kingsley's *Heroes*. He allowed his fascination to shape his interpretations of the site. When he came across the horn-shaped stone or plaster sculptures which were common in early Minoan palaces, tombs and shrines—'horns of consecration' as he called them—he insisted that they represented the horns of bulls and thus formed another element of the bull worship that he felt was so much a part of Cretan ritual. Yet they are the subject of much controversy. Are they really horns at all? They may instead be representations of the Egyptian hieroglyph for the horizon.

As Evans uncovered the central rooms and passageways of the palace, he seemed almost to believe that the Minotaur had actually lurked there. A fragment of stone with part of a bull's leg on it was interpreted as coming from the gateway to the labyrinth. Evans became especially excited about the famous bull-leaping fresco from the 'Throne Room'. Accepting the convention that figures in white were female and the one in red was male, he created the story that this was an early form of spectator sport in which the participants were being sacrificed. Thus he could link it to the tribute of youths and maidens demanded by the

Minos, falls in love with him, and helps him find his way into the labyrinth with a concealed sword. Theseus unravels a ball of string as he enters so that he can find his way out. Deep inside the labyrinth there is a brutal struggle in which Theseus triumphs. The slaying of the Minotaur is a popular theme on Greek pottery and survives into the Roman world too.

Minotaur. His interpretation is not accepted by all, however and there is still speculation over whether the scene represents an actual sport or an idealised contest between humans and bulls. The gender of the leapers is still debated, too, though when the fresco was first reassembled in 1901 it became a great favourite with suffragettes as it seemed to show men and women exercising together on a equal basis.

Mycenae

'Palace' complex of the
Mycenaeans
Flourished 1600–1100 BC

'*Crossing a barren valley, I saw the ruins of Mycenae on the side of a facing hill. I particularly admired one of the gates of the city fashioned out of gigantic blocks of stone that are set in the rock of the mountain itself and seem to form part of it. Two colossal lions carved on each side of the gate are its only ornament; these are represented in relief and stand on their hind legs … The heads of the lions are missing. Not even in Egypt have I seen such imposing architecture and the desert that surrounds it adds still further to its grandeur …*'

François René de Chateaubriand, passing in the early 19th century, was only one of many visitors who were taken by the ruins of Mycenae, its Lion Gate, the surrounding beehive tombs, and its fine walls, believed to have been built, so legend said, by the Cyclopes, the family of one-eyed giants.

Already in Homer, Mycenae, 'rich in gold', was woven into legend. Agamemnon, the leader of the Greeks at Troy, was the son of Atreus, its king. Pausanias, the author of a famous gazetteer of Greece of the 2nd century AD, tells of a 'Treasury of Atreus' somewhere outside Mycenae's walls while Agamemnon and his followers lay buried within the city. The tombs of Clytemnestra and Aegisthus, he went on, were outside, as they had not been seen worthy of an honoured burial inside. It was this legend (*see caption, left*) which inspired the wealthy speculator-turned-archaeologist Heinrich Schliemann, who had already cut through the walls of Troy, to excavate at Mycenae in 1876.

Facing page: This view of Grave Circle A at Mycenae is taken from the palace citadel. The circle had been filled with graves by 1450 BC and these were revered enough to be enclosed in newly-built fortifications, seen beyond them, when the site was strengthened in the mid-13th century BC. The famous Lion Gate (*illustrated overleaf*) was constructed at the same time.

Right: The family of Atreus was haunted by a troubled past and this was darkened further when Atreus' son Agamemnon, ruler of Mycenae, had to sacrifice his daughter Iphigenia in order to secure a good wind for his expedition to Troy to avenge the abduction of his half-sister-in-law Helen. He returned with the Trojan princess Cassandra as his captive concubine. Agamemnon's wife Clytemnestra, aided and abetted by her ambitious lover Aegisthus, murdered the king and ruled for seven years before Agamemnon's son Orestes killed his mother and her lover in revenge. This romantic early 19th-century painting by the French artist Pierre-Narcisse Guérin shows Clytemnestra, dagger in hand, egged on by Aegisthus to murder her sleeping husband.

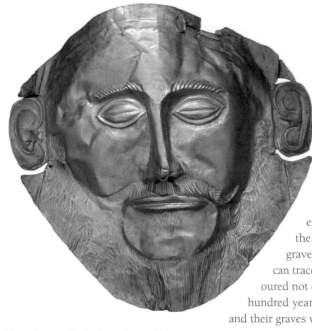

THE TOMB TREASURES

One of Schliemann's first trenches broke into a series of shaft tombs, six in total, with 19 bodies: nine men, eight women and two children. Five male warriors lay with gold masks and the finest of these was proclaimed by Schliemann, with the abandon for which he became notorious, to be the mask of Agamemnon himself. It took more scholarly assessment before the graves were dated to between 1600 and 1450 BC, long before any conceivable date for the Trojan War.

The finds of the shaft graves, now in the National Archaeological Museum in Athens, are a fitting introduction to Mycenaean civilisation, which arises quite suddenly in the 17th century BC, in a series of sites in the Peloponnese and central Greece. The earliest graves show few signs of wealth. With time, however, the burials become richer and one can trace the rise of an elite. The deceased in Schliemann's so-called Grave Circle A were honoured not only with rich grave goods, but also by being buried within walls of the citadel. Three hundred years after they had been buried, the family of Grave Circle A were still being venerated and their graves were never robbed.

Above: Just inside the Lion Gate is Grave Circle A, where Schliemann found the famous gold mask pictured here, which he proclaimed to be the Mask of Agamemnon. There were other masks in the graves but this one is especially well preserved and, unlike the others, has a distinctive upturned moustache. There has long been controversy over whether Schliemann faked it.

Right: The Lion Gate, whose colossal lintel is surmounted by a relief of a column flanked by lionesses. It forms part of the reconstruction of the citadel during the rising tensions of the 13th century and remains one of the most evocative survivals in Mycenae.

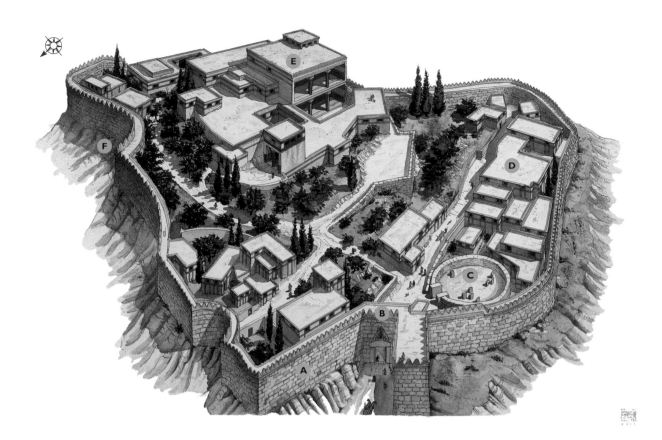

THE CITADEL

The Lion Gate, the entrance to Mycenae's citadel, dates from about 1250 BC. At the citadel's highest point stood the palace. Arriving at the palace, the visitor would have made his way through a porch, left an offering on a table of purple limestone and then gone through two entrance rooms before reaching the megaron, the hall where the king sat in honour on a throne before a ceremonial hearth. Fragments of decorated plaster show that these rooms were richly decorated. Residential quarters lay to the north of the hall.

The citadel at Mycenae was not simply the ceremonial stronghold of the ruler, it was a religious and craft centre which also acted as a storage centre for goods brought in from the fields. Though hard to interpret with any certainty, there are signs of an altar, a ritual bath for purification and small statues, probably of a warrior goddess, one of which is set up as a figure to which offerings had been made. The frescoes of the most important room show female figures which might also be goddesses. Other than showing that religious ritual was an important element of Mycenaean life—and where in the ancient world was it not?—it is hard to make much sense of this.

More is known about the economy of the palace, especially if the evidence found on the Linear B tablets at Pylos (*see box overleaf*) can be assumed to be typical also of Mycenae. While there remained some free enterprise (a house at Mycenae is known as that of the Oil Merchant), the palace controlled many artisans. Raw materials such as bronze, clay and textiles were brought in for them to work on, and the finished goods were then distributed from the palace. It is even possible to distinguish different types of cloth allocated by status among the different members of the hierarchy. Many storage jars for grain or oil have been found within the citadel. Among the most accomplished craftsmen of Mycenae must have been the stone workers, and the engineers who supported them. The Cyclopean walls needed careful planning and their survival testifies to the skill of the planners.

A rebuilding of Mycenae with strengthened walls in the middle of the 13th century BC has been seen as a response to the growing insecurity of the Mediterranean world in this period. In about 1200 a subterranean water cistern, fed by external pipes, was built into the rock, a sign that sieges might be expected. A whole series of destructions and burnings follow in the 12th century, and although survivors continued to inhabit the site for some time, by 1100 Mycenaean civilisation was dead. Only its walls survived.

MYCENAE: A RECONSTRUCTION OF THE CITADEL

A The 'Cyclopean' walls, named thus by later explorers because the stones are so massive that it was believed they must have been constructed by giants (Cyclopes)

B The Lion Gate, main entrance to the citadel

C Grave Circle A, contained within the citadel walls, and thus presumed to contain the bodies of a venerated clan

D Houses and shrines stood here, including the house where the famous Warrior Vase was found (a detail of its decoration is shown on p. 56)

E The palace itself stood on the highest part of the acropolis. Like the 'palace' at Knossos, this is more likely to have been a ritual centre and a centre for the storage and distribution of goods and commodities, not simply the residence of a ruler. Behind the palace was the so-called artisans' quarter

F An underground cistern was built into the rock here in the late 13th century BC, perhaps a sign of insecure times, when the people of Mycenae needed to secure for themselves a water supply should they have to take refuge within their walls

THE THOLOS TOMBS

Despite the splendour and seeming impregnability of the Lion Gate, it is outside the citadel, in the beehive tombs, that the finest examples of Mycenaean stonework survive. The Tomb or Treasury of Atreus is one of nine tholoi or beehive tombs surviving at Mycenae. Built around 1350 BC, it is one of the latest in a sequence of constructions of increasing sophistication. A dromos, or entrance passage, leads to a monumental doorway and the circular domed tomb beyond. The Tomb of Atreus has, uniquely, an adjoining burial chamber but otherwise it is typical of tholos tombs constructed throughout the Mycenaean kingdoms. All those at Mycenae have long been robbed, but evidence from others elsewhere which have been undisturbed show that burials here would have been very similar to those of the shaft graves.

A typical Linear B tablet. Tablets such as those found at Pylos provide an informative insight into the everyday administration of the final year of a Mycenaean palace.

LINEAR A & LINEAR B

As centres of storage and the distribution of goods, the Minoan palaces of Crete needed some form of writing system so that they could record what came in and what went out. At Phaistos, in southern Crete, clay tablets were incised with a script known as Linear A, possibly as early as 1950 BC. Each symbol stands for a syllable but the language that the syllables represent is still unknown. It may be one of the languages of the Near East brought to Crete by the earliest settlers. However, the numbering system has been deciphered and some symbols are ideograms representing the commodities being described, so it has been possible to put together some meanings. The tablets were never baked so they do not seem to have been intended as a permanent record. Linear A spread throughout Crete, and to some Minoan communities abroad, in the New Palace Period. While it was still used predominantly to record goods or the number of staff, there are also some religious texts which may contain the names of deities or places.

With the coming of the Mycenaeans, Linear B tablets appear. The Mycenaeans probably learned the idea of writing from the Minoans and adapted the script for use with their own language. It was the extraordinary achievement of Michael Ventris, a brilliant young linguist who became obsessed by the problem of decipherment when a schoolboy, to recognise that this language was Greek. He announced his findings in a BBC radio programme in 1952. The Linear B tablets, like those inscribed with Linear A, were temporary records but in centres such as Pylos in the western Peloponnese they were preserved by fire when the palace was burned down in about 1200 BC. Many again are administrative lists which can be pieced together to help reconstruct the Mycenaean economy, the officials involved in administration and the hurried orders issued from Pylos when the coast came under attack in the 12th century. They also show that Poseidon, Zeus and Athena were already recognised deities; in effect that Greek language and culture had a history unrivalled by any other in Europe.

Right: There are three main ways that human beings transcribe their language: through logograms (like hieroglyphics), where each symbol represents a thing or an idea; through syllabaries, where each sign or symbol represents a group of sounds; and through alphabets, where each symbol stands for a single sound. Linear B is essentially a syllabary, and its signs typically represent consonant-vowel pairings such as 'ti', 'za' or 'so'. It also makes use of logograms, as the examples given here illustrate. Like Egyptian hieroglyphics too, some of the Linear B signs had both phonetic and pictorial meanings.

ku—ru—so = gold

(modern Greek *chrysos*)

barley   wheel

Both these are examples of logograms which look like stylised representations of what they stand for

ewe   ram

Logograms for male and female animals often follow this pattern: the top part is the same, with two curved verticals for a female animal and a straight vertical with two crossbars for a male

Olympia

Olympia is beautifully situated and fertile, as can be seen from this view of the 3rd-century BC palaestra or wrestling ring.

'There are enough irksome and troublesome things in life; aren't things just as bad at the Olympic festival? Aren't you scorched there by the fierce heat? Aren't you crushed in the crowd? Isn't it difficult to freshen yourself up? Doesn't the rain soak you to the skin? Aren't you bothered by the noise, the din, the nuisances? But it seems to me that you are well able to bear and indeed gladly endure all this, when you think of the gripping spectacles you are going to see.'

The philosopher Epictetus, 2nd century AD
(From Judith Swaddling, *The Ancient Olympic Games*)

The ancient Olympic Games were held almost without interruption from the legendary date of their founding in 776 BC to their suppression by the Christian emperor Theodosius in AD 393. After this even the site was forgotten, as the river Alpheios, which ran alongside the original sanctuary to Zeus—in whose honour the games were held—changed course over the centuries and buried it. It was the English traveller Richard Chandler, visiting in 1766, who first realised where ancient Olympia lay, but it was not for another hundred years that German excavators began to uncover the site. It was an exciting process of rediscovery. The Greek traveller Pausanias had described the sanctuary as he saw it in his time, the 2nd century AD, and archaeologists were soon able to relate their discoveries to his description. One of the most evocative finds was the building where the sculptor Pheidias had constructed the huge statue to Zeus which had dominated the cella of the god's temple. A cup with Pheidias' name on it was among the finds.

THE OLYMPIC GAMES

A defining feature of ancient Greece was its athletic contests. The determination to honour competition based on individual excellence was the inspiration for the games which were held every four years at Olympia, with others in the years in between at Corinth, Delphi and Nemea. The Olympic Games were formalised under the supervision of the neighbouring city of Elis, and a so-called Sacred Truce was declared, allowing contestants to travel freely across the Greek-speaking world to attend them. All games were held in August or September, in the slack period of the year after the harvest. Victors were awarded a simple wreath, made of laurel at the Pythian Games (Delphi), wild olive at Olympia, wild celery at Nemea, and pine at the Isthmian Games at Corinth. The Odes of Pindar (c. 522–443 BC) celebrate the qualities of each victor and the noble cities they represent.

At Olympia, the games were held over five days and comprised a mixture of rituals, including the sacrifice of a hundred oxen to Zeus on the third day, social events, among them orations by well-known philosophers, and, of course, the contests themselves. The games began with all competitors swearing an oath before a statue of Zeus in the Bouleuterion (*see plan overleaf*). There were foot races, wrestling and a pentathlon which was made up of discus-throwing, javelin, jumping, running and wrestling events. One of the most famous contests was the *pancration*, the deadly no-holds-barred wrestling. The final day saw a procession of all the victors to the Temple of Zeus, where they were crowned with their wreaths of wild olive. The victors earned themselves great renown in their home cities and were often revered there for the rest of their lives.

Above: The glory of the Olympia sculptures are the reliefs from the Temple of Zeus, which include the Labours of Hercules and a sequence showing the battle between Lapiths and centaurs, with a regal Apollo in the centre of the pediment (pictured here). This is typical of the so-called Severe Style of the period 480–460 BC, which ushers in the Classical period. The style is restrained, though the figures do show some expression, perhaps of pain or of serenity. Often, as with the pediments from the Temple of Zeus, the viewer has to know the background story, which is only hinted at by the theatrical display of its participants.

Above left: Another example of the Severe Style: the *Discobolos*, or discus-thrower, by the celebrated 5th-century sculptor Myron, here in a Roman copy. The sculpture provided an inspiration for Leni Riefenstahl when she created her film of the 1936 Berlin Olympics for Hitler.

ANCIENT OLYMPIA: THE SITE

Olympia was an ancient place, known originally as the Altis, or 'sacred grove'. A tumulus dating from about 2500 BC still survives in the sanctuary and was honoured by later generations as the burial place of the hero Pelops, father of Atreus and grandfather of Agamemnon, who gives his name to the Peloponnese, the part of mainland Greece where Olympia is situated. Zeus was worshipped here as early as Mycenaean times but Olympia was one of many Greek sanctuaries that saw a renaissance in the 8th century BC.

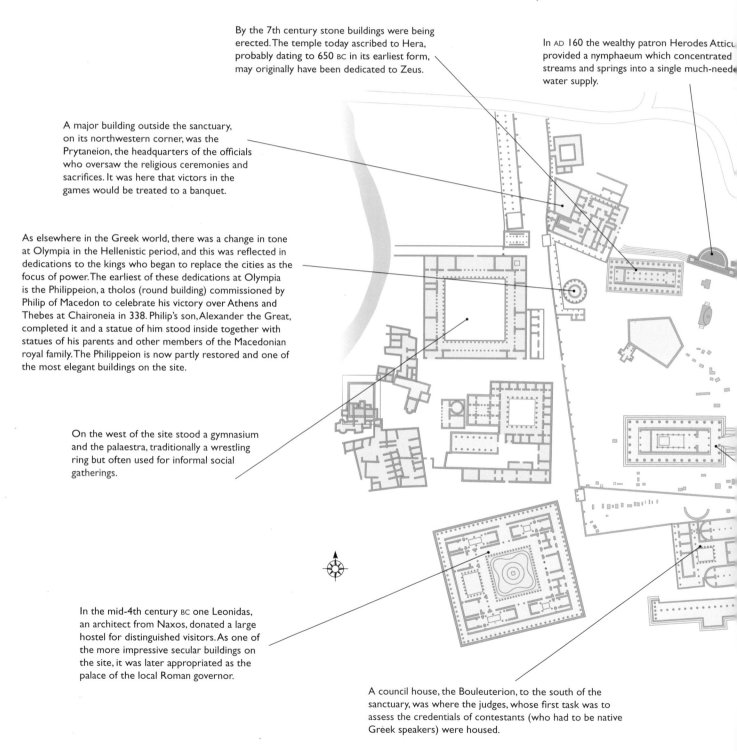

By the 7th century stone buildings were being erected. The temple today ascribed to Hera, probably dating to 650 BC in its earliest form, may originally have been dedicated to Zeus.

In AD 160 the wealthy patron Herodes Atticu provided a nymphaeum which concentrated streams and springs into a single much-neede water supply.

A major building outside the sanctuary, on its northwestern corner, was the Prytaneion, the headquarters of the officials who oversaw the religious ceremonies and sacrifices. It was here that victors in the games would be treated to a banquet.

As elsewhere in the Greek world, there was a change in tone at Olympia in the Hellenistic period, and this was reflected in dedications to the kings who began to replace the cities as the focus of power. The earliest of these dedications at Olympia is the Philippeion, a tholos (round building) commissioned by Philip of Macedon to celebrate his victory over Athens and Thebes at Chaironeia in 338. Philip's son, Alexander the Great, completed it and a statue of him stood inside together with statues of his parents and other members of the Macedonian royal family. The Philippeion is now partly restored and one of the most elegant buildings on the site.

On the west of the site stood a gymnasium and the palaestra, traditionally a wrestling ring but often used for informal social gatherings.

In the mid-4th century BC one Leonidas, an architect from Naxos, donated a large hostel for distinguished visitors. As one of the more impressive secular buildings on the site, it was later appropriated as the palace of the local Roman governor.

A council house, the Bouleuterion, to the south of the sanctuary, was where the judges, whose first task was to assess the credentials of contestants (who had to be native Greek speakers) were housed.

Dedications by visiting cities were made, as at Delphi, in the shape of treasuries. Most were from cities in Sicily and southern Italy, the richest in the Greek world and famous for their horses. 'Italian' teams tended to dominate the four-horse chariot races held for the first time in 680 BC.

Above: Pheidias' statue of Zeus, here in a 17th-century engraving, was one of the Seven Wonders of the World and amazed everyone who saw it. It was 40 ft tall—so large, one visitor noted, that it would have broken through the roof of the temple if it had stood up. It was a chryselephantine structure with an underlying wooden base covered in gold-plated bronze and ivory, and took Pheidias some eight years to assemble. The impact of the statue would have been enhanced by the cedarwood throne, itself decorated in gold and precious stones, and the pool of oil in front of it, in which it would have been seen reflected. One legend tells how it was taken to Constantinople and perished there, but it is hard to see how it could have been easily dismantled and moved. An alternative story that it was destroyed in Olympia in a fire in 425, a period when there was no longer any official protection of pagan sites, is more plausible.

The earliest athletic stadium was in the sanctuary itself. Major rebuilding took place in the 5th century, and the stadium was moved eastwards to the site where it is today. A new hippodrome, some 2,000 ft long, was constructed alongside it.

The eastern boundary of the sanctuary was enhanced by a painted stoa which became famous for its echo. The Greek rulers of Hellenistic Egypt, the Ptolemies, flaunted their status in statues placed in front of it.

A vast collection of bronze figurines has been found in the ash left by the burning of sacrifices to Zeus outside his temple. Many appear to represent Zeus or his wife Hera but there are horses and bulls as well as cauldrons, a common offering in this period. The earliest finds are local, but increasingly the influence of the Eastern civilisations is seen.

The vast temple in honour of Zeus was finished by 456 BC, and is a superb example of a Doric temple, designed with a high platform so that it dominated the buildings around it. The columns themselves were over 30 ft high—they now lie across the site, after being toppled by earthquakes in the 6th century. The chryselephantine (gold and ivory) statue of Zeus, assembled on site by Pheidias and which dominated the temple cella, was so impressive that it was listed as one of the Seven Wonders of the Ancient World. When the emperor Caligula sent men to take it to Rome, it was said to have repulsed them by a contemptuous laugh. Statues of victors clustered around the sanctuary, especially in the prestigious space in front of the temple.

Delphi

Right: View over the mountains from the remaining columns of the 4th-century Temple of Apollo, dramatically situated high on the steep hillside. The temple is reached by a winding path known as the Sacred Way, lined with the remains of commemorative monuments and treasuries, where the various city-states deposited offerings.

Above: The omphalos, a conical stone bound with a net, represents the very centre of the earth. One legend is that it represents the stone wrapped in swaddling clothes which Rhea, the mother of Zeus, pretended was Zeus himself to save him from being murdered by his father Cronos.

There can be few more stunning Classical sites than Delphi, high up on the slopes of Mt Parnassus with superb views down to the sea. The site itself clings to the mountainside with platforms for the Temple to Apollo and above that the stadium, and it was a long climb up from the coast where most supplicants to the shrine arrived.

MYTH AND EARLY HISTORY

The origins of Delphi as a shrine are lost in legend. One story tells of how Zeus, anxious to find the centre of the earth, released two eagles. They met over the slopes of Mt Parnassus and Zeus declared this to be the navel, *omphalos*, of the world. The omphalos was symbolised by a dome-shaped stone covered in a network of woollen ribbons that was kept in the inner sanctum of the Temple to Apollo.

For it was Apollo, the son of Zeus, who became the dominant god of the site. It was said that he searched the world for a home for his oracle, finally alighting on Delphi. The sacred Castalian Spring ran down the hillside, as it still does today, but it was guarded by a dragon whom Apollo killed. Its rotting body was recorded in the name *pytho* (from the Greek 'to rot') and the word stuck to the shrine. The priestess who uttered the oracle was known as the Pythia (one story suggests that she was drugged by the fumes of the rotting dragon in the fissures below her), and the games held at Delphi every four years from the 580s BC were called the Pythian Games.

Wherever these legends originated, by the 8th century BC Delphi was attracting a stream of visitors and numerous offerings were made, typically bronze cauldrons on tripods or small bronze figurines. This was the age of colonisation as Greeks began to seek more fertile land in the western Mediterranean, and the oracle gained a reputation for advising on the best sites for settlement in Sicily and southern Italy. By the 6th century BC, the shrine was especially popular with the Ionian Greeks of Asia Minor.

Right: This stunning 5th-century bronze of a charioteer serene after his victory was the gift of a Sicilian ruler after the games of 478 or 474 BC. Victorious athletes at all the ancient Greek games were revered in their home towns after the event, as is shown by this paraphrase of part of Pythian Ode 10, the very earliest written by Pindar, composed in honour of the victory of Hippocleas of Thessaly, who won the double-length foot race for boys at Delphi in 498 BC. The extract says much about Greek attitudes to death and the afterlife:

'Delphi summons me in order for me to present Hippocleas with the glorious voices of men united in celebration. Hippocleas is trying his hand in contests and the gorge of Mt Parnassus is proclaiming him to the people that live around as the greatest of the boys in the double foot race. O Apollo, the end and the beginning both grow sweet when a god urges on the work of a man. […] A god's heart should be free from pain; but as for a man, he is considered fortunate, and wise poets sing his praises, if he wins victory with his hands or the excellence of his feet, and takes the greatest prizes through his courage and strength and lives to see his young son duly winning Pythian garlands. He can never set foot in the heavens; but whatever splendour we mortals can attain, such a victor reaches the limit of that voyage.' (Tr. John Sandys, 1937, author's paraphrased selection.)

Above: The Pythian Games were held for the first time in the 580s BC. Every four years athletes from throughout the Greek world came to Delphi to compete for wreaths of laurel leaves. The stadium survives on the highest point of the site, with much of its stone seating, which could accommodate 7,000 spectators, still intact. Indeed it is the best preserved of all ancient Greek stadia.

The seating was the gift of the wealthy patron Herodes Atticus in the 2nd century AD. The theatre, where the music and drama contests took place, was below it. These contests were especially important as Apollo was the god of music. One of the most important exhibits in the Delphi museum, in fact, is the earliest known musical notation, incorporated in an inscription of hymns to Apollo.

THE SANCTUARY

The sanctuary of Apollo was always the core of the site. Legend told how the original temple had been built of laurels, the shrub always associated with Apollo. The temple whose ruins stand today was built in the middle of the 4th century BC. It was here that, after the appropriate rituals, supplicants would come to consult the oracle. It is assumed that the priestess had her house close by; a complex to the southwest of the temple has been identified as her quarters. The site has been so racked by earthquakes, however, that the remains of the underground chambers from where the prophecies emerged have been lost.

Open as it was to the Greek world and even beyond, Delphi became a place for cities to flaunt their wealth and achievements. The route up to the temple was lined with treasuries, most of them constructed in the 6th century. One of the most striking was erected in the 520s by the people of the island of Siphnos. They had discovered gold and silver mines on their island and had consulted the oracle on how to deal with the treasure. The reply was to donate a tenth of it to Delphi! The Siphnians honoured the request by building their own treasury with imported marble from Paros. The treasury frieze, preserved in fragments in the site museum, has some of the liveliest pre-Classical sculptures to survive, especially on its northern and eastern sections (*see illustration opposite*). Together with reliefs from the Treasury of Athens dating from a few years later (about 500 BC), we can see the dawn of Classical sculpture.

Few cities could resist showing off their victories, and monuments were often deliberately placed to humiliate old enemies. So after the Battle of Marathon, when Athens defeated the Persians (*see p. 58*), the

Among the ruins of Delphi is a small circular building, a tholos, below the sanctuary, dating from the 4th century, with three graceful Doric columns standing. Its purpose is unknown but it echoes the 4th-century tholos at Epidaurus (*illustrated on p. 80*), dedicated to the god Asclepius, and another at Olympia, dedicated there some 20 years later by Philip of Macedon. It has become one of the most famous symbols of the site.

Athenians used part of their spoils to honour the victorious general Miltiades, who was placed on a plinth alongside Athenian heroes. It was typical of the Spartans that, when they defeated Athens in the Peloponnesian War in 404, they should set up their own victory monument next door to it. Their triumph was short-lived. Spartan territory was invaded by the Arcadians in 370 and they, in their turn, set up their own victory monument directly opposite that of the Spartans, paid for out of the booty.

Above: The north frieze of the Siphnian Treasury (c. 520 BC) shows a battle between gods and giants, a popular theme right across the ancient world. Here one of the lions drawing the chariot of the goddess Cybele is shown attacking a giant. This is one of the most vivid surviving expressions of the sculptural art of the pre-Classical period, predating the Parthenon frieze by about 85 years.

The belief that the gods can intervene to give counsel about human affairs runs deep in ancient Greek religion, and oracle shrines, where the rituals of consultation took place, are found in several places in the Greek world. The most famous were Dodona in northern Greece, and Delphi.

The range of supplicants to oracles was wide. At Dodona, where a number of question-tablets have been found, the vast majority are from individuals. The imponderables which worry them vary from the correctness of their religious rituals (which god to sacrifice to for a particular matter) to matters of conception (will their wife have a child and will it be a son, or is the child their wife is bearing actually their own).

States could send their envoys as well, not always to get a direct yes or no but often to endorse a decision that had already been made. The oracle acted as a kind of court of appeal in religious matters too. Without a priestly hierarchy or a body of sacred texts such as would develop in Christianity, there was no other authority to approach. States would naturally be concerned about their foreign policy, whether the gods would support their decision to go to war, for example, or whether a new constitution was acceptable. It was at Delphi that colonising expeditions were planned from the 8th century onwards. Somehow (from other visitors?) the oracle seemed to know which sites in Sicily and southern Italy had not been colonised and its instructions set out which capes to sail round and which bays to enter.

At Delphi Apollo spoke through a priestess, the Pythia, apparently a middle-aged woman from the local area who practised celibacy while she was in office. Supplicants had to arrive on designated days (these appear to have become more frequent as the fame of the oracle grew) and offer a goat in sacrifice. The priestess would purify herself at the Castalian Spring and then enter an underground chamber in the Temple of Apollo and crouch on a tripod. In some way she went into a trance, perhaps self-induced or brought about by chewing laurel leaves (the laurel was sacred to Apollo) or even by inhaling vapours drifting up from fissures in the rocks. Her replies were often obscure, even incoherent, and the trick was to interpret them. One of the most famous interpretations was made by the Athenian general Themistocles, who approached the oracle as the Persian armies were massing in Asia for their invasion of Greece. He was, the oracle told him, to rely on a wooden wall. This seemed to imply building fortifications until Themistocles argued that the navy would be the saviour of Athens, as indeed it was at the Battle of Salamis.

Delphi was vulnerable to Roman imperialism. The emperor Nero, incensed at criticism from the oracle after he had orchestrated his mother's murder, looted 500 statues. Calmer times returned during the reign of Hadrian, a great admirer of Greek culture, and when the traveller Pausanias visited in the middle of the 2nd century AD, he found a sanctuary still crammed with statuary. However, supplicants were no longer kings or city states but ordinary people in search of advice on their marriages or personal affairs. There is a marked sense of decline.

The oracle was to succumb to the wave of legislation against paganism introduced by the emperor Theodosius in the late 4th century. A 'final' oracle survives, probably from this period: 'Tell the king; the fair-wrought house has fallen. No shelter has Apollo, nor sacred laurel leaves; The fountains are now silent; the voice is stilled. It is finished.'

The priestess of the Delphic oracle, perched on a tripod, worked herself up through music and fumes to the point of hysteria where she was able to utter her 'prophecies'. These in turn had to be interpreted in a way which somehow fitted the case in question. A number of such utterances and their interpretations survive.

Dodona

Oracle site, sacred to Zeus
Flourished 2nd millennium
BC–2nd century BC

Two views of Dodona, at different times of year: one in summer, the other in very early spring, when the heights of the Pindus range are still capped in snow. Beyond the theatre the plain is cultivated, but oaks of the type that once produced the oracle's answers still grow. The photograph below shows the ruins of the Temple of Zeus, with an oak growing in its centre.

Dodona is a hauntingly beautiful oracle site at the foot of the Pindus mountains. The site dates from Mycenaean times, and its original dedication was to the gods of the earth. A mother goddess was believed to live in the roots of a great oak and priests of the shrine slept on the ground around it. As Greek culture spread from the south into what was a semi-barbarian area occupied by Epirot tribes, Zeus was welcomed as a new presiding deity. Supplicants to the shrine listened to the answers to their questions in the rustling of the oak leaves in the wind. In the autumn the acorns fell into large bronze drums, and the way the sound resonated could be interpreted in the form of an answer.

Like Delphi, Dodona developed into a much bigger site, with a theatre set against the mountains and views down through the valley. It was built by the powerful king of Epirus, Pyrrhus (ruled 295–272 BC), who saw a moment of glory and unity for his people during the 3rd century when he briefly became king of neighbouring Macedonia

(his expedition to help the Greeks of southern Italy against the Romans ended less successfully when his armies, though victorious, were worn down to breaking point, hence the term 'Pyrrhic Victory', victory gained at too great a cost to oneself). Pyrrhus was also responsible for building a meeting place for delegates from the local tribes and for embellishing the sanctuary of Zeus with colonnades. The site suffered heavy damage when the Romans conquered the area and sold 150,000 Epirots into slavery. Today it is much ruined, but nothing can detract from its spectacular position.

Epidaurus

Healing centre
Flourished 6th–1st centuries BC

Like Olympia, the sanctuary of the healing god Asclepius at Epidaurus was known as a 'sacred grove'. It lies in a fertile and well-watered plain—'vine-clad' as Homer termed it—part of the territory of the coastal city of Epidaurus, whose chief magistrate presided over the site. Stories of its powers go back to Mycenaean times, and a 7th-century healing shrine to Apollo has been excavated at the nearby Mt Kynortion.

The tholos or circular building which stands in front of the abaton, where the sick visitors slept overnight, has been the subject of much speculation. Pausanias, visiting in c. AD 170, noticed it as of interest but made no further comment on its function. It seems to have enclosed an underground pit reached through series of concentric passages and it may have been that the sacred serpents associated with the cult of Asclepius were housed here, thus giving the building a key importance in healing rituals. This photograph shows the tholos in ruins but it is at present being reconstructed in old and new stonework.

INSCRIPTIONS OF HEALINGS

About 70 inscriptions are known recording cures received at Epidaurus. Here is a typical example:

'Pandaros the Thessalian had blemishes on his forehead. Whilst sleeping in the abaton he had a vision. The god wound a band around his brow He ordered him to come out of the abaton, to remove the band and dedicate it in the temple. At daybreak he arose from his bed and removed the band. His forehead was completely clear. The blemishes were stuck to the band. Then he offered it to the temple.'

An interesting development shown by the inscriptions is the rise of 'good advice'. One Apellas was suffering from hypochondria. 'As I was travelling to the sanctuary and approached Aegina, the god appeared and told me not to become very angry. When I reached the sanctuary he instructed me to cover my head because it was raining, to eat bread, cheese, celery, lettuce, to bathe unaided by a servant, to exercise in the gymnasium, to drink lemon juice, to go for walks. I left the sanctuary healthy, thankful to the god.'

ASCLEPIUS

The shrine at Epidaurus was originally dedicated to Apollo. It is only in the 6th century BC that the mythical figure of Asclepius emerges as the dominant divinity. Legends tell that Asclepius was the son of Apollo, suckled by a she-goat and protected by a dog, and that the boy grew up learned in the art of medicine. So accomplished did Asclepius become that Zeus temporarily banished him to the underworld when he began raising mortals from the dead, something his father, who was also associated with healing, had never been able to do.

A famous shrine to Asclepius was on the island of Kos and it was here that the founder of scientific medicine, Hippocrates, served in the sanctuary. The sanctuary of Epidaurus reached its peak in the 4th century and it was remarkable for banning the sacrifice of goats and for the keeping of sacred dogs. Snakes were also a part of the Asclepian cult; they often represent the underworld and their presence may symbolise the triumph of Asclepius over the forces of darkness. A snake's shedding of its skin might also symbolise rebirth. Asclepius was always shown with a staff with a snake entwined around it.

HOW THE SANCTUARY WORKED

The sanctuary at Epidaurus was separated from the world outside by the propylaia, the ceremonial gateway, whose foundations remain. No one actually at the point of death could enter, nor could women about to give birth (it is recorded that a later patron provided a building outside the sanctuary for those who had mistimed their arrival).

A sacred way led from the propylaia towards the Temple of Asclepius. Coins and reliefs survive which show how a large cult statue of the god, bearded and benevolent, dominated the inner room. Supplicants had first to purify themselves at a sacred fountain and then proceed to sacrifice on the temple's altar, which stood before it. Those coming from nearby would bring an animal—a cock, for instance, although the richest would offer something as costly as an ox. Those from further away were allowed to bring money. Respect was still shown to Apollo, the god to whom the sanctuary had originally been sacred, and every sacrifice had to be offered to both gods. Further religious rituals followed. These ceremonies must have had their emotional impact and the chants of singers, the Paianists, added to the heightened tension. It seems as if the sick were worked up to a frenzy and then taken into the abaton, the healing chamber, to sleep. Left to themselves for the night, and in a state of expectation, it is not surprising that in the morning many announced themselves miraculously cured and left offerings to record their healing.

There is good evidence that the priests did not rely solely on the power of the god but were prepared to take matters into their own hands. Surgical instruments have been found and some inscriptions show that the sick stayed longer in the sanctuary, undergoing a regime of dieting and regular exercise. Herbs were cultivated on the neighbouring hillsides. Others recorded dreams in which they had received instructions on how to treat their malady (*see box opposite*).

With time the site became more of a social centre. There had always been other activities at Epidaurus; there is a well-preserved stadium, and what used to be seen as the gymnasium is now believed to have been a banqueting centre (the rooms show how they were adjusted to fit the couches of the diners). In Roman times an odeon, for musical displays, was added to the central courtyard. At the southeastern corner of the site a guest house was built with each of its courtyards surrounded by 18 rooms. There were Greek, and later Roman, baths. South of the guest house is the famous theatre. It could seat some 14,000, making it unlikely that the sanctuary's permanent buildings could have accommodated all the visitors at once. One imagines, as with Olympia, a vast array of tents and makeshift shacks in the surrounding valley at times when the shrine was busy.

Above: Bronze statue of Asclepius with his staff and snake, the origin of modern pharmacy signs.

Overleaf: The ancient theatre at Epidaurus, dating from the 4th century BC and still in use today. It is famous for its acoustics. Studies by the Georgia Institute of Technology have established that the corrugated limestone seats filter out low-frequency sounds but reflect high-frequency ones thus creating a superb acoustic effect. A speaker standing in the centre of the orchestra can be heard perfectly on the highest rung of seats.

ANCIENT GREEK THEATRES

The 4th-century BC theatre at Epidaurus is one of the best preserved Classical buildings in Greece. A Greek theatre had three components. The orchestra was the central performance area. The records of such an area go far back in time: Homer talks of a threshing floor in Knossos which was used for dancing by Ariadne and there are other reports of dances in honour of the god Dionysus on the ground where the grapes were crushed. Dionysus was the god of wine so it is understandable that he should be so honoured, and the dedication of later theatrical performances to him suggests that the theatre originated from these dances.

The original dances were accompanied by choral singers. Tradition says that in the 530s BC in Athens one Thespis (hence 'thespian') introduced the idea of an 'actor' who explained the myths of Dionysus to the audience. The playwright Aeschylus (525–456 BC) introduced a second actor, and the two could have a dialogue with each other. From this was born the idea of a play. Gradually the chorus became less important and faded into the background, emerging only to comment on the events as they unfolded.

In Athens the first plays were probably performed in the Agora, but in about 500 BC they were transferred to the southern slope of the Acropolis where the audience could sit on the hillside, probably on wooden seats. This viewing place was known as the *theatron* (hence 'theatre'), and gradually became transformed into a set of stone seating, an arrangement which reaches its most sophisticated form at theatres such as that at Epidaurus. Many theatres in the Greek world were built in spectacular settings and they also had extraordinary acoustics.

The final architectural development was the *skene*, the building behind the orchestra (origin of our word 'scene'). This is first recorded in Athens in the late 4th century and in Hellenistic times it became much more elaborate. It could be used as an extra set of entrances and exits, could carry decorated backdrops ('scenery') or simply lend grandeur to the building. At Priene (*see p. 117*) there was a two-storey *skene* and a stage projected out from the first storey. The Romans took the final step of linking the seats to the *skene* so as to create an enclosed building.

The great days of theatre were in 5th-century Athens. There were two major festivals a year, both in honour of Dionysus, and the summer festival would attract visitors from throughout the Greek world. Selected playwrights would each produce three tragedies, all with a linked theme, which would be performed over a day. They were always rooted in myths but would develop a storyline from them that would highlight ethical dilemmas or show how fate unfolded the destiny of the characters. The three greatest of the tragedians, Aeschylus, Sophocles and Euripides, developed their themes in distinctive, highly sophisticated ways, and it must have been extraordinary to have heard their plays performed for the first time.

Then there was comedy. A day was set aside for it at the festivals and it must have provided some light relief after the draining experience of three days of tragedy. The master of 5th-century comedy was Aristophanes, in whose plays wit, bawdiness, revelry and sheer exuberant rudeness were wrapped together. No one was immune from Aristophanes' barbs, and it is a tribute to Athens' maturity as a society that even at so tense a time as the Peloponnesian War, public ridicule of its rulers was permissible.

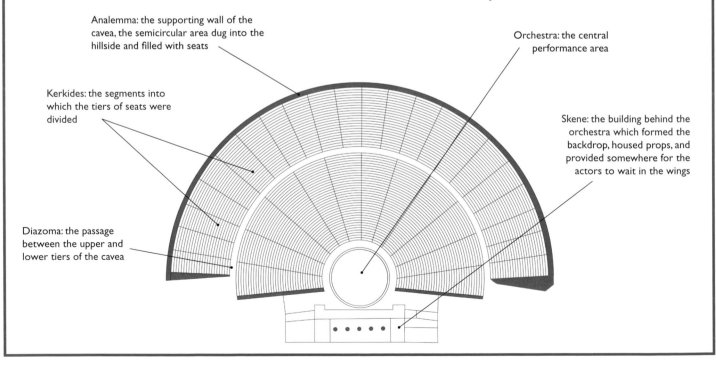

Analemma: the supporting wall of the cavea, the semicircular area dug into the hillside and filled with seats

Kerkides: the segments into which the tiers of seats were divided

Diazoma: the passage between the upper and lower tiers of the cavea

Orchestra: the central performance area

Skene: the building behind the orchestra which formed the backdrop, housed props, and provided somewhere for the actors to wait in the wings

Athens: the Acropolis

Ceremonial centre of a
powerful city-state
Flourished 5th century BC

In 479 BC, the Athens acropolis was a ruined site. The vast army of Xerxes, the Persian 'King of Kings', had swept down into Attica and sacked it in 480. The population of Athens had fled to the neighbouring island of Salamis, and in the straits between the island and the mainland the Athenian navy had defeated the Persian fleet. In 479, the Persian army was destroyed by an alliance of Greek cities. The Athenians, returning to their shattered city, made a promise that they would keep the site in ruins as a memorial to the war.

The resolution did not last. By the 440s, probably after peace had finally been concluded with the Persians, an ambitious new building programme had begun under the Athenian leader, Pericles. He was determined to create a showpiece of Classical art which would flaunt Athens' status throughout the Greek world. His opponents were many, notably from the aristocratic party, who resented the coming of Athenian democracy, of which Pericles had been a champion. They accused him of 'gilding and dressing up the Acropolis like a prostitute, hanging round her neck precious stones and statues and six-million drachma temples', but Pericles resisted all their taunts, bringing his project to a triumphant conclusion in only a few years.

Detail from the famous Caryatid Porch from the Erechtheion. Despite Roman stories of the Caryatids being women of Caryae in the Peloponnese, who betrayed Athens to the Persians and suffered the punishment of bearing burdens on their heads, it is likely these are simply priestesses of the cult of the goddess who was honoured in this temple.

THE PROPYLAIA AND ERECHTHEION

Those ascending the western end of the Acropolis rock would have been greeted by a massive gateway, the Propylaia **(A)**, constructed between 437 and 432 BC. They would move under a Doric façade, proceed through a colonnade of Ionic columns, and then emerge on the Acropolis itself through another Doric gateway. Like the Parthenon (*see overleaf*), the Propylaia is built in the finest marble from the Pentelic mines, a few miles northeast of Athens. Although white, the marble has a yellow tinge which is brought to life by the rising or setting sun. Facing the visitor was a monumental statue of Athena Promachos, the patron goddess, 'resolute in war' (already in place by the 450s), and a series of temples covered the hill.

Pericles was, of course, building on an ancient and revered site. The most sacred spot was the Erechtheion **(D)**. Legend told of how the smith-god Hephaistos had tried to rape Athena but his semen had only reached her leg and Erechtheus had been born from it. Athena had raised him and he had become king of Athens. The two were commemorated together in the temple, where an olive-wood statue of Athena was honoured by being clothed in a woven cloth, the *peplos*, every four years at the Panathenaic Festival. The rebuilding may have begun in the 430s but was then put into abeyance while all energies were transferred to the new Parthenon. Finally completed only in 395, the Erechtheion is a complex temple, ingeniously designed to fit the rocky site, with the famous Caryatid Porch facing outwards to the south.

Today as one reaches the summit of the Acropolis, one is greeted with bare rock and only two significant buildings, the Erechtheion and the Parthenon. This is the result of a cleansing of later buildings which took place in the 19th century as Athens celebrated its revived status as capital of Greece and wished to revitalise her heroic past. At the near end is the ceremonial entrance gate, the Propylaia (A), and perched on the promontory to the right the exquisite small temple of Athena Nike (B), dedicated to the goddess in her role as victor. The Parthenon (C) dominates the southern side of the Acropolis. The Erechtheion (D) is the complex on the northern edge. To the right of the Erechtheion is the base of an earlier temple to Athena (E), demolished by the Persians and never rebuilt. Beyond the Acropolis, in the top right-hand corner of the photograph, are the ruins of what was once the largest temple in all Greece, dedicated to Olympian Zeus (F). It was begun in the 6th century BC but only finally completed by Hadrian in the 2nd century AD. In front of it to the left, visible against a clump of trees, is the Arch of Hadrian (G), built during the Roman period and dividing the ancient city from its new extension.

Above: A piece of the 'Elgin Marbles' showing a detail of the battle between Lapiths and centaurs. The sculpture of the Classical period after 460 is intensely realistic and more relaxed than that of the earlier Severe Style (*see p. 71*). The body is more integrated, as if coordinated movements are better understood. Although the sculpture is still pure and concentrates on ideal bodies, there is more awareness of emotions. This approach is preserved into the 4th century but by the end of the century a much more ornate style develops with the Hellenistic period. The range of characters increases, young and old and complex groups emerge with the body no longer idealised. Though Hellenistic sculpture is often superb, many observers mourn the loss of the purity of earlier styles. For a comparison, see the battle between gods and giants on the Pergamon frieze on p. 110.

THE PARTHENON

The Parthenon (**C**) was constructed on the base of an earlier temple to Athena, with its original entrance on the east as was customary, and thus facing away from those approaching it. It is possible that the Parthenon gained its name from the opulent chryselephantine (gold and ivory) statue of Athena in her role as *parthenos*, 'virgin', which the sculptor Pheidias created for it. It may even be that the building was created as a showpiece for the statue itself, with a treasury in the back room where much of the city's gold, silver and spoils of war were stored. Unlike a typical Greek temple, the Parthenon had no altar for sacrifices in front of it, and there is no record of a cult priestess. Its size suggests that it was deliberately planned to surpass the recently completed temple to Zeus at Olympia.

The Parthenon's design may seem typical of a Greek temple but the refinements that its architect, Ictinus, introduced were meticulously planned. Curves in the platform, steps and columns, which swelled slightly at the centre, had been a feature of temple architecture for a century, but the sophistication of such adjustments reached a climax in the Parthenon. The columns along the sides lean slightly inwards and a line drawn from them would meet one from the opposite side six and a half thousand feet above the floor of the building. The columns on the two façades also lean backwards but at a lesser angle, so that they would meet about 16,000 ft above the floor.

If its size, as the largest building yet constructed on the Greek mainland, and its sophistication were not enough, the sumptuous decoration of the Parthenon completed the whole as the most astounding creation of Classical Greece. The pediment sculptures and the famous internal frieze (much of which was taken off to England by Lord Elgin in the early 19th century) have a vitality and overall sweep which show how much Greek sculpture had liberated itself from the Severe Style, shown on the pediments of the Temple of Zeus at Olympia (*see p. 71*) only a few years before.

TEMPLE OF ATHENA NIKE

Behind the southern wall of the Propylaia is one of the most exquisite of the Acropolis' buildings, the temple to Athena Nike (**B**), Athena in her role as victor. A temple had stood here before, but it was destroyed like all others by the Persians. The replacement was not built until the 420s BC, probably to fit with the completion of the Propylaia itself. Its sculptures are among the finest of the Classical period to survive, with the relief from the parapet of Nike adjusting her sandal especially acclaimed. The temple looked out on the city as if in a public proclamation of Athens' great victories over the Persians, but only twenty years after it was completed, its glory was tarnished by the ignominious defeat of Athens by Sparta.

FROM PLUTARCH'S *LIFE OF PERICLES*

Plutarch describes the Acropolis building programme, especially the speed with which it was carried out:

'Pericles' works are especially admired as having been made quickly, to last long. For every particular part of his work was immediately, even at that time, for its beauty and elegance, antique; and yet in its vigour and freshness looks to this day [2nd century AD] as if it were just executed. There is a sort of bloom of newness upon those works of his, preserving them from the touch of time, as if they had some perennial spirit and undying vitality mingled in the composition of them...

When the orators, who sided with Thucydides and his party, were at one time crying out, as their custom was, against Pericles, as one who squandered away the public money, and made havoc of the state revenues, he rose in the open assembly and put the question to the people, whether they thought that he had laid out much; and they saying, "Too much, a great deal." "Then," said he, "since it is so, let the cost not go to your account, but to mine; and let the inscription upon the buildings stand in my name." When they heard him say thus, whether it were out of a surprise to see the greatness of his spirit or out of emulation of the glory of the works, they cried aloud, bidding him to spend on, and lay out what he thought fit from the public purse, and to spare no cost, till all were finished.' (*Tr. John Dryden*)

For many people the elegance of the Classical period is beautifully exemplified in this relief from the balustrade of the Temple of Athena Nike, showing the goddess adjusting her sandal. The way in which the drapery is composed so as to cover but not conceal her body makes this figure truly exceptional.

Athens: the Agora

*Political and commercial
centre of a powerful city-state
Flourished 5th–4th centuries BC*

If the Acropolis was the ceremonial centre of Athens, the Agora, its market place, was the ancient city's political and commercial heart. Completely lost to view after centuries of later occupation, the Agora has gradually been uncovered in a continuous series of excavations conducted since 1931 by the American School. For much of its history, the core of the site was left clear for market stalls, and finds of over 100,000 coins show just how busy it must have been: the comic plays of Aristophanes are full of shouting stall-holders and unscrupulous traders. Quarters of potters and terracotta-workers have been found, and along the western boundaries the foundries of metalworkers clustered around the temple to their god, Hephaistos, which still stands, the best preserved Greek temple anywhere in the world.

EVOLUTION OF THE AGORA

The Panathenaic Way **(1)**, the processional route to the Acropolis which began at the western gate of the city, ran across the Agora and was kept clear throughout its history. Yet, like the Forum in Rome, political and ceremonial affairs began to intrude. By the 5th century, restoration work after the Persian sack saw the building of a fountain house, shrines to the gods and the famous Painted Stoa **(2)**, where the victory over the Persians at Marathon (490 BC) was commemorated in paintings. The stoa was also a favourite place for discussions and gave its name to Stoicism, the philosophy founded in the late 4th century. Then, along the

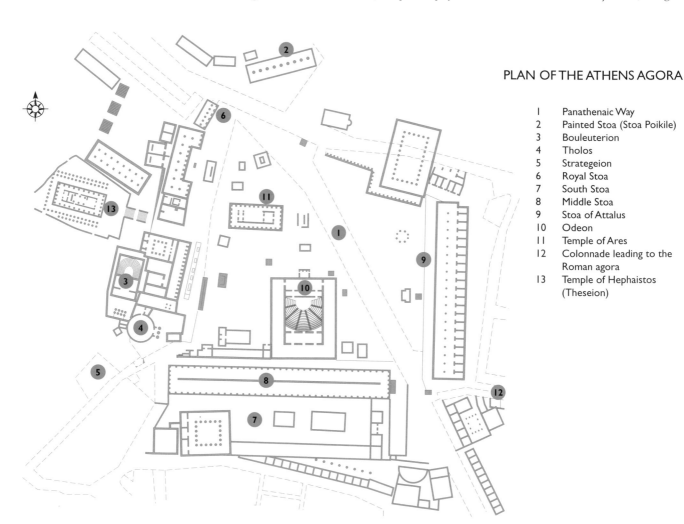

PLAN OF THE ATHENS AGORA

1	Panathenaic Way
2	Painted Stoa (Stoa Poikile)
3	Bouleuterion
4	Tholos
5	Strategeion
6	Royal Stoa
7	South Stoa
8	Middle Stoa
9	Stoa of Attalus
10	Odeon
11	Temple of Ares
12	Colonnade leading to the Roman agora
13	Temple of Hephaistos (Theseion)

western edge of the Agora, the buildings of democracy appeared. The first city council chamber, the Bouleu-terion **(3)**, housed the elected Council of Five Hundred, which prepared all official business for the citizen assembly before its meetings on the Pnyx hill. Fifty members of the council were on duty by rotation day and night, and were allocated their own building, the Tholos **(4)**, where they could eat and sleep. The original circular building, nicknamed 'the Sun Hat', was built next to the council chamber soon after 480 BC and its foundations remain. Just south of the Tholos was the Strategeion **(5)**, where the ten generals of the city had their headquarters. They were important figures, elected from year to year, and it was his sustained general-ship which helped give Pericles his prominence. This southwestern corner of the Agora housed a range of buildings identified as law courts and the state prison.

Close to the Painted Stoa was the Royal Stoa **(6)**, a legacy of the days when Athens had a king. The post of royal archon (magistrate) still existed: the archon supervised all the religious activities of the city including many of the ceremonial processions. A variety of official business took place in the building and the official copy of the city constitution was stored there. It was here that the philosopher Socrates was indicted in 399 BC for corrupting the young (*see overleaf*). Another stoa **(7)**, for commercial activities including money changing, was built about 420 BC on the southern edge of the Agora. The official who enforced weights and measures had his office here and measures for grain and oil have been found. An inscription details the procedures of handing on the post from one year to the next. The city's own mint was in the far eastern corner of the Agora.

In the 4th century BC, the Agora was still closely tied to the political, legal and commercial activities of the city, but by the 3rd century Athens' importance as a centre of trade was in decline and the city was living on her past. A new commercial stoa in the southern Agora, known as the Middle Stoa **(8)**, was much larger than the old one, and encroached into space that had traditionally been kept open, but it was of far lower quality than earlier buildings. It was now that outsiders began to boost their cultural creden-tials by honouring Athens. Along the eastern side of the Agora, where private houses had stood among shops, a vast new stoa **(9)** was donated by King Attalus of Pergamon, in about 150 BC. Just over a hundred years later, the Roman aristocrat Agrippa donated an Odeon **(10)**, a small covered theatre for musical performances. By now much of the re-maining open space in the Agora was filled. In the remaining area a 5th-century BC temple, apparently dedicated to the war god Ares **(11)**, was brought into the city for re-erection here. There was now no space for new buildings but the Romans built their own ceremonial agora to the east and linked it to the Greek one by a colonnade **(12)**.

Above: On a hillside west of the Agora is the most complete ancient Greek temple to survive. Dedicated to the blacksmith god Hephaistos (in an area where the bronze-workers were based), it is often known, incorrectly, as the Theseion, from the relief sculptures of Athens' ancient hero Theseus which adorn the frieze. Its survival is the result of conversion into a church. Excavations have shown that plants were arranged around it in antiquity and these have been restored.

Below: The stoa was a quintessentially Greek building. It provided shelter from the sun while allowing the cooling breezes to circulate. Behind the colonnade it could house shops or administrative offices. The re-erection of the stoa donated by Attalus II, king of Pergamon, 159–138 BC, was financed by Rockefeller money in the 1950s and it now houses a museum of artefacts found in the Agora excavations. Note the fine head of Nike, the personification of victory.

CLASSICAL GREEK PHILOSOPHY

The word philosophy comes from the Greek meaning 'love of wisdom' but this gives little idea of the enormous range of the Greek intellectual tradition. In the first instance, it depended on questioning the nature of the physical world, trying to see whether there were underlying laws from which predictions could be made. The idea of natural laws was important, because it was an alternative to the view that the gods intervened in the order of things—that thunder, for instance, was a manifestation of Zeus' anger.

In the 5th century BC the centre of philosophical activity was Athens. The rise of democracy sparked off an intense interest in public speaking and the construction of an argument, and these skills were taught by the Sophists, men who charged fees in return for passing on their expertise. The Sophists spawned many new ideas but also resentment from more austere philosophers, who felt that knowledge was not something that could be traded for money. The man who steered philosophy in a new direction was Socrates (469–399 BC). Socrates was self-absorbed and unashamed in his intellectualism. He took little care of his own appearance but was ruthless in his exposure of shoddy thinking. He would confront even passers-by, ask them what they believed and then break down their replies to show how inadequate their ideas were. This destruction of conventional thinking meant nothing, of course, without something more constructive to put in its place and Socrates speculated on how one could define concepts such as Truth, Beauty and Justice in unchallengeable ways. However, at a time of great tension in Athens at the end of the Peloponnesian War, he aroused too much distrust and he was put on trial for 'corruption of the young'. He argued his case so arrogantly that the jury found him guilty and passed a death sentence. Socrates' most faithful follower was Plato, a young aristocratic Athenian (429–347 BC) who was determined to find a foundation for absolute truth that could be grasped by reason. He argued that 'Forms' or 'Ideas' of Beauty, Justice, Goodness and so on, did exist but on a plane above the material world. Through a long and disciplined search a few selected individuals could reach an understanding of the Forms, memories of which are actually imprinted on our souls waiting for rediscovery. These 'Guardians', as Plato called them, then had the right to impart these ideas to the masses. His Republic, or the ideal society as he envisaged it, was to be an authoritarian state which would ban poetry and sensual living and concentrate instead on attaining the ultimate value, the Good. His austerity was offset by the way in which he presented his ideas, taking the figure of Socrates and involving him in dialogues with opponents. These works are so readable and show up the weaknesses of conventional thinking so effectively that they remain important to this day.

Plato set up his Academy as a school within which his ideas could be taught and explored further. His most famous pupil, Aristotle (384–322 BC), placed much greater value on the material world than Plato did and he had little time for speculating about what could not be apprehended by the bodily senses. He was the first great natural scientist, a founder of the disciplines of zoology and botany.

One could not gather information and relate it in a coherent system, however, without knowing how to use logic. Aristotle established that any theory was only as good as the empirical evidence on which it was based. He also developed systems of more formal logic. 'All men are mortal, Socrates is a man, therefore Socrates is mortal' makes logical sense. 'All dogs have four legs, all cats have four legs, therefore all cats are dogs' does not and Aristotle lays down the rules to show us why.

In the early Christian centuries Plato was preferred over Aristotle. Like Plato, Christians distrusted the senses and wished to understand the nature of the world beyond. However, Christianity came to rely too heavily on faith at the expense of reason and the restoration of Aristotelian reason by the 13th-century Dominican theologian Thomas Aquinas brought Aristotle into the forefront of Christian thinking. The different approaches to knowledge of Plato and Aristotle have led to a creative tension which has been of immense importance to the history of philosophy.

Facing page: The oldest of the Athenian teaching schools was Plato's Academy, founded in the 4th century. This mosaic of the 1st century BC, found in a villa at Pompeii, is believed to represent it. The Academy survived until closed down by the emperor Justinian in AD 529.

ATHENIAN DEMOCRACY

Athenian democracy can be said to have come of age in 461 BC when a coup led by one Ephialtes and an ambitious thirty-year-old aristocrat named Pericles seized power on behalf of the citizen assembly. The assembly could now make policy on almost any issue, including religious matters, foreign affairs and civic administration. It was made up of all male citizens over eighteen once they had completed two years of military service. There may have been some 30,000 men eligible, although only a small proportion would have been able to attend the assembly regularly. By the end of the 5th century it was meeting some 40 times a year on the Pnyx, the hill above the Agora.

Certainly there were powerful speakers, many of them aristocrats such as Pericles himself, all trained in rhetoric, but it needed enormous skill to dominate what were often raucous debates. During the Peloponnesian War, when tensions were acute, the historian Thucydides complained that unscrupulous speakers were manipulating the assembly. On occasions, when emotions rode high, the assembly would pass a harsh sentence of which it would later repent. A notable example was the decision to execute all the men of the city of Mytilene who had rebelled against Athens, a decision which was rescinded when emotions had cooled. A trireme arrived at the city just in time to stop the executions.

The first European literature was created when the Greeks mastered the Phoenician consonantal alphabet, added vowels and began to record the epics of Homer, which had been preserved in the memories of wandering poets. The earliest surviving examples of Greek writing are texts scratched on pottery dating from the first half of the 8th century BC. The example here is an *ostrakon*. Athenians developed a system by which any disruptive or otherwise undesirable citizen could be expelled from the city by a vote. The name of the man chosen was scratched on a piece of pottery (an *ostrakon*) and placed in an urn. Here the name of Themistocles, the architect of the victory of Salamis, can be seen. Despite his success he was caught up in the power politics of his city, offended many by his arrogance and was ostracised in 472 or 471 BC.

Those citizens aged thirty, perhaps 20,000 of them, were eligible to be selected by lot for jobs in the city administration. Whether it was supervision of the prisons or street cleaning, conducting religious rituals, organising the law courts or keeping the city accounts, all this was done by unpaid citizens. It was a remarkable system and carefully supervised. At the end of each year's service, accounts were checked to make sure there had been no corrupt activity.

There were also the citizen juries. Again the pool of jurors was drawn from those over thirty, with 6,000 being selected for service each year. Juries could be as large as 2,000, and sittings might take up to 200 days a year. As a result Pericles introduced payment. The law courts were very lively. Citizens could be accused—often, it appears, for political reasons—of breaking any law, and then had to defend themselves before the jurors. The most ribald taunts were acceptable. The orator Demosthenes faced accusations from a political rival that he had betrayed his friends, had been the passive partner in a homosexual encounter, behaved as a coward in battle and had failed to respect the gods. The most celebrated case is that of Socrates, who outraged the jurors by claiming that he should be supported at public expense for his philosophical activities. His accusers were eventually goaded into ordering the death penalty.

The system certainly had its flaws. Yet despite the attacks of philosophers such as Socrates' pupil Plato (who compared democracy to a ship without a captain), the Athenians were proud of their achievements. It has been argued that the success and prosperity of the city was the result of the effective use of talent and the resolution of social conflict through the safety valve of the law courts. It is remarkable that even during the most horrific days of the Peloponnesian War, tragedians such as Euripides were still able to question the validity of war and comedians such as Aristophanes ridicule the city's leading politicians. There has perhaps never been another such example of direct democracy—citizens being involved in their government simply by virtue of their citizenship—in history.

Delos

'Delos, if you would be willing to be the abode of my son Phoebus Apollo and make him a rich temple—for no other will touch you, as you will find: and I think you will never be rich in oxen and sheep, nor bear vintage nor yet produce plants abundantly. But if you have the temple of far-shooting Apollo, all men will bring you hecatombs and gather here, and incessant savour of rich sacrifice will always arise, and you will feed those who dwell in you from the hand of strangers; for truly your own soil is not rich.'

Homeric Hymn to Delian Apollo (Tr. Hugh Evelyn-White)

Island sanctuary (of Apollo) and commercial centre Flourished 6th–3rd centuries BC and c. 250–88 BC

The island of Delos, in the centre of the Cyclades, is not an obvious place to find one of the most important cult centres of antiquity, but it is home to the greatest of all of the sanctuaries to Apollo, and the island's location may well have influenced the choice: as one sails eastwards from the Peloponnese towards the coast of Asia, it provides the last and the best anchorage, just halfway through the passage. It is well sheltered by the islands surrounding it. It was also a haven for those making their way between Crete and the Dardanelles, which connect the Aegean to the Sea of Marmara and thence to Byzantium.

From earliest times Delos was sacred to Apollo, son of Zeus, who was said to have been born here: at his birth the barren island responded with an outburst of fruitfulness. Apollo, known also as Phoebus, the Shining One, was god of light and reason, lord of the swift bow. All the Olympians represent the triumph of order over brute nature—as the friezes of battles between gods and giants on so many temple friezes show—but this is perhaps especially true of Apollo. Also venerated here was another son of Zeus, the god

Delos has a stunningly beautiful setting and was always to be a centre for commercial and ritual activity, as sailing routes converged on this scatter of islands.

Above: The procession of lions at Delos echoes similar processions of rams and sphinxes in Egypt and the idea may well have been brought to Delos by Naxian traders, whose influence was felt early here, and who had trading links with Egypt. The lions certainly date from the period of Naxian rule, before Athens came to control the island in the 6th century BC.

Dionysus, in many ways the antithesis of Apollo. Born in the East, he came in triumph to Greece, mounted on a leopard, with satyrs and maenads in drunken, frenetic attendance. Dionysus is the god of abandon, through which man can come at wisdom (*see p. 178*).

The Naxians were the first people to control Delos and they instituted a festival, the Delia, which was open to all Ionian Greeks (Hellenes from the Aegean and Asia Minor). Several monuments survive from this period, including the base of a great statue of Apollo which stood inside the sanctuary.

As Athens rose to power and prosperity in the 6th century, it gradually increased its hold on Delos, carrying out purification rituals, including the removal of all bodies buried there. The city maintained her control over the island by fostering a festival to Apollo, in effect a revival of the Delia. Apollo was always feared as the god who brought disease, and the foundation of the festival in the 420s may be a propitiation after the plague which had swept Athens in 431. Everything had to be brought in for the festivals, and a long line of ships, led by the Athenian delegation in an ancient vessel, *Theoris*, which was believed to have been used by the great Athenian hero Theseus, carried the priests, choirs and sacrificial victims. The rituals were followed by games and oratory competitions, and music, as befitted Apollo's own interests (the historian Xenophon records that the Athenian choirs always won). Athenian dominance of the island came to be so resented that one of the first acts of the Spartan generals after the defeat of Athens in the Peloponnesian War was to make their own dedications in the sanctuary.

THE SITE

The Sanctuary of Apollo **(1)**, a large complex with the remains of three temples, lies close to the shore. When completed in the 3rd century, it would have been an impressive sight to pilgrims as they approached by sea. To the north there is a Sacred Lake **(2)**, now dried up, where the sacred geese and swans of Apollo would have had their home. There are distinct echoes of Egypt (notably Karnak), not only in the presence of a sacred lake, but also in the famous procession of lions **(3)** which lines the route and which is very similar to those found protecting Egyptian temples. Five of the original twelve lions remain (*see illustration above*).

In front of the lion terrace is the columned Agora of the Italians **(4)**, built by the Italian residents of Delos towards the end of the 2nd century BC. A Temple to Dionysus **(5)**, the god who frees mankind from his troubles through frenzy, ecstasy and wine, and who would have presided over the choruses at the festivals, is honoured by a series of now damaged phalluses (*see example opposite*).

To the south of the sanctuary a theatre was built in the 3rd century BC. Here was the residential quarter **(6)**. The 3rd century saw the emergence of much more comfortable homes, with corridors leading in from the street to enclosed courtyards. Floors were decorated with mosaic, of which excellent examples remain. The so-called

House of the Masks **(7)**, which may have acted as a hostel for visiting actors, is full of references to Dionysus, and the god himself is shown riding a leopard (*pictured opposite*).

The best preserved series of religious buildings on the island are the Sanctuaries of the Foreign Gods **(8)**. The breakdown of the Greek city-states with their traditional gods had led to an enthusiasm for the cults of Egypt and the Near East. Scrapis (*see p. 109*) and Isis (*see p. 178*) were adopted from Egypt, while the orgiastic rituals of the Syrian goddess Atargatis and her consort Hadah could be watched from a small theatre **(9)**. It was said

PLAN OF ANCIENT DELOS

1	Sanctuary of Apollo	7	House of the Masks
2	Sacred Lake	8	Sanctuaries of the Foreign Gods
3	Lion terrace	9	Small theatre (odeon)
4	Agora of the Italians	10	Macedonian stoa (Stoa of Antigonus)
5	Temple of Dionysus	11	Commercial harbour
6	Residential quarter		

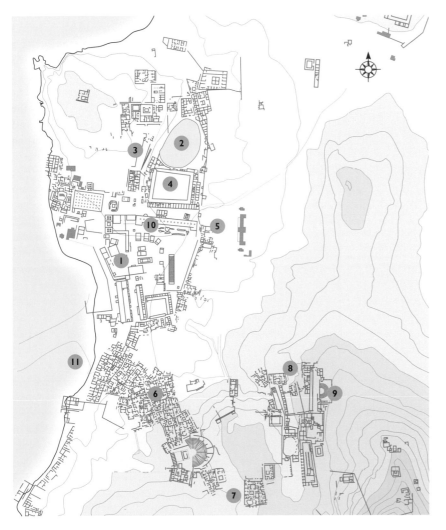

Above: The phallus, here one of a row, was a common symbol of Dionysus, whose orgiastic rites were linked with fertility and regeneration.

Facing page: Dionysus was always the god of excess and abandon. This fine mosaic from the House of the Masks shows the god in a typical pose, seated on a leopard. His legend describes him riding such a beast on his progress to Greece from his birthplace in India.

In this fine Hellenistic sculpture of c. 100 BC, dedicated in Delos by a trader whose family came from Berytus, the modern Beirut, Aphrodite is shown as a serene goddess of love, repelling an advance by the god Pan by slapping him with her sandal. Eros hovers between the two.

that an Athenian priest was brought in to bring some order to the proceedings by incorporating the more sober cults of Aphrodite.

DELOS AS A COMMERCIAL CENTRE

Athenian control over the island had ended by the 3rd century BC, when Macedonia became the dominant power in the Aegean. The northern side of the sanctuary was given a fine stoa by the Macedonian general Antigonus **(10)**, and over the next two centuries Delos came into its own as a commercial centre. It ran itself as a democracy, with a presiding magistrate, senate and assembly. Roman merchants began visiting in about 250 BC and after Roman control was asserted over the eastern Mediterranean the Romans allowed the Athenians to return as nominal overlords. When Corinth was sacked by the Romans in 146 BC many Corinthian merchants set up their business on the island. The granaries and warehouses whose remains line the shore of the commercial harbour **(11)** date from this period. Delos also became the centre of the slave trade, and the geographer Strabo records that there were some 10,000 transactions a day in its markets. All this came to an end in 88 BC when King Mithridates of Pontus, a powerful enemy of Rome, attacked the island, massacred or enslaved its inhabitants and sacked the city. The Romans regained control but somehow the island never recovered its prosperity. When Pausanias visited in the 2nd century AD he found the only inhabitants to be the temple guards. With few resources of its own, the island remained largely deserted.

SHIPPING IN ANTIQUITY

During the summer months the Mediterranean is a stable sea and navigation is facilitated by the mass of small islands, especially in the Aegean. Over 13,000 years ago traders were reaching the island of Milos to mine its obsidian. By 1600 BC, the Minoans had established a trading empire, their slender vessels relying on a combination of sail and oar, vital in a sea where the winds are so variable and the entrances to bays and harbours tricky to negotiate.

The famous 14th-century BC shipwreck of a merchantman at Uluburun (southern Turkey) shows just how sophisticated the trading networks were at this date, with cargo (some standard such as copper, some luxury such as Egyptian jewellery) being picked up and dropped off as the ship made its circuit from the Nile around the eastern Mediterranean.

Homer's epics are full of the sea: the exhilaration of sailing with the wind behind the sail, driving the ship onwards, or the safe arrival on shore as the vessel beached, anchored in earliest times with heavy stones. In frescoes of Minoan sea battles, we can see that the ships have no special defences and rely on arrows and lances to disable each other's crews. By 850 BC we have our first evidence of a revolution in naval warfare: the ram. Instead of ships coming close together with their crews fighting it out by hand, they were now required to manoeuvre towards an enemy ship, set up a burst of speed, crash against its hull and move away fast. The head of the ram was specially shaped to minimise the risk of it getting stuck in the hull of a rival.

This revolution meant that crews had to be highly trained and their strength consolidated by their seating arrangements in the hull. The historian Thucydides tells us that it was the Corinthians who first developed the trireme, perhaps around 650 BC, but it was the Athenians who perfected it in the 5th century. The Athenian navy had two hundred triremes—some 34,000 rowers—at the Battle of Salamis in 480 BC. It was an extraordinary achievement to be able to organise so many men and coordinate them in

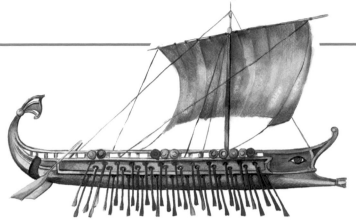

Facing page: The earliest ships were constructed by knocking planks together with mortice and tenon joints and then adding a frame to give the whole strength. It was a method which continued for centuries: it is not until well into the 1st millennium AD that an alternative approach, constructing the frame first and then adding on the planks, began to take over.

Left: The drawing here shows a trireme under sail, its ram clearly visible at the front. As the name trireme suggests, the rowers were arranged on three levels. There were 27 oarsman on each side of the ship on the lower two levels and 31 on the top. To this basic crew of 170 oarsman were added some 30 more (officers and sail-handlers). The oars were banked so that the ship could be rowed without any clashing but, as modern experiments with the trireme *Olympias* have shown, coordination had to be meticulous (the rhythm was maintained by a musical beat).

battle formation. A major problem was how to provide a supply of fresh water for so many crews rowing in the heat of a Greek day. It is said that it was this common sense of purpose of the mass of rowers that impelled Athens towards democracy in 461.

Triremes continued in operation in the navies of the Mediterranean but in the 3rd century BC a range of much larger warships began to be built. Termed supergalleys, penteres (Greek) or quinqueremes (Latin), they were a response to the intense rivalry between Alexander the Great's generals as they battled for dominance over the eastern Mediterranean. The Romans celebrated the capture of ships by prising off their rams (*rostra*) and installing them as trophies on the speakers' tribune in the Forum (hence the word rostrum for a speaker's platform).

After the great naval battle of Actium in 31 BC, when Octavian (the future emperor Augustus) defeated Antony and Cleopatra, there was no Mediterranean navy able to challenge Rome. It was more a matter of defending the coastlines from pirates or, later, fighting off barbarian raids. Smaller manoeuvrable ships manned by well-trained soldiers were all that was needed. As the *pax romana* spread across the Mediterranean the large galleys were replaced by merchantmen. Grain, wine and olive oil were the major trade staples, carried in sailing ships steered by quarter rudders, like large oars, on either side. Their capacity was considerable. One 1st-century BC wreck contained 6,000 amphorae (the standard way of carrying wine or oil). Even more remarkable were the vast blocks of stone conveyed to Rome and other major cities from Egypt and north Africa. The eight Egyptian granite columns of the Pantheon are almost 50 ft high. All this collapsed as the Empire disintegrated in the 4th century. Trade dropped dramatically and with it the spread of goods across the empire. It has been argued that Roman levels of trade were not reached again in the Mediterranean until 1600.

Above: The quinquereme became the standard warship of any state able to man them. The Carthaginians adopted them and when their empire went to war with Rome in the 3rd century BC they had an immediate advantage over a city-state with little experience of the sea. Legend tells how the Romans quickly learned to copy the Carthaginian model from a captured ship and soon had a hundred supergalleys in service. Because training

crews to ram would take too long, they fitted a platform, the *corvus* (or 'crow'), to the prow of the ship and used it as a boarding plank. This proved successful in battle but not so helpful in storms when its weight caused ships to capsize. The Romans went back to training up crews. They eventually defeated the Carthaginians by a combination of victories on land and at sea.

Segesta and Selinunte

Greek colonies in Sicily
Flourished 6th–5th centuries BC

The landscape of Sicily is fertile and agricultural, and was an important source of grain for the ancient Greeks and after them the Romans. The island was an important centre of cults of the earth deities. Demeter, the goddess of the harvest, and her daughter Persephone, were particularly honoured here (*see overleaf*).

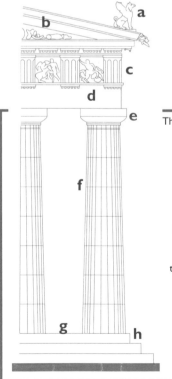

The main features of the Doric order:

(a) acroterion, the wedge-shaped plinth and ornament at the edge of the roof; **(b)** the pediment, formed of a horizontal and two raking cornices framing a triangular space (the tympanum), filled with a relief; **(c)** the frieze, made up of alternating decorated panels (metopes) and triple vertical grooves (triglyphs). The frieze and the architrave **(d)**, the horizontal stone lintel above the columns, make up the entablature. The capital **(e)** sits on top of the column, whose shaft **(f)** is fluted. The column has no base, but rests immediately on the top level of the temple platform, the stylobate **(g)**. The platform is stepped, and is known as the crepidoma **(h)**.

The Greeks in Sicily

The Greeks first landed in Sicily in the 8th century BC: the Euboeans put down a toehold in 734 at the first landfall on the island from the eastern Mediterranean, the modern Giardini Naxos. The Corinthians soon followed, setting up a colony at Syracuse, which had a fine harbour and fresh water. It was to become the largest of the Greek cities in Sicily. Once the best sites on the eastern coast had been occupied, the Greeks spread along the south to Gela (688) and from Gela to Agrigento (580). Native populations were broken up or pushed inland, and before long the colonists were cultivating grain so successfully that they were exporting it back to the less fertile lands of their native Greece. The wealth they gathered went towards the building of opulent cities and vast temples.

THE DORIC ORDER

The Doric order as developed by the Greeks, and which flourished in Sicily, gave a simplicity to their temple construction which is immediately attractive (although there was originally much more decoration and colouring than appears in surviving ruins today). Despite its apparent regularity, temple-building does not seem to have proceeded from a drawn plan. The base or stepped platform (the crepidoma) was laid first, with a slight slope outwards so that rain would run off. The columns would be built next. An irregularity, the entasis, was built in so that sometimes the outer columns were wider or all the columns bulged slightly outwards. This added to the impact of the building and corrected any optical illusion of curvature. It is one reason why Greek temples are so aesthetically satisfying. Only when the basic shape of the temple was in place would the naos be built inside: it can be assumed that the relationship between the completed columns dictated all the other relationships in the rest of the building.

THE TEMPLES

The great Doric temples of the Greek colonies of Sicily stand serene and confident today, but the impression of solidity is an illusion, for they were built in turbulent times when the cities were fighting bitterly amongst each other and against the encroaching Carthaginians. No one can forget their first sight of the great temple at Segesta, which dominates the landscape as one ascends from below. The city's ancient rival, Selinous (the modern Selinunte), constructed three equally massive temples alongside each other, a display of pride and status to impress any visitor approaching from the east. Yet both cities were more vulnerable than they appeared. At the end of the 5th century BC the Carthaginians carried out a major sacking of Selinunte. The temples were reduced to ruins and the city's inhabitants sold as slaves. Segesta continued its existence as a subject of Carthage. After this, although there was some revival of Greek power under a series of impressive leaders, notably Dionysius of Syracuse (ruled 405–367), the Carthaginians could not be dislodged from western Sicily. Their expansion brought its own reaction from the Roman empire, and, as was usual with Rome, no city, Greek or Carthaginian, was ultimately able to sustain its independence. Segesta became the first Sicilian city to declare allegiance to Rome; by the end of the 3rd century the entire island had become a province of the empire. The surplus of Sicilian grain was now diverted to the hungry masses of Rome itself.

The great Doric temple at Segesta, which was never finished (the columns have no fluting), and perhaps was never intended to be. It is possible that it was planned as a prestige project to awe and intimidate other cities.

Agrigento

Greek colony in Sicily
Flourished 480–410 BC

The outline of the temples of Agrigento, on a ridge as one enters the valley below the modern town, is stunning. This was the ancient Greek Akragas, in a fine position on the coast, well able to exploit both trade and the fertile hinterland. One of the city's 5th-century inhabitants, the poet Pindar, talked of 'a splendour-loving city, the most beautiful on earth, home of Persephone'. Its population at its height has been estimated at 200,000.

The greatest moment in Akragas' history came in 480, when the Greek forces of Akragas and Syracuse defeated the Carthaginians at Himera, a city on the northern coast of Sicily that the Carthaginians were trying to prise from Akragas' control. The 70 years of peace that followed led to a period of enormous prosperity for the Greeks. When the Carthaginians returned, however, the short period of Akragas' greatness was at an end. In the 3rd century BC the city became entangled in the Punic Wars between Rome and Carthage, and was finally conquered by the Romans in 210. It was renamed Agrigentum, and survived in reduced form for 500 years, until the Roman Empire collapsed, at which point its position on the coast made it all too vulnerable to raiders. The inhabitants gradually withdrew from their ancient city to higher ground, where the modern town still stands.

CULTS OF THE EARTH GODS

In the temple area at Agrigento is an enclosure known as the Sanctuary of the Chthonic Divinities, sacred to the gods of the earth, Dionysus, Demeter and her daughter Persephone. Human civilisation depended on the growth of corn, and Sicily was a bountiful producer. Demeter, goddess of the harvest, was an important deity on the island, and many sanctuaries were dedicated to her and to her daughter, who had been snatched away into the underworld. The world had been in mourning while Persephone was missing, but sprang into life again at her 'resurrection', when she was granted leave to return to her mother for six months of each year. The seasons were the result: at each annual return of Persephone, the earth would show its bounty again. The best documented mystery ceremonies of the ancient Greek world, in fact, were those held in Demeter's honour at Eleusis near Athens, the site where, by legend, the goddess had been reunited with her daughter. We have only a sketchy idea of what went on at an initiation ceremony at Eleusis, but it is clear that the rites offered some comfort to the initiate, who was guaranteed a better fate in the afterworld. 'Thrice blessed are those mortals who have seen these rites and thus enter into Hades: for them alone there is life, for the others all is misery', is how the tragedian Sophocles put it. The mysteries continued well into Roman times: Cicero wrote that they offered 'a way of dying with greater hope'. Clay tablets with images of Demeter and Persephone were commonly used as grave offerings.

Above: Temple in the Sanctuary of the Chthonic Divinities at Agrigento, dedicated to the gods of the earth and fertility, the harvest, growth and renewal.

Left: Carthaginian coin of the 4th century BC showing a head of Persephone with a garland of corn in her hair.

THE TEMPLES

The main part of ancient Akragas was in the fertile valley below where the modern town now stands. Just inside the southern wall there was a ridge, an ideal vantage point on which to build a series of temples. The largest, dedicated to Olympian Zeus, is the biggest temple ever known in Sicily. Unusually, the normal rows of columns were replaced by walls with half-columns placed against them. Built into the walls were vast male statues (telamones) who appeared to be holding up the roof (there were 38 in total and a reconstruction of one is in the city's museum). Both these temples were on raised knolls and they must have inspired the city to flaunt its wealth by building more along the ridge. Another five temples were put in hand. All are in the local limestone, but as this was easily eroded they were cased in painted stucco. Now this has gone, the warmth of the original stone makes their aspect especially romantic.

The most spectacular of the temples are those on the east. The first, the Temple of Concord (*illustrated opposite*), is the best preserved of all the Greek temples after the Temple of Hephaistos in Athens. The name comes from a Latin inscription found nearby; it is unlikely to have been the original dedication. It was begun about 450 BC, when temple-building was at its most sophisticated, and this temple has its own refinements, notably in the gap between the outer two columns of the porch, which is narrower than that in the centre. In the 6th century AD the temple was converted into a church. Its first priest, Gregory, records how he chased away the pagan demons which still haunted the site. Walls were built inside the temple and there were

Facing page: The Temple of Concord, the most famous of all the Agrigento temples, built in the mid-5th century BC and converted into a church in Christian times, hence its excellent state of preservation.

Above: The Temple of Hera at Agrigento clings to the eastern end of the ridge and gives some idea of how impressive the temples must have been for visitors approaching the city.

Right: Christians were always suspicious of ancient temples as they felt they might still be haunted by pagan demons. Many were destroyed but others—the Temple of Hephaistos and the Parthenon in Athens, and the Temple of Athena in Syracuse—were converted into churches. Here the inner wall of Agrigento's Temple of Concord provides a vivid picture of its conversion to Christian use.

statues of St Peter and St Paul. A Christian cemetery is nearby. The building was thus preserved until the late 18th century, by which time there was a new passionate interest in ancient Greece. The German poet Goethe, visiting in 1786, enthused over the beauty of Girgenti, as Agrigento was then known, especially as the sun rose over the valley. Two years later, the Bourbon king of Naples and Sicily, Ferdinand, decided to restore the temple to its original state. Statues and other additions were taken away, though the inner walls of the nave remain in place (*illustrated below*) and an inscription on the façade records the temple's transition back to its Classical origins.

Right at the end of the ridge is another temple, also Doric (*pictured above*), which has traditionally been seen as a dedication to Hera, the wife of Zeus. Impact was everything for such a proud city as Akragas, and the commanding position on the edge of the city wall was exploited to the full. The foundations had to be built up to support it, and to make it even more impressive there are four steps leading up to it rather than the usual three. The temple still bears marks of a fire and so records the devastating revenge of the Carthaginians. A Carthaginian army besieged the city for eight months in 406 and when it fell there was widespread destruction.

Paestum

Greek colony in southern Italy
Flourished 6th–5th centuries BC

The Greeks in Italy

The earliest Greek settlement on the southern Italian mainland was Cumae, founded in 740 BC. Like many of the Greek cities of the region it became very prosperous and began founding its own colonies. Neapolis, the modern Naples, was one of them, first settled c. 600 BC. Another important early foundation (c. 720 BC) was Sybaris, with settlers from the northeast Peloponnese. It was especially successful in trading with the Etruscans and became so fabulously wealthy that the word 'sybaritic' still denotes luxury. It aroused the jealousy of its neighbour Croton and was destroyed by it in 510 BC, but not before it too had founded colonies, among them Poseidonia, more usually known by its Roman name, Paestum.

The Greek colonies of southern Italy were collectively known as Magna Graecia, 'greater Greece', a term which was sometimes extended to include Sicily as well. Their cities, like those of Sicily, were modelled on those at home but they had far greater resources. They also made their own contributions to Greek culture. Pythagoras, for instance, was a migrant from Samos to Croton (about 530 BC) and he attracted an impressive school of followers there. Legends credit him with many teachings: the transmigration of souls, the theorem of the right-angled triangle that bears his name, and a belief that numbers and ratios underpin the musical scale. Pythagoras was said to be the only mortal able to hear the 'music of the spheres', the notes produced by the circular motions of the stars. He founded a tradition of mystical meditation on philosophical issues which continued in southern Italy long after his death. Vegetarianism was one prominent Pythagorean practice.

The 6th-century Temple of Hera at Paestum is enormously impressive, even in ruin. Seeing the way the sun sets through its columns it is hardly surprising that a highly romanticised picture of ancient Greece developed in the minds of the 18th-century Grand Tourists. It is sobering to remember that much of the temple would have been gaudily painted and that there would have been a great stench of burning entrails from the blood sacrifices on the altar in front of it.

THE TEMPLES

Poseidonia, about 35 miles southeast of Naples, was a Greek colony that grew rich on the fertile soils of Italy. Its original walls were three miles in circumference and they enclosed a grid-planned city which was further developed when the Roman colony, Paestum, was set up. Poseidonia's most famous cultural contribution in the early period of its long history was three superb temples. The first was built between 550 and 530 BC and there is some archaeological evidence of a dedication to Hera, the wife of Zeus. The Doric columns are rather heavy but impressive nonetheless. The outer colonnade had nine columns along the front and twice that number, 18, along the sides, enclosing a naos which, unusually, had a row of columns running down its centre (it may have had a double dedication). There were further decorative refinements around the tops of the columns in the shape of floral motifs, and attractive terracotta sheathing along the eaves complete with animal-head waterspouts.

The second temple, the Temple of Ceres, was built, like the first, out of local limestone with sandstone additions. It is by far the smallest of the three and was built for effect on a limestone outcrop in the northern part of the city. It is revolutionary in being the first Greek temple to mix Doric and Ionic elements. The external columns are Doric; the inner shrine is fronted by Ionic columns. The Ionic influence is believed to have come from Miletus in Asia Minor, with which Poseidonia had close trading links (*for more on the Ionic order, see p. 120*).

The third temple, in chronological order, the so-called Temple of Poseidon, is aligned with the Temple to Hera and may have been on the site of what was in effect the earliest Paestum temple of all. It was built c. 460 BC but the quality of the limestone was poor and the columns are thicker than they would have been if the temple had been built, like many of its contemporaries, in marble. Inside the shrine were two rows of columns, an early use of a design which became common in Sicily and southern Italy.

When Goethe came this way in 1786 he found the temples disappointing at first, but they grew on him. 'Our eyes and, through them, our whole sensibility have become so conditioned to a more slender style of architecture that these crowded masses of stumpy conical columns appear offensive and even terrifying. But I pulled myself together, remembered the history of art, thought of the age in which its architecture was in harmony, called up images in my mind of the austere style of architecture—and in less than an hour I found myself reconciled with them … It is only by walking through them and round them that one can attune one's life to theirs and experience the emotional effect which the architect intended.' (*Italian Journey*, March 1786)

Two of Paestum's three magnificent temples, the Temple of Hera in the foreground (550–530 BC) and the Temple of Poseidon behind (c. 460 BC). The base of the sacrificial altar can clearly be seen in front of the latter temple.

The Tomb of the Diver, discovered in the necropolis just outside Paestum, is the only example of Greek painting with figures in its scenes to survive in its entirety from the period 700–400 BC (it is dated to c. 470 BC). The four inner walls of the coffin show a symposium, the Greek drinking party, well known from similar scenes on Greek pottery. The men have their drinking cups and some share a couch with younger boys in poses suggestive of homoeroticism. The inside of the coffin lid (shown here) is painted with a diver heading towards a still lake. This unique scene has been interpreted as a symbol of the transition from the security of life (the tower from which the diver leaps), through water to death.

THE GREEK TEMPLE

The idea of sacred space is a very old one, and in Greece the temenos, or sanctuary, within which cult worship took place, was certainly a feature of religious observance by the 8th century BC and probably much earlier. Greek cult centred on ritual sacrifice, and elaborate ceremonies were developed by which animals—anything from a bull to a chicken—could be brought to the temple, killed and cut up in a prescribed way, the meat distributed to the assembled worshippers and feasting enjoyed by all. Worship was not congregational, as we understand worship in a church, mosque or synagogue. The faithful remained outside the temple, which was strictly the domain of the priests. The sacrificial altar would be outside too, typically at the east end (the temple entrance faced the rising sun). A cult statue of the deity to whom the sanctuary was devoted, originally in wood, was housed within the temple itself, in an inner chamber known as the naos (cella in Latin).

Early temples were rudimentary and it seems that their roofs were held up by wooden posts grouped around the naos. The roofs were designed with a considerable overhang, which had the practical purposes of taking the weight from the walls and allowing rain to run off clear. The naos could be given an extra chamber, back to back with that housing the statue (*see diagram*), and with no entrance except from within, in which valuables and other dedications could be kept. Such was the genesis of the temple.

The key development was building in stone. Stone, whether in limestone or the harder marble, is common in Greece, while wood is rare. Inspiration for carvers could be found in Egypt where the Greeks were trading by the 7th century. Here sophisticated stone-working skills had been developed over millennia. The columns of Hatshepsut's temple at Deir el-Bahri near Luxor (c. 1460 BC; *illustrated on p. 29*) seem an obvious model for the thickset Doric colonnade.

The greatest age of Greek temple-building was the 6th century BC, largely because of the larger numbers of temples being built both in Greece itself and in Magna Graecia. In these areas the impetus is sustained into the 5th century but drops off in Italy and Sicily during the tensions in the region with the rise of Rome and inter-tribal fighting. On mainland Greece itself, building continues at a reduced level in the 4th and 3rd centuries BC.

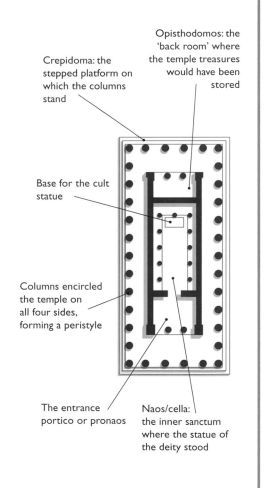

Crepidoma: the stepped platform on which the columns stand

Opisthodomos: the 'back room' where the temple treasures would have been stored

Base for the cult statue

Columns encircled the temple on all four sides, forming a peristyle

The entrance portico or pronaos

Naos/cella: the inner sanctum where the statue of the deity stood

The ancient
HELLENISTIC
world

' "Then verily, having crossed the narrow strait of the Hellespont,
The devastating host of the Gauls shall pipe; and lawlessly
They shall ravage Asia; and much worse shall God do
To those who dwell by the shores of the sea
For a short while. For right soon the son of Cronos
Shall raise them a helper, the dear son of a bull reared by Zeus,
Who on all the Gauls shall bring a day of destruction."

By the son of a bull she meant Attalus, king of Pergamon…'

Pausanias, 2nd century AD, commenting on an oracular prediction
concerning Attalus, whose dynasty glorified itself through the defeat of the
Celtic tribes (Gauls) who had invaded Asia Minor

Historical overview

The Hellenistic Age is the period between the death of Alexander the Great in 323 BC and the addition of Egypt, the last of his successor kingdoms, to the Roman empire by Octavian, the future emperor Augustus, in 30 BC.

Alexander's vast dominion was brought into being by his destruction of the Persian empire, which had extended as far east as modern Afghanistan. But he had made no plans for the long-term survival of his conquests, and after his death they fell prey to rival generals. By the early 3rd century three kingdoms had emerged, one centred on Alexander's own monarchy, Macedonia; one under the Seleucids (named after one of Alexander's generals, Seleucus), which extended over much of Asia; and one centred on Egypt, under the Ptolemies (named after another general and former bodyguard), which also expanded into the eastern

THE HELLENISTIC WORLD

Antigonids   Seleucids

Attalids   Ptolemies

Mediterranean. Greek culture no longer revolved around independent city-states as it had in the earlier Classical period, and rulers now took on a semi-divine status. This was a much more fluid and opportunistic world—the Greek cities of Egypt attracted newcomers from at least 200 cities outside Egypt. The mingling led to the disappearance of dialects and the emergence of a common Greek, *koine*.

The influx of booty from the East also made for wealthier societies. Homes became larger and more comfortable and mosaics widespread. The richer rulers flaunted their patronage on libraries and showcase building projects, especially shrines, temples and the open colonnades known as stoas. The simple purity of Classical art was no longer fashionable and art became more flamboyant. Typical prestige projects of the age were the Colossus of Rhodes, a massive bronze statue of Helios the sun god at the entrance to Rhodes harbour; the Lighthouse of Alexandria; and the great Altar of Zeus at Pergamon.

The intellectual powerhouse of the Hellenistic world was Alexandria, where there were major developments in science and mathematics. This was the age of Euclid, Archimedes and Hipparchus, the great astronomer and mathematician. Alexandria's library was the greatest in the Greek world (*see p. 116*).

As in any fast-changing world, new cults grasped the imagination of restless minds. Religious beliefs were marked by spiritual exuberance and diversity. Tyche, Fate, personified as a woman, became a popular city god, while many joined mystery cults surrounding the Egyptian deities Serapis and Isis. Serapis was an amalgamation of Osiris, the Egyptian god of the afterlife, Apis, the Egyptian bull-god, and a number of other deities. He is commonly shown with a grain measure on his head, a symbol of fertility. He was patronised by the Ptolemies in one of the greatest temple complexes of the ancient world, the Serapeum in Alexandria, but his cult spread widely, certainly to all the major Greek cities of the period.

Above: The second great battle between Alexander the Great and the Persians took place in 333 BC and resulted in a devastating defeat for the Persian king Darius. This mosaic from Pompeii, with the youthful Alexander on the left heading towards a routed Darius right of the centre, shows the powerful impact of the battle even on the Roman imagination.

Previous page: Detail of a marble statue of the 2nd century BC showing a defeated Gaul. The exaggerated brow and deep eye sockets are typical of Hellenistic sculpture.

Compared to sculptors of the Classical period, those of the Hellenistic Age thrust their onlookers into drama. For the frieze of the Pergamon altar (c. AD 160) they may have adopted the idea of a narrative from the Parthenon and other Classical buildings but the narrative they show is a cosmic battle between gods and giants which goes well beyond any calm Classical equivalent (in total there are 34 goddesses, 20 gods, 59 giants and 28 animals shown). The whole has been planned by a single mind but the mythology is intricate. The ruler, Eumenes II, was advertising his knowledge of Greek culture. Here the goddess Athena is shown seizing a winged giant by the hair. His mother, Gaia, the earth, representing the original, untamed forces of creation, pleads for his life.

The borders of the Hellenistic kingdoms were always fluid. The Seleucids steadily lost territory to the Ptolemies, while at Pergamon the Attalid dynasty carved out its own independent realm. But by the late 2nd century all these kingdoms faced the growing power of Rome. Macedonia was the first to succumb, at the Battle of Pydna in 168 BC. The cities of the Greek mainland vainly sought refuge in confederations but these were easily outmanoeuvred by the Romans. In 146, the wealthy trading city of Corinth was brutally sacked to show the others the futility of resistance, and 50,000 men, women and children were sold into slavery. The Attalids wisely bequeathed their territory to Rome in 133 BC.

The Ptolemies held out. The last of their queens, Cleopatra, attempted to manipulate Roman alliances to her advantage but her relationship with the Roman general Mark Antony ended in disaster when Octavian destroyed their combined fleets at the Battle of Actium in 31 BC and Egypt became a province of Rome.

KEY DATES IN HELLENISTIC GREEK HISTORY

334 BC: Alexander the Great chases the Persians from Priene and Ephesus, going on to destroy the Persian empire

305 BC: The general Seleucus establishes the empire of Babylonia. Ptolemy declares himself king of Egypt as Ptolemy I Soter ('Saviour')

c. 300 BC: Ptolemy builds the famous Library at Alexandria

263 BC: Pergamon shakes off the Seleucids and founds its own ruling dynasty, the Attalids

323 BC: Death of Alexander the Great, aged 32. His generals battle with each other for control of his empire

302 BC: Lysimachus receives Lydia and Phrygia, on the west coast of modern Turkey

281 BC: Seleucus kills Lysimachus and takes control of his territory

240s: The Ptolemies expand into the eastern Mediterranean

STOICS, SCEPTICS & EPICUREANS: PHILOSOPHY OF THE HELLENISTIC AGE

Stoicism was born in Athens in the late 4th century BC, when the philosopher Zeno created his own school of followers who walked and talked in the colonnade of the Painted Stoa. The most important follower of Zeno is Chrysippus, who arrived in Athens c. 260. He appears to have been a powerful mind, and he may be the true founder of Stoicism as we know it today. There is a record of one scholar having a library of 700 papyrus rolls of Chrysippus' works, but no single complete text survives today.

The Stoics believed that the material world is moving providentially forward in a series of cycles, each of which will eventually end in a conflagration and then a rebirth. There is an underlying force, the *logos*, which underpins its movement. The world is a material whole, each part dependent on others, a point continually stressed in the famous *Meditations* of the Stoic emperor Marcus Aurelius in the 2nd century AD. It is important for the Stoic to live in harmony with a world to whose movements he is subject, not to try and see it for his own use.

Nevertheless, the Stoics thought deeply about what human beings are capable of. They deplored emotion, believing that one should learn to bring one's feelings under control in a world where one's influence is limited. The understanding and following of virtue is in itself sufficient for happiness. Stoics applauded reason as it allowed human beings to operate with some degree of free will. One could and should involve oneself in public affairs and serve others with honesty and sober judgment. Much Stoic writing is about the means by which one can transcend the bustle of everyday life without turning one's back on it. Yet dignity must be maintained. Another famous Stoic, Seneca, committed suicide in AD 65 when he felt no longer able to serve the dictatorial Nero as a minister.

The Stoics would resist the Christian idea that humanity has been given a privileged place by God, above and apart from the rest. Nevertheless, Stoic values did persist into the Christian era, for many other Stoic precepts proved attractive to the new religion: the stress on sober living, for example, and the readiness to face death unflinchingly in the name of virtue.

Stoicism faced two challenges from rival schools. The first of these were the Sceptics, who saw themselves as the heirs of Socrates in that they delighted in questioning all conventional knowledge. They were rooted in Plato's Academy and from the 3rd century engaged in a passionate and often highly erudite debate with the Stoics, particularly over whether anything of certainty can be said about the natural world. The arguments and counter-arguments of this enduring dialogue (it can be traced over 200 years) go right to the core of philosophical enquiry and are still alive in discussions on the nature of reality today.

The other great school, the Epicureans, drew their inspiration from Epicurus, a native of Samos, who came to Athens as a young man and remained there until his death in 270 BC. Epicurus was a materialist, believing essentially that what we see is what there is. He was prepared to accept that there might be gods, but they had no impact on human life and could safely be disregarded except in so far as their idealised lives could provide a model for those seeking eternal peace. What mattered above all was the cultivation of the mind as a route to happiness. 'We say that pleasure is the beginning and end of living happily.' Although often accused of simply being a pleasure-seeker, Epicurus in fact believed that the search for true happiness was a serious intellectual task and he and his followers were fully aware that happiness is not necessarily consequent on the mere fulfilment of desire.

Many despised the Epicureans, often in the belief that their lives were pure hedonism (they welcomed women and slaves into their entourage and it appears that the women were shared among them). They challenged the Stoic ideal that a man should be involved in public life as a matter of duty (it was, they said, far too stressful). For Christians their views were abhorrent. The great Christian philosopher-theologian Origen, who was ordinarily very open-minded in his reading of the pagan Classics, excluded the Epicureans. Yet there remains something of value in the more austere forms of Epicureanism: withdrawal from the world for philosophical contemplation on the nature of peaceful living is not without its attractions.

220s: Attalus I of Pergamon defeats the Gauls (Galatians)

146 BC: Rome advances through Greece and takes Corinth

31 BC: Battle of Actium. The fleet of Octavian (Augustus) defeats Antony and Cleopatra

29 BC: Augustus visits Asia Minor and chooses Ephesus to be capital of the new Roman province

168 BC: Battle of Pydna. Rome conquers Macedonia

133 BC: Seeing the way things are going, the Attalids of Pergamon bequeath their city to Rome

30 BC: Egypt is annexed to the Roman dominions

Pergamon

Pergamon had a fine site, far enough inland to be safe from opportunistic raiders while close enough to the sea to be able to communicate with the outside world. Its impressive citadel, with views over the surrounding countryside and a fertile valley beneath, ensured that the city was defensible as well as self-sufficient. Local resources included the fruits of the fertile soil, building stone (grey-blue andesite) and parchment (from the skins of sheep, goats or cattle). The latter is so identified with Pergamon that the word parchment itself derives from a Latin corruption of the name.

The strength of the site was the reason why one of Alexander the Great's generals, Lysimachus, chose to entrust a treasure of some 9,000 talents to one of his officers, Philetairus, to hoard there. For 15 years Philetairus proved a faithful custodian but when Lysimachus was defeated by Seleucus, the founder of the Seleucid dynasty, in 281, he submitted to the new rulers. The assassination of Seleucus shortly afterwards meant that Philetairus was, in effect, able to rule independently and he survived to the age of eighty, dying in 263 BC. The treasure remained his. His nephew and successor Eumenes I chanced his luck and successfully declared Pergamon independent.

The dynasty he founded is known as the Attalids, after Philetairus' father Attalus, and it soon took on the mantle of a champion of Greek culture. Philetairus had fortified the citadel and dedicated a temple to Athena there. Eumenes I was known to have patronised philosophers. His successor, Attalus I, probably a cousin, brought a new dimension in the 220s when he successfully defeated the Celtic tribes known as the

Pergamon is a dramatic sight. This aerial view shows the terraces up which one ascends (from the right) towards the citadel, where the columns of the later Temple of Trajan stand in the sanctuary of the earlier temple to Athena. On the hillside below the citadel is the theatre with, as is common with Greek theatres, stunning views of the valley below.

Pliny in his *Natural History* mentions Sosus of Pergamon as the most famous mosaicist of his day (2nd century BC), and certainly Pergamon

was known as a centre of mosaic-making. Sosus is credited with the *Asarotos oikos*, or 'Unswept Room', where discarded food and other debris are shown scattered on a floor. Roman copies exist of it as well as of another famous Sosus creation of doves drinking from a bowl of water. The most notable example of the latter comes from Hadrian's Villa at Tivoli (*illustrated on p. 183*).

Galatians, who were ravaging central Asia Minor. The Attalids now proclaimed that they had defeated the barbarians in the name of Greek civilisation just as the Athenians had defeated the 'barbarian' Persians 250 years before. Attalus made sure the Greek world knew of his success by dedicating trophies at Delos, Delphi and Athens as well as commemorating his victories with monuments in Pergamon itself. The famous *Dying Gaul* (*pictured below*) and *Celtic Chieftain with his Wife*, which today can be seen in Rome, are probably Roman copies of Attalus' dedications in his capital.

Attalus I died in 197 BC, just at the moment when Rome was beginning to confront the Greek world. His successor, Eumenes II, wisely kept in with the Romans, and survived their ever-growing power. This was partly because his three brothers stood loyally beside him even when Rome tried to involve one of them in a plot to depose him. The eldest of the three, Attalus II, succeeded in 159. He proved more ready to compromise with Rome, even providing troops to help in the sack of Corinth in 146. His successor, Attalus III, lacked the vigour of his predecessors and was soon embroiled in intrigues. The only way that he saw of keeping his kingdom intact was by bequeathing it to Rome, which he did on his death in 133.

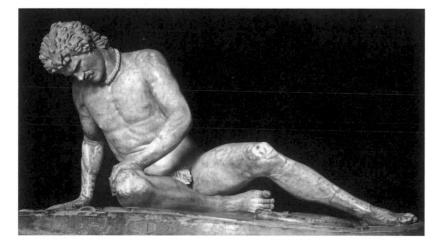

The sculpture known as the *Dying Gaul*, here in a Roman marble copy of the bronze original of c. 225 BC, reveals the respect with which the Attalids treated the Gauls whom they defeated. Nudity is always a mark of heroism: this, therefore, was an honourable enemy. The figure is recognised as a Gaul by the torc round his neck and, being beardless, he is probably a chieftain. The statue is typical of Pergamene art in that it exaggerates anatomical features, here the bulges on the brows and the muscles on the abdomen.

Right: Artist's reconstruction of the Altar of Zeus at Pergamon

Below: The inner frieze around the altar itself shows the life and exploits of Telephus, son of Hercules, and legendary founder of Pergamon. The scenes are represented in lower relief and in a much calmer narrative style than the clash and mêlée of the outer frieze.

Bottom: Just as today one might hang a reproduction of Van Gogh's *Sunflowers* in one's living room, so in Roman times copies of Greek and Hellenistic masterpieces adorned villas throughout the empire. This Roman version of a scene from the Telephus frieze comes from Herculaneum.

THE CITADEL

There are few sites which show the drama of Hellenistic architecture more completely than Pergamon. The ruins are essentially those of the city of Eumenes II, enclosed by walls and extending into the valley, leaving the higher ground free for the glorification of the Attalid dynasty. The royal palace, its barracks and service buildings were at the northern end of the citadel, where the steep slopes made them impregnable. The only access to the citadel was from the south, and the land was terraced so that one ascended from one section to the next, each level offering a more impressive vista.

First came the commercial agora, as if in acknowledgement of the founding wealth of trade. The next terraces were dedicated to gymnasia, each catering for an older age group as one climbed higher. The highest was fitted out for visiting philosophers with its own lecture hall. Rhetoric was an essential part of cultured life and here it was provided for in style. The whole gymnasium complex is the biggest and best preserved to survive from antiquity—though for all this there is no evidence of any great philosophy coming from Hellenistic Pergamon.

The next terrace contained another porticoed agora, possibly commercial in origin but which appears to have been adapted as a forum for legal and political affairs. Passing through this one reached the terrace on which stood the massive Altar of Zeus. Having been stripped bare by German archaeologists in the 19th century—350 tons of the altar were carted off to Berlin in 1880 alone—the space is now rather forlorn. Beyond it lay the Sanctuary of Athena, the original religious core of the city and host to a Panhellenic festival in honour of the goddess, which Eumenes founded in 182. Very little remains of the temple today; within its colonnade was housed the city's famous library (*see overleaf*). On the western edge of the site is the theatre, held in by a massive retaining wall which was embellished as yet another portico. Very much later, in the reign of Hadrian, a Roman temple was built on the northwestern edge of the citadel. It was dedicated to Hadrian's predecessor, the deified emperor Trajan.

THE ALTAR OF ZEUS

The Altar of Zeus is Pergamon's most celebrated monument, even though one now has to visit Berlin to see it. It was set out on what was an almost square base. One side was left open, the other three enclosed. A plinth of five steps led up to reliefs that ran round the sides and back of the altar in a continuous frieze of 400 ft showing the Olympian gods locked in combat with giants, whom they defeat and banish (*see illustration on p. 110*). This type of scene, known as a gigantomachy, was used often in Greek art as an allegory of Greek defeat of barbarians. Here it can be seen to stand for the Attalid triumph over the Galatians. Above the frieze was a colonnade, reached by a flight of steps up the open side of the complex. The altar itself was enclosed in the centre of the colonnade. The whole was the achievement of Eumenes II. The altar is dedicated to Zeus, although his daughter Athena is also given prominence. Yet the dedicatee might also be seen as the hero Telephus, son of Hercules, and hence grandson of Zeus, whom the Attalids claimed as the founder of their family. Telephus' story is told in a smaller, inner frieze around the altar itself (*see illustration opposite*).

THE WATER SUPPLY

Getting water in and out of Pergamon was a major concern. In Philetairus' city all the streets on high ground were provided with channels so that rainwater could drain away easily without disrupting everyday life. In this period, there was enough water for the city to survive on but as Pergamon grew more extensive new sources had to be found. It was Eumenes II who was responsible for the famous Madradag aqueduct. This began as a conventional water course, holding three pipes which between them could carry a million gallons a day. Just under two miles from the city the water was running at a height of 1200 ft. However, there was a valley below it, from which the citadel rose again to a height of slightly under 1100 ft. Overall there was a drop of over 100 ft between the heights. If an airtight pipeline, an inverted siphon, could run between the two heights, water would gush out on the citadel (*see diagram*).

The problem was making this siphon airtight. The engineers of Pergamon were not daunted. They used lead pipes between four and six feet long. The joins were sealed with collars and held in place by stone slabs with round holes bored through them. The pipes have all disappeared (their existence is only known through the lead content of the soil) but many of the stones are still in place. To hold the enormous pressure of the water, which reached 400 lb per square foot at the bottom of the valley, the pipes had to be thick, 12 inches externally with an internal diameter of 7 inches. What is extraordinary is that as the pipeline crossed the valley, it had to bend to cover two small hills. This could have been avoided by digging the pipeline

into the hills, and it has been suggested that the height of the hills was used deliberately to reduce the water pressure in parts of the line.

There is no known comparable example of such a highly pressurised piping system anywhere else in the Greek or Roman world. The pipes in the best-known Roman example, on the Gier aqueduct at Lyon, experienced only a quarter of the pressure found at Pergamon (*see illustration opposite*).

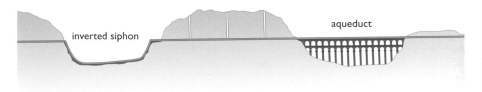

inverted siphon   aqueduct

Above: Diagram of an aqueduct showing two ways in which water could be brought across a valley. On the right the water channel is raised on arched piers. In the case of the left-hand valley, the water is piped underground via an inverted siphon. This is, in essence, a U-shaped pipe through which the pressure from water entering at one height pushes out the water at the other, lower, end.

Left: The remains of the Madradag aqueduct, which once fed water to Pergamon.

THE LIBRARIES OF ALEXANDRIA & PERGAMON

The greatest library in the ancient world was at Alexandria. It was set up by Ptolemy I, possibly as early as 300 BC. Ptolemy had wanted to encourage scholarship in his capital and his Mouseion, 'the House of the Muses', was a place where scholars could come and study at state expense. The library was to be their major resource. Although it has disappeared completely, its fame lives on.

There was no shortage of Egyptian texts—on papyrus, of course—but the Ptolemies wished to accumulate everything in Greek they could find, even cookbooks. They had the resources and energy to do so and their agents were sent off through the Greek world to find works. They always went for the oldest texts, as purists knew that errors tended to creep in with each new copying. There is a famous story of Ptolemy II approaching Athens for copies of the great tragedians, Aeschylus, Sophocles and Euripides. Athens agreed to send them but only after a large surety was lodged to ensure their return. Ptolemy had them copied—but kept the originals, even though this meant he had to lose his surety. Another important work commissioned for the library was a Greek translation of the Hebrew scriptures. This was known as the Septuagint after the legend that 72 scholars had worked independently on it and had miraculously come up with the same text. The apostle Paul and the evangelist Matthew always refer to the Septuagint translation when they quote from the scriptures, and it was the text used by the vast majority of early Christians.

Parchment, made from stretched and dried animal skins, and said to have been invented at Pergamon. It could be used for scrolls but it was not until the codex, the book as we know it, made up of pages, developed in the 3rd and 4th centuries that parchment was widely used. It was vastly more expensive than papyrus. A large codex might require the slaughter of a hundred calves. The Romans called parchment *charta pergamina*, 'paper from Pergamon'.

The rolls in the library totalled some 490,000 with perhaps another 42,800 in a smaller library in the Serapeum nearby. Something is known of their arrangement. Each papyrus roll would have its author and title on a tag. The rolls were stored alphabetically. In addition, there was a catalogue, itself running to 120 books, compiled in the first half of the 3rd century by one Callimachus, probably the director of the library. In this the books were listed by categories. The prose writers were divided, for instance, into groups such as philosophers, orators, historians and writers on medicine.

Scholars worked in the library to produce the authoritative text of any work, to write commentaries on major works and to compile glossaries of unusual words. The whole enterprise marks one of the peaks of Greek scholarship and it is tragic that the library was destroyed, probably in bitter fighting in AD 270 under the emperor Aurelian in the face of a revolt by Zenobia, queen of Palmyra (*see p. 194*). The smaller library must have perished when the Christians sacked the Serapeum in 391.

The library building at Pergamon was located within the sanctuary of Athena and was one of the projects of Eumenes II. By that date the Alexandria library had been collecting for a hundred years and Eumenes had to be ruthless if he was to get hold of early texts. Any of his subjects who had a library of their own (one apparently had a set of Aristotle's works) had to conceal it from his searches. Many sources speak of the intense rivalry between Pergamon and Alexandria. One celebrated story tells how the Ptolemies refused to export papyrus to Pergamon, and in order to survive the library there had to invent parchment, dried animal skins which could be written on. Another story, albeit from a late source, claims that Mark Antony gave 200,000 rolls from the library at Pergamon to his lover Cleopatra.

The Pergamon library consisted of four rooms, one of which was a reception room dominated by a statue of Athena. Around the statue were busts of famous literary figures such as Homer and Herodotus. The other three rooms held the rolls, stacked on wooden shelving. Readers were allowed to take them out into the colonnade. It is possible that 200,000 rolls could have been stored in these spaces, so the story of Antony is not implausible (Pergamon had by this time lost its independence and Antony was supreme ruler of the East so he could not be prevented from helping himself).

Priene: the planned city

The *polis*, the independent Greek city-state, was not simply an assembly of citizens, it was a planned showpiece of buildings. However, the older cities of the Greek mainland had grown up piecemeal and always with the needs of defence in mind so that there was little chance of working to a formal plan. For new colonies it was different. Even as far back as the 8th century BC, there are examples of new settlements dividing up their territory into sacred, commercial and residential areas before building had even begun. These are the seeds of urban planning.

The architect who brought this approach to fruition was Hippodamus of Miletus. Hippodamus was born about 500 BC and was active through much of the 5th century. Miletus was a major port on the western coast of Asia Minor with extensive trade networks. It had already shown itself a pioneer in rational thinking with the philosophy of Thales, the first man to understand the patterning of the stars in such a way as to predict an eclipse (in May 585), and Hippodamus certainly followed in the tradition. According to Aristotle, writing in the next century, he had a vision of an ideal city, of some 10,000 male citizens, added to which, of course, there would be women, children and slaves, perhaps to a total of 50,000. The separation of religious, public, commercial and residential areas would be preserved, but the whole would be enclosed within a grid pattern. As a young man Hippodamus was credited with such a grid in Miletus and after the Persian Wars he was asked to replan the Piraeus, Athens' harbour, in the same way. It is said that he lived there in a show house open to interested citizens who wished to see his plans. The idea of a grid within which all houses were of equal size fitted well with the democratic ideals of Athens.

THE SITE

Priene is a good example of a medium-size city, very much of a Hippodamian ideal, although its population was perhaps half the size he recommended. It was built as a new city by settlers who moved up the slope of Mt Mycale as their harbour silted up. A foundation date of about 352 BC seems likely. The city's big mo-

Example of a Hippodamian city Flourished 4th century BC

Left and below: Priene was a democracy in that all decrees were issued in the name of the people. Day-to-day administration took place in the Council House, whose ruins are shown left. The marble 'armchair', shown below, is from the theatre, one of what was originally a row of seats (*prohedrai*) for distinguished spectators. The existing *prohedrai* are decorated with lions' claws and have inscriptions recording that they were dedicated to Dionysus by Nysios, son of Diphilos.

Priene benefits from its comparative unimportance in Roman times—it has none of the grandiose buildings that transformed Ephesus, for example (*see p. 121*), so it is easier to understand as a typical city of the Hellenistic age.

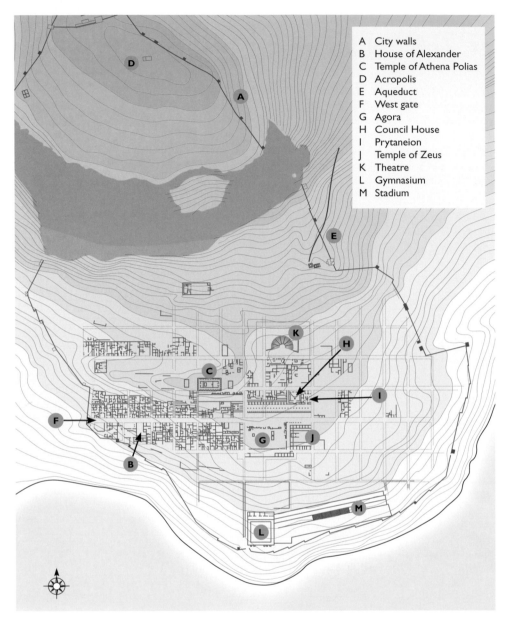

A City walls
B House of Alexander
C Temple of Athena Polias
D Acropolis
E Aqueduct
F West gate
G Agora
H Council House
I Prytaneion
J Temple of Zeus
K Theatre
L Gymnasium
M Stadium

ment came in 334 BC when Alexander the Great visited after having 'liberated' the city from its Persian overlords: a house (**B**) is shown as the one occupied by him at this time. By now building of the city's main temple, to Athena Polias (**C**), Athena as goddess of the city, was well under way and Alexander agreed to pay for it. The plaque recording his patronage is now in the British Museum. The city grew prosperous on trade and the houses are of good size, typically with internal courtyards. There was an acropolis above the city (**D**) and the water from streams on higher ground was collected in cisterns and then siphoned downwards. Many of the homes had their own internal water supplies while sewage was swept out in pipes along the streets. This was sophisticated living, and city government appears to have been democratic, as befitted the ethos of a planned Greek city.

Much of Priene's immense attractiveness as a site lies in its position on a slope so that its grid of streets is laid out along a series of terraces, with four houses in each block. The grid plan might seem unnecessarily restrictive but in practice it was not. Very few cities were situated on level ground so there were always slopes, descents and high points to break up uniformity. A number of grid squares could be joined into a single larger space for prestige projects. There was also the use of gateways and façades at the beginning and end of each street so that there would be impressive vistas. The grander streets would also have colonnades, fountains and a mass of statues, so the overall impact was far from monotonous.

Priene is enclosed within walls. The main streets run between the east and west gates (**F**). Its administrative and commercial quarter is in

the centre. Although the deserted nature of the site now makes it difficult to visualise, this must have been a bustling place in its heyday. There was an agora, of course (**G**), and this was backed by a graceful stoa which uses both Doric and Ionic styles. At the back of the colonnade is the very well preserved Council House (**H**), the seats arranged on three sides around the speaker's platform. The Prytaneion (**I**), the seat of the city's day-to-day administration, is right beside it. In the same central complex, next to the agora, is a temple to Zeus (**J**). Like any self-respecting city of the period, Priene has its own theatre (**K**), with a capacity of some 5,000. The seats for the city magistrates are still in place. Along the southern wall of the city are a gymnasium (**L**) and a stadium (**M**).

THE TEMPLE OF ATHENA POLIAS

The temple's architect was Pytheos, probably a native of the city, who was also credited with work on the Mausoleum at Halicarnassus, the great building project of the mid-4th century (*illustrated opposite; inset*). Pytheos wrote extensively about architecture and while his original works are lost, some of his ideas are preserved in the famous treatise *De Architectura* by the Roman architect Vitruvius. Pytheos lauds his profession for its ability to transcend the arts and sciences, but in practice he shows himself to be rigid in his pursuit

This woman's head of c. 350 BC (now in the British Museum) was found in the cella of the temple to Athena Polias. It is similar to dynastic portraits found in the Mausoleum at Halicarnassus and it may have been brought from there by the architect Pytheos when he moved back to Priene. One suggestion is that it is of Ada, the sister and, with her brother, successor of Mausolus.

of excellence. Unable to work out how a Doric temple's corner triglyphs should fit in, a well-known difficulty because any arrangement involved breaking up the symmetry of the frieze, he banned the Doric altogether and, whether or not due to his influence, it certainly disappeared from the repertoire of Greek architecture.

The Temple of Athena Polias, then, was Ionic in style and, in line with the rest of Priene, it was given a grid plan, this time based on a square of six Attic feet. The plinth of each column took up exactly this space and the gap between the columns was the same. A similar square separated the columns from the side wall of the temple. The inside of the cella was six squares wide by 16 long. The columns and the entablatures above them were equal to half the length of the cella and other measurements were similar multiples. While the temple has been criticised for its simplistic design, there is an elegance to it and its modest size, 65 by 125 ft, is a relief after the more monumental constructions of Ephesus and elsewhere. This was a city that kept a sense of proportion.

Priene was 'raided' by the Society of Dilettanti in the 1860s and the sanctuary of Athena Polias was robbed of much of its surviving sculpture. It is now in the British Museum. Now that the fragments have been studied, it can be seen that they come from the ceiling coffers above the peristyle and, like the frieze of the altar of Pergamon (*see p. 110*) represent a battle between the gods and giants. The whole is of high quality. The temple also had a cult statue of Athena modelled directly on Pheidias' in the Parthenon, but about two thirds the size. It was clearly a prestige object and can be seen on Priene's coins.

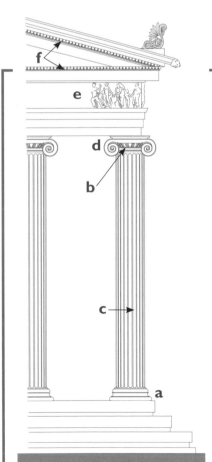

THE IONIC ORDER

The first Greek temples were made of wood: building in stone began about 600 BC. The inspiration for stoneworking came from Egypt and it is possible that columned buildings such as temple of Hatshepsut (*illustrated on p. 29*) provided a model for the Doric column as it emerged on the Greek mainland. The Doric order is simple: the earliest examples had rather squat columns which rested on the temple platform. It could be said that, in their original form, they showed a down-to-earth functional approach to architecture which did not attempt to be innovative. The order is seen at its best in the 5th-century Parthenon in Athens, where its simplicity makes it highly effective and attractive.

It is interesting that a very different style, within the same model of a colonnaded temple, emerges in the cities of Ionia, along the coast of Asia Minor, in the first half of the 6th century BC. This 'Ionic' style is consciously more refined than the Doric. The slimmer columns rest on a base **(a)** and have a 'cap' **(b)** which is often decorated with egg and dart moulding. The fluting **(c)** is much deeper. Over the top of the 'cap' curls the volute **(d)**, the trademark of the Ionic style. This can be produced in such a way as to offer a facing on the façade and sides of the temple even at the corners. The Ionic entablature does away with the Doric triglyphs (*see p. 98*), leaving space for an unbroken frieze **(e)**. The cornice of the Ionic order normally has a boundary of dentils **(f)**, in contrast to the plainer form of the Doric.

Egg and dart moulding.

Ephesus

The extensive ruins of Ephesus are the most impressive in Asia Minor. The city is important for its range of surviving buildings and for the way it shows how a Greek city could continue to flourish under the patronage and stable living conditions of the Roman Empire, of which it became a part.

HISTORY OF THE CITY

Ephesus was founded by Ionian Greeks at the mouth of the Kayster river on the west coast of Asia Minor. Tradition speaks of an oracle that told the would-be settlers to search for 'a fish and a boar'. They came across a group of fishermen roasting their catch. Their fire spread to a nearby bush out of which charged a boar. There was no hesitation by the Ionians now. Excavations show the first signs of Greek occupation to date from the 8th century BC. A good harbour, fertile surrounding land and access to trade routes into Asia Minor allowed the city to flourish. Yet Ephesus was also a vulnerable site. It was conquered by the Lydians and then by the Persians. A liberation from Persian rule by Alexander in 334 was followed on Alexander's death by subjugation to one of his generals, Lysimachus. By now the sea levels had risen leading to flooding of the original city and the river was also silting up the harbour. Lysimachus moved the core of the city to the southwest, onto the slopes of Mt Preon, where parts of his walls still stand.

When another of Alexander's generals, Seleucus, defeated and killed Lysimachus, Ephesus became incorporated into the Seleucid kingdom. When the Attalids of Pergamon freed themselves from Seleucid rule, Ephesus fell within their territory. Pergamon was bequeathed to the Romans in 133 BC (see p. 110), and Ephesus found itself part of a much larger empire. Augustus spent some months here in 29 BC, and he chose Ephesus, not Pergamon, to be the new capital of his Roman province covering western Asia Minor. It is from the Roman period that many of the surviving ruins date.

Cult centre (of Artemis) and a Romanised Greek city
Flourished 4th century BC and 1st century BC–2nd century AD

These exuberant swags and the Medusa head, here on the side of a sarcophagus, are typical of the Roman imperial art to be found at Ephesus. Portrait busts of the deceased appear to left and right.

PLAN OF ANCIENT EPHESUS

Facing page: View of the Library of Celsus through the archway from the Tetragonus Agora.

(1) The administrative quarter, commissioned by Augustus on higher ground in the southern part of the city, included the Prytaneion **(a)**, the seat of the city's administration which also housed the sacred fire of the city, and the city's council chamber, the Bouleuterion **(b)**, in the shape of an odeon, or small theatre. The colonnaded agora **(c)** had a temple in honour of Rome and Julius Caesar (Augustus' adoptive father) in the centre. Ephesus certainly benefited from imperial Roman patronage, though the cost of building was financed largely by wealthy local citizens, many of whom were freedmen.

(2) Between the administrative quarter and the harbour stood a second agora, the so-called Tetragonus Agora. Originally part of Lysimachus' Hellenistic city, it was rebuilt by the Romans in a much grander form. This was a commercial rather than an official space and its colonnades were occupied by shops.

(3) Just as the administrative area had been set out on a grid system, so an attempt was made to impose the same order on the old city around the harbour. A tree-lined arcade **(d)** led from the harbour to the theatre **(e)** so that the building provided a focal point for visitors arriving by sea. From the theatre a street known as the Plateia (today's Marble Road) ran north towards the temple of Artemis and south to meet Curetes Street.

(4) The beginning of Ephesus' most opulent age came in the 80s AD, when the city was awarded the honour of dedicating a large new temple to the Roman emperors. With this honour went the right to hold games, and the city responded in style. There was a large open space down by the harbour and this was made into an arena, the Xystoi, for the running races. West of it were built a new gymnasium **(f)** and baths **(g)** dedicated to the imperial cult.

(5) Augustus had ordered two aqueducts to be built and there were two more by the early 2nd century AD. This meant that there were extravagant supplies of water. In the square at the top of Curetes Street, a large decorated fountain was erected at the end of the 1st century. Water also allowed for a number of bath houses, always a symbol of a civilised and prosperous city. The Scholasticia baths, named after the patron who restored them in the 5th century, are off Curetes Street.

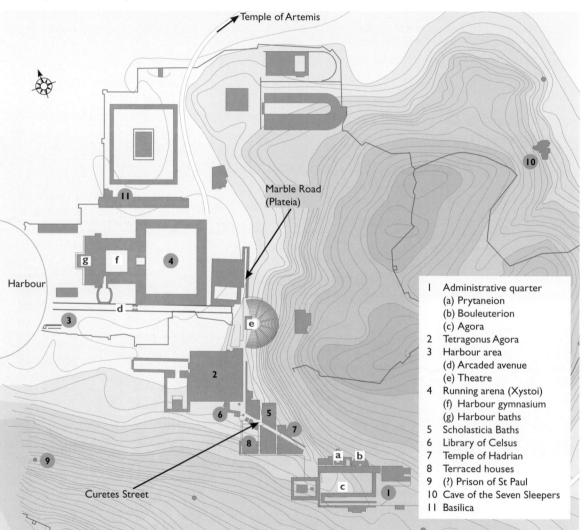

Temple of Artemis

Marble Road (Plateia)

Harbour

Curetes Street

1	Administrative quarter
	(a) Prytaneion
	(b) Bouleuterion
	(c) Agora
2	Tetragonus Agora
3	Harbour area
	(d) Arcaded avenue
	(e) Theatre
4	Running arena (Xystoi)
	(f) Harbour gymnasium
	(g) Harbour baths
5	Scholasticia Baths
6	Library of Celsus
7	Temple of Hadrian
8	Terraced houses
9	(?) Prison of St Paul
10	Cave of the Seven Sleepers
11	Basilica

(8) The terraced houses at Ephesus, with their mosaics and painted walls, reveal the high standard of living of well-to-do Ephesians. When restoration is complete they will be among the finest surviving examples of Roman domestic architecture.

(7) Like many Greek cities, Ephesus reached its peak in the mid-2nd century AD, partly thanks to the patronage of the Hellenophile emperor Hadrian. The era is marked by a temple erected in honour of Hadrian and the divinities of the city.

(6) The celebrated Library of Celsus stands at the bottom of Curetes Street. It was erected by a consul, Gaius Julius Aquila, as a memorial to his father, Celsus, a former governor of the provinces, who was buried in the complex. He must have enjoyed exceptional popularity and respect to deserve this honour. The columns and statues on the library façade represent the peak of Graeco-Roman architecture of the period (c. AD 135). It is estimated that the library held some 12,000 scrolls. The square which the library dominates is given even greater opulence by the gate which fronts the adjoining agora.

Right: There are many versions of the Artemis of Ephesus, shown in the Asiatic pose with protuberances adorning her gown. Even before the Ionians arrived at Ephesus there were settlements here, and it is likely that the Greek goddess Artemis merged her cult with the Anatolian one of Cybele. Cybele was always associated with fertility and nurturing, and the origins of her 'breasts' may be her mothering role. However, Cybele was also associated with the bull, and other (Roman) legends make bull's testicles one of her attributes, another obvious symbol of fertility.

'I have set eyes on the wall of lofty Babylon, on which is a road for chariots, and the statue of Zeus at Olympia, and the hanging gardens of Babylon, and the Colossus of the Sun [at Rhodes], and the huge labour of the high pyramids in Egypt and the vast tomb of Mausolus at Halicarnassus, but when I saw the temple of Artemis that mounted to the clouds, those other marvels lost their brilliance, and I said, Lo, apart from Olympus, the Sun never looked on anything as grand.' (Antipater of Sidon, 2nd century BC.) It is hard to believe that the scant ruins shown here are all that is left of such magnificence, one of the Seven Wonders of the Ancient World. In 401 the bishop of Constantinople, John Chrysostom, urged the Ephesians to destroy their temple and he has gone down in history as its overthrower. In the 6th century, the domed basilica to St John the Evangelist was built from its rubble, and the site of the temple itself stands desolate.

THE TEMPLE OF ARTEMIS

The sanctuary to Artemis, the twin sister of Apollo, lies on a floodplain outside the original city walls. Even when the temple was built, it was an ancient site. There had been two earlier temples there; the second, dating from the 6th century, had been burned down in 356 BC. When Alexander passed this way 20 years later, he offered to rebuild it on condition that his name could be recorded on an inscription. The Ephesians, sensitive to any loss of their independence, refused and found the money from other donors. Tactfully they told Alexander that it was not fitting for one god to dedicate a temple to another.

The new temple, in the Ionic style as was typical in the cities of central Asia Minor (*see box on p. 120*), measured 170 ft by 360 ft. It was made even more imposing by its positioning on a base of ten steps, primarily to preserve its core from flooding. Thirty-six of the columns had sculpted drums at their bases (one survives in the British Museum). These were placed on square plinths which were themselves carved with reliefs. The names of donors are modestly recorded here on the columns.

The temple had other remarkable features too. There was an extensive front porch with two rows of columns which served both as a treasury and as a meeting place for city councillors. There were three door openings on the pediment, with the largest in the centre. On feast days of the goddess, her statue would be exhibited here. There are echoes of the public appearances of the gods in Egyptian festivals and of the Windows of Appearance in Egyptian sanctuaries (*see p. 37*). Inside the temple, the cult room of the goddess was left open to the sky. Roman coins of the early 2nd century AD show the temple with its pediment door and a cult statue of the goddess, in the 'Asiatic' pose (*illustrated above*) standing between the central columns.

CHRISTIAN EPHESUS

Ephesus was typical of the large trading cites of the Roman empire within which Christianity secured an early toehold. An early tradition linked the city to the apostle John, who was said to have brought the Virgin Mary here for her final years. There was already a Christian community when Paul arrived in the early 50s (*Acts 19:1*).

Paul's first visit was short but he returned and seems to have preached for two years in a meeting hall, which was separate from the city's synagogue. It was a precarious existence. Paul was imprisoned once—a site is identified as his possible prison—**(9)** and his denunciation of idols led to a riot by the silversmiths who prepared images of Artemis for the pilgrims (*Acts 19*). Even though this was calmed down by the city authorities, Paul left the city never to return.

The Letter to the Ephesians, attributed to Paul, makes no specific reference to the city nor to any individual Ephesians. This is untypical of Paul and scholars now tend to date it later, perhaps to the 80s AD and to attribute it to a follower of Paul. The attribution of texts to 'a founding figure' is common in the Greek world; Pythagoras and Hippocrates are good examples of authorities who were credited with the authorship of much later texts, and the same seems to have happened here.

The Seven Sleepers were Christians from Ephesus. During the persecution of the emperor Decius in AD 250 they sought refuge in a cave near the city **(10)** but were discovered and walled up inside. Some hundred and fifty years later, when Ephesus had become a Christian city, the cave was broken into and they were found asleep. They believed that they had only slept for one day. The story of their miraculous survival became especially popular in the medieval West.

In 262 a devastating earthquake struck Ephesus and the loss was made greater by barbarian raiders taking advantage of the wider disruption of the empire in the 3rd century. The Terrace Houses, the Tetragonus Agora and the theatre all collapsed.

There was no major revival in the city's fortunes until the 5th century, when Christian energy saw the destruction of pagan buildings and the construction of churches from the looted stone. Ephesus was also the venue for two Church councils, which met to discuss the relationship of Jesus' humanity to his divinity. Both ended unsatisfactorily. The first (431), which probably met in the great basilica to Mary **(11)**, built within the ruins northeast of the harbour, was discredited when proceedings were rushed through by Cyril, bishop of Alexandria, before opponents of his views had even arrived in Ephesus. The second (in 449), where Cyril's successor, Dioscorus, used force to get bishops to sign up to his formula, was denounced by Pope Leo I as 'a robber council'. It was only at the Council of Chalcedon in 451 that a lasting statement on the relationship was agreed (*see p. 218*). It was at the Council of Ephesus of 431 that the Virgin was declared Theotokos, 'Mother of God', and this remains the standard terminology in the Greek world up to this day.

Ephesus was never to regain her importance, however. Decline set in in the 7th century, and the grandest city of Asia Minor was no more than a village for hundreds of years.

There are many records, both in texts and, increasingly, from archaeological finds of pagan buildings which were ravaged by Christian mobs. This defaced column from the Library at Ephesus is possibly one such victim.

The ancient ROMAN world

'Others will cast more tenderly in bronze
Their breathing figures, I can well believe,
And bring more lifelike portraits out of marble;
Argue more eloquently, use the pointer
To trace the paths of heaven accurately
And accurately foretell the rising stars.
Roman, remember by your strength to rule
Earth's people—for your arts are to be these:
To pacify, to impose the rule of law,
To spare the conquered, battle down the proud.'

Virgil, *Aeneid*, Book VI. Tr. Robert Fitzgerald

Vindolanda   Hadrian's Wall

Eboracum
(York)

BRITAIN

Aquae Sulis
(Bath)

Atlantic

Ocean

Rhine

**GALLIA
BELGICA**

Augusta Treverorum
(Trier)

Danube

G A U L

Lugdunum
(Lyons)

Mediolanum
(Milan)

Nemausus
(Nimes)   (Pont du Gard)
Arelate   Aquae Sextiae
(Arles)   (Aix-en-Provence)
Massilia
(Marseilles)

Ravenna

Rubicon

PANNONIA

I L L Y R I A

E T R U R I A

D A L M A T I A

Salonae
(Split)

I B E R I A

Tarquinia

AD 312   Tivoli
Rome
Ostia   Alba Longa

L A T I U M

*Adriatic
Sea*

Mt Vesuvius

Herculaneum   Pompeii

Sardinia

Tyrrhenian

Sea

M e d i t e r

MAURETANIA

Utica

Thagaste   Carthage

Lambaesis

Thamugadi
(Timgad)

N U M I D I A

146 BC

Thysdrus
(El Djem)

SICILY

Piazza Armerina

*Ionian
Sea*

T R I P O L I T A N I A

A F R I C A   P R O C O N S U L A R I S

Leptis Magna

*r a n
a n*

THE ROMAN EMPIRE IN AD 200

Sirmium

DACIA

Danube

Black Sea

THRACE

MACEDONIA

Byzantium
(Constantinople)

Bosphorus

BITHYNIA

PHRYGIA

ASIA MINOR

THESSALY

Aegean Sea

LYDIA

Euboea

Meander

CARIA

Actium
31 BC

Athens

Aphrodisias

Halicarnassus

Cnidos

Rhodes

Crete

Cyprus

ean   S e a

Cyrenaica

Alexandria

Nile

EGYPT

Caspian Sea

PERSIA

Euphrates

Tigris

Antioch

Apamea

Palmyra

Babylon

S
Y
R
I
A

Damascus

Jerusalem

GILEAD

JUDAEA

Moab

Gaza

Dead Sea

Petra

A
R
A
B
I
A

0	100	200	300 miles
0		250	500 km

Historical overview

Previous page (p. 127): The initiate is dressed as a bride. Detail from the cycle of wall paintings in the Villa of the Mysteries, Pompeii, thought to illustrate a Dionysiac initiation ceremony.

The story of the rise of Rome to supremacy over an empire which stretched throughout the Mediterranean and beyond is an extraordinary one. At first sight, the city's position on the open plain of Latium in central Italy makes it vulnerable to any attacker. Yet left to itself the city had its advantages. It was on a river crossing, a few miles from the sea, surrounded by higher ground. The site could thus be protected while taking advantage of passing trade. The traditional founding date of 753 BC may be an accurate record of scattered hilltop settlements coming together as one, just as this part of Italy was making contact with Greek traders. The Etruscans, whose civilisation was by now well established in the north (*see opposite*), certainly recognised the potential of the site, and legend records a series of Etruscan kings seizing control and bringing the first public buildings to Rome in the shape of paved areas, palaces and temples.

In 509 BC the Romans expelled their kings and exulted in a new republican freedom, governed by magistrates elected by the citizenry on an annual basis. The key to Rome's success lay in stable government and in its recruitment of new citizens. The gradual conquest of the cities of Latium brought in their manpower, which was then used to expand the armies for new conquests. From early days there was an exaltation of military victory.

The years from 400 to 280 BC were tough ones. Italy is mountainous, hard to rule effectively, and the more warlike of its native peoples proved resistant to takeover. It was sheer grit which led Rome to wear down the Etruscan cities and then the mountain tribes, and these wars set the foundations for future conquest: impressively trained legions, a refusal to accept defeat, acceptance of those who acquiesced in Roman supremacy, and the brutal punishment of those who resisted. By 270 BC Rome was secure enough in the north to expand southwards to confront the opulent Greek cities which had existed there for centuries (*see p. 103*). The collision of traditional Roman austerity with the indulgent exuberance of Greek civilisation brought a new maturity to the culture of the expanding empire.

KEY DATES IN ANCIENT ROMAN HISTORY

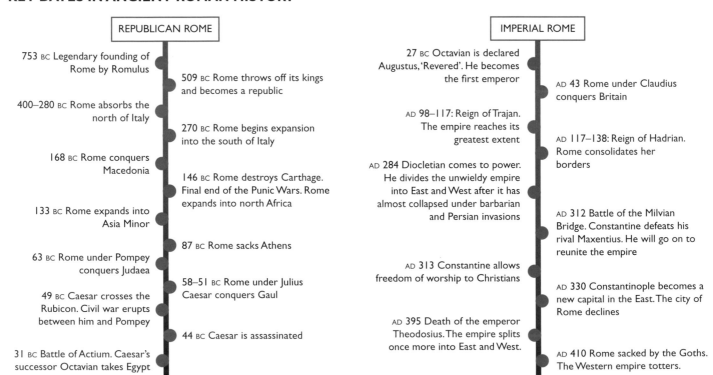

REPUBLICAN ROME

753 BC Legendary founding of Rome by Romulus

509 BC Rome throws off its kings and becomes a republic

400–280 BC Rome absorbs the north of Italy

270 BC Rome begins expansion into the south of Italy

168 BC Rome conquers Macedonia

146 BC Rome destroys Carthage. Final end of the Punic Wars. Rome expands into north Africa

133 BC Rome expands into Asia Minor

87 BC Rome sacks Athens

63 BC Rome under Pompey conquers Judaea

58–51 BC Rome under Julius Caesar conquers Gaul

49 BC Caesar crosses the Rubicon. Civil war erupts between him and Pompey

44 BC Caesar is assassinated

31 BC Battle of Actium. Caesar's successor Octavian takes Egypt

IMPERIAL ROME

27 BC Octavian is declared Augustus, 'Revered'. He becomes the first emperor

AD 43 Rome under Claudius conquers Britain

AD 98–117: Reign of Trajan. The empire reaches its greatest extent

AD 117–138: Reign of Hadrian. Rome consolidates her borders

AD 284 Diocletian comes to power. He divides the unwieldy empire into East and West after it has almost collapsed under barbarian and Persian invasions

AD 312 Battle of the Milvian Bridge. Constantine defeats his rival Maxentius. He will go on to reunite the empire

AD 313 Constantine allows freedom of worship to Christians

AD 330 Constantinople becomes a new capital in the East. The city of Rome declines

AD 395 Death of the emperor Theodosius. The empire splits once more into East and West.

AD 410 Rome sacked by the Goths. The Western empire totters.

Far left: As a result of their close contacts with Greek traders, the Etruscans borrowed many ideas from Greece, including the structure of the temple. The platforms at the front tended to be higher than their Greek counterparts as they were used by priests to scan the skies for portents of unfolding events. Moreover, the columns of an Etruscan temple did not extend all the way round the building. Temple roofs were richly embellished with terracotta figures, both on the cornice and along the ridge. Both the high platform and the limited use of a peristyle were adopted by the Romans for their temples.

Above left: The terracottas of reclining couples are the most attractive creations of Etruscan funerary art. This late 6th-century example from a tomb in Cerveteri, north of Rome, is remarkable for the affection the couple show to each other. The wife pours scented oil onto her husband's palm, a gesture familiar from the tomb decorations of ancient Egypt.

THE ETRUSCANS

The Etruscans emerge in central Italy in the 8th century BC, probably immigrants from the Near East. Their settlements formed a loose confederation of towns whose chieftains indulged in heroic combat, and—if we are to rely on their tomb paintings—revelled in banqueting and horse racing. One of the chief cities of the confederation was Tarquinia, from where, according to legend, came the house of Tarquin, two of whose members ruled as kings of Rome.

The glory of Tarquinia is its painted tombs, which follow the custom of providing an underground room in which the sarcophagus of the deceased could lie surrounded by pictures of an ideal life or afterlife—a tradition that has echoes in the world of ancient Egypt. The earliest tomb chambers are painted to represent houses. Later a Greek influence becomes marked, and scenes from Greek mythology appear.

In the 5th century, banqueting, hunting, horse- and chariot racing are common themes. Some frescoes show abandoned dancing, as if the rituals of Dionysus (*see p. 178*) have been adapted to Etruscan life. In contrast to Greek custom, where only courtesans are shown in drinking scenes with men, the Etruscans relax on couches with their wives. From other Etruscan burial sites come marvellous life-sized terracotta sarcophagi of couples reclining together on couches.

It is always unwise to read too much into scenes such as these. Did they represent the real world or just the world one hoped to find in an afterlife? Were the portrayals of rituals of death or sacrifice designed to ward off evil spirits so that the deceased could enjoy a carefree passage to the next world? There does, however, seem to be a change of tone by the 4th century. In one of the later Tarquinia tombs, demons are shown apparently

Left: The Greek idea of athletic contest was adopted into Etruscan society, as illustrated in the image two wrestlers found in one of the tombs at Tarquinia (c. 510 BC). The Romans also adopted Etruscan rituals, among them the gladiatorial contests. Under the Etruscans these had been held at the funerals of heroes. The Romans turned them into mass spectator sports.

threatening a woman who moves from this world to the next. On both sides of the divide her family, those still living and those deceased, take leave or greet her. Does this reflect new fears—the decline of the economy, the emergence of Rome as a hostile power—which were permeating Etruscan society? The southern cities of the Etruscan confederation were vulnerable to the expansion of Rome. Unable to mount a common resistance, the cities were absorbed one by one.

ROME EXPANDS BEYOND ITALY

With Italy subdued, the 3rd century BC saw the beginnings of overseas expansion. Conquests in Sicily drew Rome into conflict with the Carthaginians, whose own empire stretched from north Africa to western Sicily and Spain. The so-called Punic Wars forced the Romans to create their own navy (*see p. 97*), which they did with such imagination that it was soon able to take on the hardened Carthaginian seafarers as equals. Defeat of the Carthaginians came on African soil in 202 at the hands of the great commander Scipio, dubbed 'Africanus' in honour of the victory. The destruction of their capital, Carthage, in 146 BC, by Scipio's adopted grandson, saw Rome dominant in the western Mediterranean. First in Sicily and then in Africa and Spain, she established the system of provinces. Each province was assigned to a governor, who kept overall order. Only the more troublesome provinces or those with vulnerable borders had legions stationed on a permanent basis (*for more on the administration of the empire, see the box overleaf*).

The 2nd century BC saw the absorption of the Greek east. None of the Hellenistic kingdoms was able to stand up to the Roman armies. Here again provinces were set up, but several independent kingdoms were allowed to survive so long as their rulers acquiesced in Rome's supremacy.

Above: Mounted Roman warrior from a sarcophagus of the 2nd century BC, a time when Rome was steadily expanding its dominions into the eastern Mediterranean and Gaul.

Below: Roman sculpture was known for its realistic portraiture. These two busts, of Scipio Africanus (who defeated Hannibal outside Carthage in 202) and Julius Caesar, the conqueror of Gaul and 'dictator' of Rome, are remarkable in two ways. Not only do they show what the men looked like—Scipio bald, burly and full-lipped, Caesar lean and sinewy—but there is also psychological portrayal. One can clearly see in both the ruthlessness and determination of the successful warrior.

POMPEY AND CAESAR

The expanding Mediterranean-wide empire led to increasing tensions at home. Annual magistracies were no longer adequate when commands had to be extended for several years on the frontiers. Not only that, but successful commanders had the wealth and troops to become a political threat. By the middle of the 1st century BC, two generals were competing for power: Pompey the Great had added much of the ancient Near East, including Judaea with its capital Jerusalem, to the empire. Julius Caesar had been enjoying similar success in Gaul (modern France). In 49, Caesar moved beyond his sphere of official command back into Italy—his famous crossing of the Rubicon—and a civil war was under way. It raged across the whole empire before Pompey was defeated.

Julius Caesar returned to Rome but his position was insecure. He now had no rivals, but this was a city which still treasured its ancient traditions of republican liberty. Opposition to him grew as he began to absorb the power of the magistracies. It was feared that he would claim the hated title of king. A group of determined patricians decided to assassinate him, and he was stabbed to death in March 44.

Far from there being an outburst of enthusiasm, the populace was stunned. They turned against the assassins, who fled, and Caesar's popularity was assured when it was found he had left money in his will for the citizens of Rome. The political system was still in chaos, however, and soon a new civil war broke out, between Caesar's fellow consul Mark Antony, who had unwisely entangled himself with Cleopatra, queen of a still independent Egypt, and Octavian, Caesar's great nephew, whom Caesar had adopted as his son in his will. In 31 BC, at the Battle of Actium, off the western coast of Greece, Octavian defeated Antony and Cleopatra and pursued them to Egypt. When both had committed suicide he added this rich country to the Roman dominions.

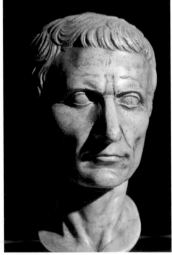

THE REPUBLIC BECOMES AN EMPIRE

Octavian had been brutal in achieving power but he was now beyond challenge and could relax. He turned into a cunning politician, flattering the senate into believing that they still mattered and waiting until they had, inevitably, to recognise that he was the only arbiter in Roman politics. In 27 BC the senate accorded him the title of Augustus, 'Revered', and acquiesced in his gathering of the ancient magistracies under his control. He was soon appointing provincial governors, arranging where legions were to be stationed and receiving the embassies of foreign kings. Augustus was a master of propaganda: his statue was to be found throughout the empire and his public monuments exuded images of peace and prosperity. By the time he died in AD 14, he was in effect an emperor: henceforth Rome was to know no other system of government.

The empire depended on efficient central control, on the appointment of competent provincial governors, on the use of the legions to quell disorder and on the gradual building up of loyal provincial elites from the many cultures that the empire ruled. There were appalling emperors—Caligula and the increasingly unbalanced Nero, for instance—but the 2nd century AD saw a series of exceptional rulers. Trajan (ruled 98–117) was a wise and moderate emperor and he added the last province to the empire when he conquered the Dacians north of the Danube and brought back immense booty to Rome (*see illustration on p. 140*).

Trajan's successor, the complex Hadrian (ruled 117–138), refused to extend the empire further and focused on consolidation. He was a vigorous builder: the Pantheon, his vast villa at Tivoli, and his Wall, which marked the northern limits of the empire in Britain, show the range of his undertakings. His successor, Antoninus Pius (ruled 138–161), was able to rule peacefully from Rome at a time when the balance between centre and provinces seemed perfect. Cities in both East and West were embellishing themselves, trade was flourishing and in the countryside landowners were extending their villas.

Such peace could not last. There was always the threat of the Persians on the eastern borders, while population growth on the borders of the Rhine and Danube was increasing the threat of raids from the north. The emperor Marcus Aurelius (ruled 161–180) spent much of his reign on the Danube containing the barbarians. By the mid-3rd century the empire was facing attacks on both fronts.

Clockwise from the top: Augustus, Hadrian, Marcus Aurelius. The emperors used busts and full-size statues as propaganda tools. Augustus, here shown in youthful guise with a wreath of victory, was particularly successful at this. Hadrian (always recognisable by his creased ear lobes, a sign of heart trouble) wears the beard of a Greek philosopher as does Marcus Aurelius, author of the famous *Meditations*, which he wrote in Greek. He spent much of his reign fighting to preserve his empire, and is shown here in military dress.

Below: Augustus was a superb propagandist and the Ara Pacis, the Altar of Peace, unveiled in Rome in 13 BC, trumpeted the achievements of his reign. This goddess, perhaps symbolising peace, the earth or even Italia herself, shows off the restored fecundity of a world where civil war had ended. The altar deliberately copies 5th-century Greek friezes.

It was the emperor Augustus (reigned 27 BC–AD 14) who established the professional Roman army as it was to last until the late empire. He began by disbanding surplus troops and giving them land and bounties. The settling of veterans became an important part of Roman policy—many were sent out to *coloniae*, Roman citizen settlements in strategically important areas, where they could be relied on to defend their newly granted land if attacked. New recruits to the armies joined between the ages of seventeen and twenty-three and, from AD 5, were required to serve 20 years. While originally most legionaries were Italian, as Roman citizenship spread to other provinces, recruitment became empire-wide.

This was now a standing army of 25 legions (by the 3rd century it had grown to 33 legions). In practice we are talking of some 150,000 men, who consumed some 70 percent of the empire's annual income. At full strength each legion had a core of 5,400 infantry backed by 120

Rome was never shy of parading her victories. The scene here, from a sarcophagus of the 2nd century AD, shows a defeated barbarian doing homage before a Roman commander.

cavalry. The commander was normally of senatorial status, aided by six tribunes from the equestrian class with the centurions as the main professional officer class, often recruited directly from the ranks. The centurion was an important and well-paid post that carried social benefits (a senior centurion might be given equestrian status on his retirement). The emperor remained supreme commander, and often led his men into battle.

Each legion had its own name and traditions (much as a British regiment does) and many would have a semi-permanent base in the empire. Over half the army was stationed on the Rhine and Danube, for example, as this tended to be the most volatile border, subject to sudden raids. Some bases were so settled that civilian towns would grow up around them and provincial governors could request that the skilled surveyors and engineers attached to each legion be farmed out for local building projects.

The infantrymen had bronze helmets with an iron skill-plate inside. The upper body would be covered by a cuirass. Each had two javelins to throw at the start of a confrontation and the gladius, a short stabbing sword for hand-to-hand fighting. Training in basic fitness and the use of weapons was relentless, and as a result the legions were hard to defeat in open battle—their cohesion and experience was formidable. The defeats that are recorded were often ambushes.

The legions were backed by local auxiliary troops, who often retained their own customs and weapons. They were usually employed on garrison duties or were sent on in front of a marching legion as skirmishers. On retirement an auxiliary soldier would be granted full Roman citizenship.

The long-term problem of the empire was that its frontiers were simply too long to defend adequately. One of the drawbacks of Hadrian's refusal to expand the empire further was that the men started to get slack, and Hadrian maintained a constant round of visits exhorting the legions to keep up standards. By the end of the 2nd century, however, constant warfare had returned.

THE LATER EMPIRE

The pressures on leadership proved immense in the 3rd century and there was a rapid succession of emperors as battles were lost, rival armies declared their own emperors, or men simply cracked under the pressure. This was the moment when the empire seemed doomed.

Yet, as so often at crisis points in history, a saviour was found: Diocletian, a tough general from the Balkans, seized power in 284. He recognised that complete reform was needed if the empire was to survive. He divided it into four and appointed two senior emperors, the Augusti, and two junior ones, the Caesars, each with their assigned territory. The provinces were reorganised into smaller units and military command was separated from tax gathering. The economy was stabilised and the tax system planned more efficiently. There was now the money to finance border fortifications and well-trained armies. A massive victory over the Persians in 297 brought peace on that border for a hundred years.

Another transformation took place under Diocletian's successor, Constantine, who between 306 and 324 defeated his rival emperors and reunited the empire. Constantine recognised that Rome was by now too far from the borders to use as a base and so he created a new capital, Constantinople. Its site, overlooking the Bosphorus, on the eastern edge of a peninsula in Thrace, was so impregnable that it was not to be taken until 1204, during the Fourth Crusade, when it was conquered by the Franks.

Diocletian and his co-emperors had been increasingly concerned about the growth of Christianity. The Christians had their own hierarchy of bishops, independent of imperial authority, and they refused to honour the traditional gods at a time when many felt that their favour had been lost. In the early 300s, a wave of persecution was launched. Constantine, however, took a completely different tack. He realised that the bishops could be used to support his authority and so offered patronage and toleration to the Christian church. He linked this initiative to the battle at which he had conquered his rival Maxentius, at the Milvian Bridge outside Rome in 312. The Christian God had promised him victory, and victory had come. By the end of the 4th century, Church and state were to be closely aligned. The new structure was not able to save the empire in the West, which became separate from the East again after 395, but in the East, the Byzantine empire was to last until its final overthrow by the Ottoman Turks in 1453.

The story of the discovery of the True Cross by Helen, the mother of Constantine, on pilgrimage in the Holy Land, was a popular medieval legend and is the subject of Piero della Francesca's magnificent frescoes in Arezzo, Tuscany (completed by 1466), a scene from which is shown here. Constantine, sleeping before the Battle of the Milvian Bridge (312), receives a vision telling him that he will conquer his rival Maxentius through the power of the Cross. Constantine went on to outlaw the persecution of Christians, and shortly before his death was received into the Church, becoming the first Christian emperor.

THE ADMINISTRATION OF THE ROMAN EMPIRE

The government of the Roman empire was originally in the hands of three levels of annually elected magistrates: the consuls, commanders of the armies; the praetors, in charge when the consuls were on campaign; and the quaestors, who oversaw financial matters. The senate acted as a body of elder statesmen, mostly retired magistrates. The tribunes were popularly elected citizens' representatives. The system became increasingly vulnerable to the power of military commanders, who retained their commands from year to year independently of elections. Julius Caesar was an example: he seemed on the verge of abolishing the system to make himself king, and was assassinated by supporters of the old regime in 44 BC. It was the genius of Augustus that he acted much more subtly, gradually accumulating the magistracies in his own name, with the senate acquiescing in the loss of republican institutions. Key posts were handed out as an honour to the emperor's associates and supporters.

The wider empire was divided into client kingdoms and provinces. A client kingdom could be brought to an end if a ruler was seen as unreliable or disloyal. Thus in AD 6, Augustus deposed Archelaus, king of Judaea, and made the territory into a province. The provinces were allocated to governors, who served for two to three years. A governor would hear cases brought to him (only he could pass the death sentence) and summon armed help if there was serious unrest. His main purpose, however, was to encourage local rulers to keep their own order and to channel their taxes to Rome.

Some cities were colonies, founded by veteran soldiers, and these had a superior status over the smaller provincial towns. If these became sufficiently important they would be granted *municipium* status, in effect a recognition of their right to govern themselves. Many cities, especially those in the East, were far older than Rome itself. Their local system of government was usually recognised by the Romans and their city councils continued to sit. The emperor presided over the whole system, showering patronage on the cities he favoured. The imperial cult flourished across the empire, with many cities dedicating new temples and public buildings to the emperor and to Rome.

Rome: the Forum

The historic centre of Rome grew up alongside two low hills, the Capitoline and the Palatine, close to the River Tiber. The Palatine Hill had permanent settlers as early as the 9th century BC, long before any urban development, and Roman tradition held that the original hut of Romulus, the founder of the city, had stood there. A hut was kept restored in his memory. Before the 1st century BC, the Palatine had been a ceremonial area with major temples to the goddess Cybele (the Great Mother, originating in Asia Minor) and to Victory, always an important cult in a militaristic city. The hill was also the site of patrician houses, including those of the orator Cicero and the consul Mark Antony. When Octavian, later the emperor Augustus, returned victorious from his wars against Mark Antony, this was the obvious location for his own house. It was a modest one, built close to the temple to Augustus' favourite god, Apollo.

Right: The Capitoline She-wolf has been in Rome's Capitoline Museum since the 15th century, when a 'Romulus and Remus' was added to it. While it has traditionally been seen as an Etruscan bronze of the 5th century BC, scientific tests suggest that it might, in fact, be medieval.

Below: Detail of the Altar of Romulus and Remus at Ostia. In one of many 'found in a basket in the river' stories, the twins Romulus and Remus, sons of the Vestal Virgin Rhea Sylvia by Mars, the god of war, were rescued by the river god Tiberinus (the reclining figure here), brought to the Palatine Hill and suckled by a she-wolf. After a quarrel over the foundation of Rome, Remus was killed and the city was founded by Romulus.

Across the valley at the foot of the Palatine, the Capitoline Hill is the likely home of the first permanent Roman community. The hill, with steep slopes on three sides, was readily defensible and legends claim that Romulus founded a temple there and allowed refugees from other cities to settle. The most important moment in the history of the hill came with the founding of the great temple to the Capitoline Triad, Jupiter, Juno and Minerva, just at the time when Rome threw out its ruling Etruscan kings and declared itself a republic (509 BC). The temple and the freedom of the city from royal control went hand in hand. It was on the steps of this temple that a victorious general would lay his wreath after his triumph, the procession along the Via Sacra (the ceremonial route through the Forum) in which the prisoners and booty from the conquest would be paraded. The two consuls, in effect the generals of the state, would receive their commissions for the year ahead while governors set out from here for the far-flung provinces they were to administer.

THE VALLEY OF THE FORUM

The Oppian Hill, site of the surviving remains of Nero's vast Domus Aurea, which stretched all the way across the valley of the Colosseum and up the Palatine Hill.

The vast Basilica of Maxentius was begun by Constantine's rival emperor, whom Constantine defeated at the historic Battle of the Milvian Bridge in AD 312.

The circular Temple of Vesta housed the sacred fire, kept perpetually alight as a symbol of the perpetuity of the Roman state.

Ruins of the Temple of Mars Ultor, dedicated by Augustus in his new forum after Caesar's assassins had been defeated.

The Colosseum, the largest Roman amphitheatre ever built.

The Arch of Titus, embellished with reliefs of his greatest victory: the sack of Jerusalem in AD 70.

In the lee of the massive monument to Vittorio Emanuele stand the remains of the Temple of Venus, built by Julius Caesar and dedicated to the goddess from whom he claimed descent.

On the summit of the Capitoline Hill stood the greatest temple in all Rome, dedicated to Jupiter. It was to this temple that a victorious general would process in triumph.

Trajan's Column dominates the ruins of the fora built by successive emperors after the Roman Forum had become too crowded.

On the site of the Arx, the ancient citadel of Rome, stands the vast white monument to Vittorio Emanuele II (1911), first king of a united Italy.

The Palatine Hill, from which the modern word 'palace' is derived, was a favourite residential area for patrician Romans and emperors.

THE ROMAN FORUM AND IMPERIAL FORA

The Roman Forum served two purposes: as a market and as a gathering place for political and legal activities, especially after the founding of the Republic in the late 6th century BC, when the citizen assemblies became closely involved in electing the consuls and city magistrates. The Curia (senate house) was here **(1)**, as were the law courts and the Comitium **(2)**, the assembly place for citizens. However, as the city expanded and the spoils of war poured in, temples began to be built as well. One of the oldest was to Saturn **(3)**, the god identified with bringing a golden age to Rome and commemorated each year in the festival of the Saturnalia. Another, in the centre of the then open space, was the temple to Vesta **(4)**, which enclosed a symbolic sacred hearth whose fire was kept burning by the Vestal Virgins, who had their own enclosed house nearby.

The booty pouring in from the conquest of southern Italy and Sicily, and later of the Carthaginian empire, in the 2nd and 3rd centuries BC, saw the building of the first great basilicas, the all-purpose meeting halls. After his successful return from civil war in the 40s BC, Julius Caesar created the large Basilica Julia **(5)**. Accepting that the area had now become so cluttered with buildings that it needed an extension, he also created the first of the

Scene of an emperor riding into Rome in triumph with his quadriga through a triumphal arch (*see p. 142*), as seen through the eyes of two French artists, Jacques Grasset de St-Saveur and L.F. Labrousse (1796).

so-called Imperial Fora, which extended the Forum to the north. Caesar's forum was dominated by a new temple to Venus **(6)**, honoured as the founder of his own family. It was probably here that he summoned the senate to attend him instead of going himself to the senate house, thereby arousing suspicions that he was transforming himself into a king. His assassination in the name of *libertas*, the ancient republican liberties of the state, followed in 44 BC. Caesar's adopted son Octavian, the future emperor Augustus, dedicated the Temple of Divus Julius **(7)** in honour of the now deified Caesar, in the original Forum on the spot where Caesar's body had been cremated.

Augustus followed Caesar in buying up land to the north of the Forum for his own. Here he built a temple to Mars Ultor **(8)**, Mars in his role of avenger of the murder of Caesar, after the assassins Brutus and Cassius had been defeated. Augustus also began another tradition. In Republican days the Triumph marked the end of a general's career: now Augustus commemorated his in a permanent form, the triumphal arch (*see p. 142*). One of his arches celebrated the victory at Actium (over Antony and Cleopatra), another a defeat of the Parthians. Both have disappeared but two later triumphal arches still stand within the Forum, one erected by the emperor Titus **(9)** to commemorate his victory over the Jews and the destruction of the Temple in Jerusalem in AD 70, and the other built by Septimius Severus in AD 203 **(10)** to celebrate another victory over the Parthians.

MONUMENTS IN THE FORUM

1 The Curia, the ancient senate house
2 The Comitium, where the citizens' assembly met
3 Temple of Saturn, one of the oldest sacred buildings in the Forum
4 Temple of Vesta, where the holy fire was kept perpetually alight
5 Basilica Julia, the civil magistrates' court built by Julius Caesar
6 Temple of Venus, built by Julius Caesar in honour of the founding goddess of his family
7 Temple of Divus Julius, built by Augustus in honour of Caesar after his assassination
8 Temple of Mars Ultor, built by Augustus in honour of the god of war, who had avenged the murder of Caesar by granting defeat in battle to his assassins
9 Arch of Titus, built after the conquest of Jerusalem
10 Arch of Septimius Severus, built after a defeat of the Parthians (in modern-day Iran)
11 The lower slopes of the Palatine Hill
12 The Valley of the Colosseum, where the colossal statue of Nero once graced his opulent 'Golden House'. The vast amphitheatre known as the Colosseum was built on the site after Nero's death
13 Forum of Trajan
14 Temple of Venus and Roma, designed by Hadrian
15 Temple of Antoninus and Faustina
16 Basilica of Maxentius
17 Column of Phocas

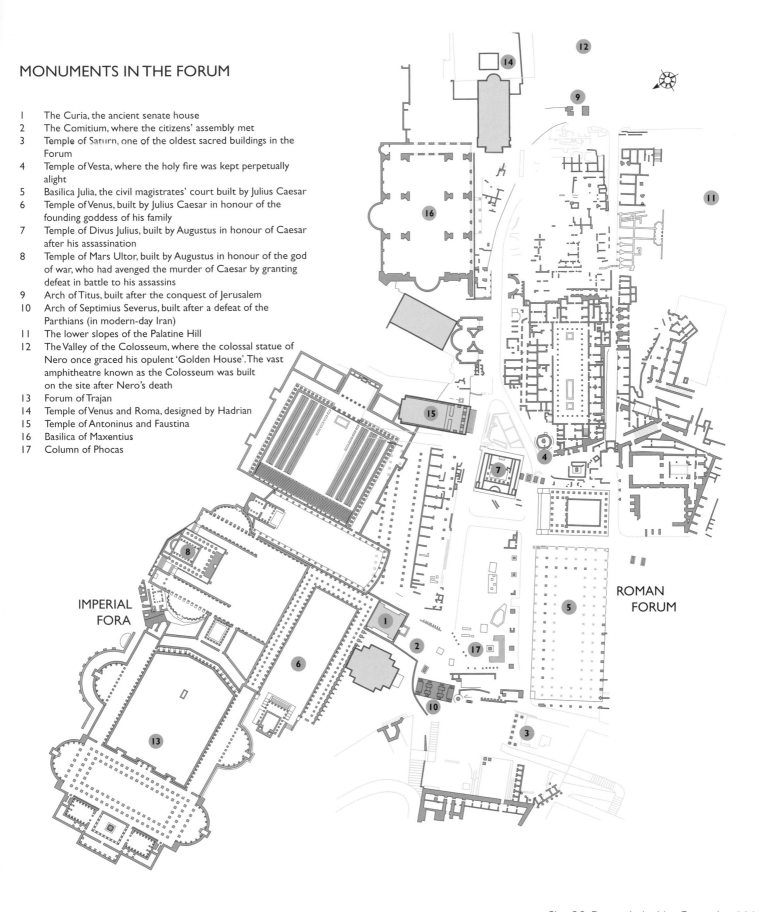

IMPERIAL FORA

ROMAN FORUM

Above: One of the most exciting moments in the history of Renaissance art came when Nero's vast Domus Aurea was rediscovered and artists such as Raphael were lowered down into the ruins to see the frescoes. These were of elegant, idealised, ornamental designs and set the taste of the day. Similar designs appear in the wealthier homes of Pompeii from the same period. Art historians term them 'Fourth Style' to distinguish them from earlier fresco styles found at Pompeii.

THE PALATINE HILL AND DOMUS AUREA

Augustus' immediate successor, Tiberius, was the first to conceive of the Palatine (11) as a site for the imperial palace, and his own was on the slope running down to the Forum. The foundations are still intact on the hillside. Tiberius was totally outclassed by Nero, who created an enormous private palace for himself to the east of the Forum, stretching all the way across the valley and up the eastern end of the Palatine. This was the Domus Aurea, the Golden House, where 'everything was covered in gold, decorated with gems and shells', as the historian Suetonius tells us. It had porticoes a mile long, an artificial lake in the centre 'almost a sea', and a statue of Nero, the Colossus, 120 ft high, at the entrance (12). It was built between AD 54 and 64.

With the suicide of Nero in 68, there was a powerful reaction against his usurpation of the centre of Rome. His successor, the emperor Vespasian, saw the opportunity to return the land occupied by the Domus Aurea to Rome. The baths of the Domus now became public ones and Vespasian began to construct a vast amphitheatre in the centre of the site. Its name, the Colosseum, derived from the very statue of Nero which stood there.

If Vespasian had shown himself ready to pander to the instincts of the people to sustain his popularity, his son Domitian, emperor AD 81–96, was more dictatorial. His legacy was a great palace built over the eastern end of the Palatine Hill. At the centre was a huge audience hall and it was clear that Domitian, who styled himself 'Lord and God', and who had himself described as 'eternal pharaoh' in Egyptian hieroglyphics on an obelisk, expected to preside there. The palace complex (the word 'palace' itself derives from Palatine) recognised the power of the emperor by bringing together, for the first time, all the functions of imperial government into one structure. The emperor was still expected to respect the people, and Domitian paid for his tyrannical attitude by being assassinated in the very palace he had built. The building nevertheless remained the Roman home of the emperors for the rest of the empire.

Soon after Domitian's death, another major transformation took place across the valley on the northern side of the Forum. The emperor Trajan returned from the Danube border in AD 107 with immense booty from his victory over the Dacians, booty which he poured into the glorification of himself and Rome. His architect, Apollodorus of Damascus, began by carving a huge chunk out of the neighbouring Quirinal Hill. It is recorded that the top of Trajan's Column marks the original height of the hill.

The forum which Trajan now constructed (13) was probably the greatest single monumental complex in Rome and overawed visitors for centuries to come. It was 1,000 ft long by 600 ft wide. Its entrance gateway was surmounted by a figure of Trajan in a six-horse chariot and in the enormous piazza inside there was a famous equestrian statue of him. At the far end of the piazza was another massive building, the Basilica Ulpia (Trajan's full name was Marcus Ulpius Traianus). This,

Right: The height of Trajan's Column equalled the depth of the excavation of the hillside needed to make space for it and the adjoining forum. It may even have been intended as a form of reparation for the destruction involved, but its siting between Greek and Latin libraries is also a recognition of Trajan's written account of the Dacian Wars which it illustrates. Some of the higher levels of the frieze would have been visible from adjoining buildings, now vanished. The frieze is the most complete depiction we have of a Roman military campaign. Here booty from the defeated Dacians (from modern Romania) is being stuffed into saddlebags.

the largest basilica in Rome, was used for the display of plunder from Trajan's campaigns but also for judicial and commercial functions. This was traditionally the site where slaves were freed and this ancient practice appears to have continued in the new building.

The best preserved monument of Trajan's forum is the column on which he recorded his campaign against the Dacians in a continuous frieze. Trajan followed Julius Caesar in writing an account of his campaigns and the 650-ft frieze is a pictorial representation of this account. It is thus an accurate document of the campaign rather than a propaganda show as was normally the case with public sculpture. The main purpose of the column, however, was to provide a resting place for the urn containing Trajan's ashes.

The most important building in the Roman Forum associated with Trajan's successor Hadrian is the Temple of Venus and Roma **(14)**, dedicated to Venus and to the city itself in AD 135. Hadrian himself designed it using Greek rather than Roman models. His efforts aroused the fury of Apollodorus who, one account suggests, was put to death by Hadrian for his protests. The temple was built over the entrance to the Domus Aurea and was one of the largest cult centres in the city. Nero's Colossus, already recast as a sun god, had to be moved, by 24 elephants.

The Forum was by now so fully packed that few new buildings could be fitted in. One exception was a temple erected to Faustina **(15)**, the wife of the emperor Antoninus Pius, who was deified by him after her death in 141 (*see box right*). After his own death, in 161, his name was added to the dedication. The columns of Greek marble, brought from the island of Euboea, are 55 ft high (those fronting the Pantheon are only 45 ft) while the high podium of the temple is reminiscent of the earliest Roman temples.

THE APOTHEOSIS OF EMPERORS

When Augustus' body was being burned on the funeral pyre, a senator claimed to have seen the emperor's spirit ascending to heaven and the claim was sufficient to that ensure Augustus was declared a god.

After that the idea of apotheosis, literally the act of 'becoming a god', was represented in pictorial form on monuments to deceased emperors. Here, in a relief of AD 161, the emperor Antoninus Pius and his wife Faustina are seen being carried to heaven, borne on the wings of a large nude figure. To the right is the goddess Roma. The reclining figure to the left may be a personification of Mars, as it was in the Field of Mars in Rome that imperial funerals took place. Normally an apotheosis would be declared by the senate, but Hadrian himself declared that his dead lover Antinous was a god and should be accorded cult worship.

In 305, after the death of Diocletian, the empire was split by rival claims to power. A usurper, Maxentius, seized power in Italy and made his capital in Rome. The previous hundred years had seen the efflorescence of monumental vaulted buildings, especially the great bath complexes, which had been the most important legacies of the later emperors. Maxentius used the central hall of a large bath as his model, and his basilica **(16)** has a nave 260 ft long with an aisle either side. Inside the surviving walls are niches for statues, and the brick would have been clad in marble. The basilica is believed to have served as the city prefecture. One room is known to have been set aside for trials of senators, who claimed the privilege of judging themselves.

Maxentius' ambitious project was left unfinished when he fell fighting against the emperor Constantine at the Battle of the Milvian Bridge in 312. Constantine took over the basilica and placed an enormous statue of himself in the western apse. Parts of it have been found (*see illustration on p. 208*); the head and neck alone measure eight feet. Within a few years, Constantine was scattering his patronage elsewhere, on monuments to the new faith, Christianity. The last monument in the Forum is the Column of Phocas **(16)**. A reused column from the 2nd century AD dedicated to the Byzantine emperor by the exarch of Italy in 608 AD, it contains the inscription 'Phocas, general in perpetuity, crowned by God, triumphator, always Augustus'. Alas for his hopes, Phocas, who had come to power through a violent *coup d'état*, was deposed and murdered in 610.

Rome: the Arch of Constantine

Commemorative monument to
an imperial victory
Built AD 315

Right: Circular relief from the Arch of
Constantine showing the moon goddess
in her chariot. The symbolism is clearly
pagan and carries no hint that the emperor
who erected this arch was soon to adopt
Christianity as his own religion.

Below: Carving from the arch of Septimius
Severus, erected in AD 203 to celebrate the
emperor's victory over the Parthians. It
shows a captured Parthian prisoner with a
Roman soldier behind him.

It was the habit of Etruscan chieftains to celebrate their victories by processions of booty and captives, and the Roman triumph was adapted from these models. In Rome it assumed a political purpose in that it was seen as the final culmination of a general's success, after which he retired from public life.

In some cases the trophies of the victor seem to have been commemorated in an arch with the statue of the victor on top, but none of these has survived. The triumphal arch as we know it today is essentially a display of propaganda from imperial times. Augustus erected a number of arches in the 20s BC, marking northern Italian conquests. In 19 BC he built one in Rome to commemorate the safe return of Roman standards captured by the Parthians.

In most cases a quadriga, a four-horse chariot, with a figure of the emperor inside, would have stood on the summit of a triumphal arch. The arches are also important records of imperial iconography and reach their culmination in the Arch of Titus, which stands in the Roman Forum. It celebrates Titus' victory in Jerusalem in AD 70 and shows his triumphal procession into Rome complete with the sacred objects he had looted from the Temple (*see illustration on p. 212*). Inscriptions fill the central façade, recording the arch as a gift of the senate and people of Rome to both Vespasian (who had born the brunt of the fighting in Judaea before his accession as emperor) and Titus.

By the 2nd century AD triumphal arches are commonly found throughout the Western empire. They might mark the end of a new road, be an offering of respect to a new emperor or recognition of his patronage—the elegant arch marking the boundary between Hadrian's Athens and the Classical city, for instance (*'G' on the plan on p. 85*). The north African provinces were especially enthusiastic and here one finds examples of the *arcus quadrifrons*, the arch which stood in the centre of a crossroads and had four equal faces. Septimius Severus' arch at Leptis Magna is a famous example (*shown on p. 191*).

An even grander form of triumphal arch had three openings instead of a single one. The most famous is that of Constantine in Rome (*see illustration opposite*). Another, also in Rome, is that of Septimius Severus, erected in AD 203 to commemorate his victory over the Parthians. Large panels over its smaller side arches contain a series of images from the Parthian campaign while at the foot of the columns reliefs show Romans with their Parthian prisoners. The great central arch has personifications of Victory in spandrels on either side. The arch is famous for its rewritten inscription in which the name of Septimius' son Geta has been obliterated after his murder by his brother Caracalla and the words 'to the best and bravest of emperors' substituted. This arch certainly did have a quadriga on top—it is shown on a contemporary coin.

ICONOGRAPHY OF THE ARCH OF CONSTANTINE

The Arch of Constantine was erected in 315 in honour of Constantine's defeat of his rival emperor Maxentius in 312. The victory is credited to the 'inspiration of god and the greatness of his mind', terminology which was acceptable to pagan and Christian alike. There is no hint of the announcement of toleration for Christians that Constantine had promulgated in Milan in 313. Such a commitment could hardly be shown in the pagan centre of the ancient capital, and all the reliefs show traditional pagan iconography, including roundels of Sol, the sun god and Luna, the moon goddess.

Constantine's arch shares many features with that of Septimius Severus, and it has even been argued that its origins are closer to that arch in date but that it was adapted to its new role after Constantine's victory. Certainly many of the panels come from earlier monuments, dating from the reigns of Trajan and Hadrian. This may be because the capital now lacked the craftsmen to create new ones or it may have been a deliberate attempt to link Constantine with successful past emperors. Many of the reliefs from Constantine's own time show the campaign leading up to his victory over Maxentius and his triumphal entry into Rome. Some are especially interesting because they show Constantine facing forward, his men acclaiming him from either side. These are sometimes cited as forerunners of the front-facing imperial and divine figures of Byzantine art. Naturalism in portraiture gives way to the impulse to portray the ruler as a remote or semi-divine being.

The Arch of Constantine was dedicated to the emperor by the senate in 315 after his victory over his rival Maxentius. Reliefs of his campaign surround the arch, which is also remarkable for the recognition of the 'supreme deity' which had inspired the emperor.

Rome: the Colosseum

Amphitheatre
Heyday: 1st–2nd centuries AD

The Colosseum still remains one of the most prominent of the ruins of ancient Rome. In this engraving of 1839, Lord Byron mounts a romantic pose in front of it. In his *Childe Harold's Pilgrimage* Byron had famously imagined a Dacian gladiator slain within these walls, 'butcher'd to make a Roman holiday'.

The earliest Greek theatres date from the 5th century BC, but in southern Italy in the 1st century BC there was a revolutionary new development: two theatres were placed facing each other with an arena in the centre (the word comes from the sand, *arena*, that was scattered to soak up the blood), the spectators sitting on tiered seats all the way round. The oldest known amphitheatre is that at Pompeii, built just after 80 BC. After that amphitheatres began to spring up across the empire, though they were always more common in the West. There are about 230 known, some 90 of these in Italy, 35 in Gaul and 40 in northern Africa. There were only two known in Greece, where the traditional theatre (*see p. 82*) persisted.

The Colosseum in Rome, built by Vespasian in the 70s AD, was an extraordinary architectural and engineering achievement, built on marshy land. With seating for 50,000, it is the largest amphitheatre known, and was clearly a major inspiration for others. These free-standing structures were major undertakings—show-off buildings erected by cities anxious to display their status.

The amphitheatre could be used for any kind of spectator entertainment, which might be tied in with festivals, the recognition of new magistrates (who would foot the bill), imperial victory celebrations or simply the inauguration of the amphitheatre itself. Financing games was an easy, if expensive, way for a local magnate to gain popularity. Permission had to be gained from the emperor before games could be held.

Gladiator fights developed from Etruscan funeral rituals where pairs of warriors fought each other. In Rome the custom developed into public entertainment. There are records of eight major games thrown by Augustus, which between them used 5,000 pairs of gladiators. Trajan's victory games at the conclusion of his war with the Dacians involved a similar number. The different kinds of costumes and weapons added to the variety of combats. A well-trained gladiator was a valuable commodity, and the 'sport' held a fascina-

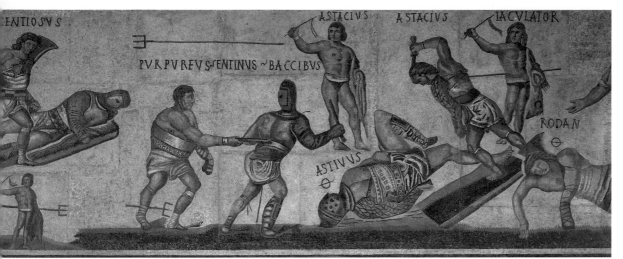

Left: This mosaic scene of gladiators in combat shows details of their different weapons and armour, and each gladiator is named, a sign that in their day they were minor celebrities. Note the Greek letter Θ, which stands for *thanatos*, 'death', above the head of the fallen gladiators.

Below right: The amphitheatre at El Djem in modern Tunisia is, like the Colosseum, an astonishing survival.

Below left: Mosaic detail from the grand villa of Piazza Armerina in Sicily (see *p. 198*) showing the loading of an ostrich onto a ship bound for Rome and the games.

tion for many high-class Romans (to such an extent that laws were passed restricting who could become a gladiator). Many gladiators were, in fact, slaves. The death rates were far lower than might be expected and the lives of wounded gladiators were often saved in the hope that they could fight again. Gladiator schools existed alongside amphitheatres.

A major development, recorded for the first time in 186 BC, was the introduction of wild animals. Hunts of panthers, bulls, hippopotamuses, lions and elephants had always been part of an aristocratic lifestyle and this activity was now transferred into the arena. The empire was scoured for examples—often a provincial governor was given the task of hunting out exotic creatures so that ever more bizarre contests could be staged. When the Colosseum was inaugurated, the games included 5,000 wild and 4,000 tame animals while Trajan's victory games saw the deaths of 11,000 more. Animal fights were increasingly tied in with the public execution of criminals, which was usually one section of a day's entertainment. In some venues, Christians were considered criminals, especially if they refused to sacrifice to the traditional gods. It is no mere myth that Christians were among those thrown to the lions, and their martyrdom accounts provide a substantial record of this part of the 'games'.

Having such large crowds together could easily lead to disorder. An amphitheatre was designed so that different classes would enter by different staircases and tunnels and so that they could be easily dispersed, but peace did not always hold. Pompeii was a local centre for games, drawing in spectators from the surrounding towns, and in AD 59 serious rioting broke out between the native Pompeians and rival crowds from nearby Nuceria. Several died in the fracas and the emperor Nero asked the consuls to investigate. There followed a ban on all games, other than athletic contests, in Pompeii for ten years, though the ban was lifted by Nero in 64.

The holding of games diminished as the difficulties and expense of providing gladiators and animals became more prohibitive. The enormous amphitheatre at El Djem, the Roman Thysdrus, in modern Tunisia, second only to the Colosseum in size, was constructed in the 230s but may never have been fully completed or used. When Constantine banned most kinds of games in the 330s there seems to have been little protest. Patrons must have been relieved that they did not have to incur so many expenses. It was the chariot races in the hippodromes which remained as the main spectator sport, especially in Constantinople, where racing went on for centuries.

Rome: the Pantheon

Supreme example of Roman architecture
Built AD 118–125

The inscriptions in the photograph below are from different eras but remarkably similar in style and mood. 'M. Agrippa, consul for the third time, built this' was inscribed on the porch of the Pantheon at the time of Hadrian, in honour of Agrippa, who built the first temple on this site. The fountain commemorates the munificence of a pope, Clement X (1670–76), who claims as one of his honours the office of 'Pont. Max.' (Pontifex Maximus), chief priest, a position originally held by the Roman emperor.

The Pantheon is the best preserved ancient building in Rome. This is largely due to the skill of its builders, who created its vast dome out of concrete so effectively (*see box opposite*) that it has stayed in place for nearly 2,000 years. It was also lucky to be bequeathed to the papacy by the 7th-century Byzantine emperor Phocas; it was converted into a church and thus preserved. It remains one of the most extraordinary feats of ancient engineering.

The Pantheon lies within what was once the Campus Martius (Field of Mars), originally a large uninhabited area inside the loop of the River Tiber, north of the Forum and Capitoline Hill, used for military training and elections. It was inevitable that, as the city expanded northwards, it would encroach on the open space. The key figure in its development was Marcus Agrippa, right-hand man and later son-in-law of the emperor Augustus. Effective both as a politician and as a general (he commanded the fleet that defeated Antony and Cleopatra), he earned himself great popularity in Rome in the 20s BC by buying up a large area of the Field of Mars and constructing public buildings on it. One of these was a temple to the twelve Olympian gods, later known as the temple to all the gods ('pan-theon'). Statues of Augustus and Agrippa stood flanking the doorway; their empty niches remain. In the early 120s the emperor Hadrian decided to rebuild the temple entirely. The date stamps on the bricks tell of a building programme between AD 118 and 125. Hadrian even switched the façade from the south to the north but he modestly preserved Agrippa's name in the inscription (it was almost unknown for Hadrian to use his own name on his buildings).

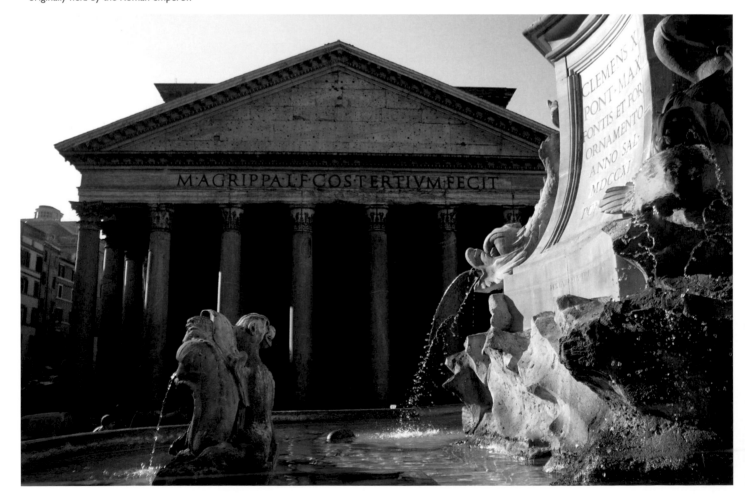

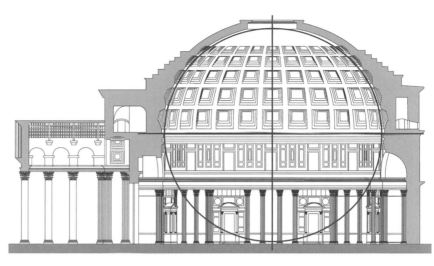

The porch of the Pantheon is faced with eight giant columns, each some 45 ft high, of rose and grey Egyptian granite. The outer columns and the third one on each side are backed by two more columns so that one has a sense of walking through an aisle towards the bronze doors which may, at their restored core, be the originals. At night, when the doors are closed and there is only the glow from the street, the vast columns provide an intensely evocative sense of the Roman past.

The impact of entry through the portico and great doors into the interior is still stunning. Grand Roman temples were never left bare, and the Pantheon was cloaked in marble. The floor is still the original and the same range of coloured marbles was used on the walls (the originals were removed in the 18th century but a small section has been restored). Niches show where the statues of the twelve Olympian gods were placed.

The Roman engineers constructed a solid circular foundation some 15 ft deep and then superimposed a wall on it which rose in three sections with a diameter of 142 ft. Exactly half this distance up, they built a huge wooden frame and the concrete dome was put up layer by layer over it. By narrowing the width of the dome as it rose, the weight was kept manageable. Further weight was saved by carving out coffers, which may originally have been decorated with rosettes as was the case in other buildings of the period. For centuries this was the largest unreinforced concrete dome in the world. The proportions are so harmonious because the distance from the floor to the centre of the oculus, the 'eye' in the centre of the dome, is exactly the same as the building's diameter. The interior contains, in fact, a perfect sphere.

The dome of the Pantheon with its unglazed oculus, almost 30 ft in diameter.

DOME CONSTRUCTION & CONCRETE

The Romans' 'invention' of concrete was one of their most ground-breaking technological achievements. A building material of like quality was not known again until the 20th century.

Making concrete involves binding together a core of stone or brick fragments with a lime mortar. The Romans were lucky in that such a mortar could be made from a volcanic ash which was available at Pozzuoli near Naples (the ash is known as *pozzolana*). It had the property of setting right through the mix, not just on the surface, and it even hardened under water, making it an indispensable ingredient of harbour walls. Before this, concrete had only been used as a thin (stucco) facing for buildings, as only the surface dried.

A great deal of trial and error was needed to arrive at exactly the right consistency. One can see the growing sophistication of the process beginning in 150 BC (the Stabian Baths in Pompeii are an early example). The first really successful use of free-standing concrete is usually seen to be the central octagonal dining room of Nero's Domus Aurea (c. AD 65). Sixty years later the dome of the Pantheon was completed. Here the builders introduced another refinement, the use of lighter pumice in the concrete as the building rose so that the dome's centre was less heavy.

By AD 200 really massive vaulted buildings such as the Baths of Caracalla were possible (*see overleaf*). The walls were covered by stucco that could be painted. It was not simply the durability of concrete that was important (although, of course, only those buildings where it was used successfully have survived); it was the speed with which buildings could be erected. The Baths of Caracalla went up in just five years.

Rome: the Baths of Caracalla

The Romans had a passion for bathing, and the bath house was often one of the largest public buildings in a city. The Greeks had added baths to their gymnasia, but in the western part of the Empire baths often grew up around existing hot springs—the Romans may have taken the idea from those Greek cities of southern Italy which exploited such springs. The Roman Aquae Sextiae, the modern Aix-en-Provence, was one town where the spring might have provided the lure of settlement. So too at Aquae Sulis, the modern Bath in England, where the springs provided 250 thousand gallons of hot (48°C/120°F) water a day.

A bath which had to provide its own water supply took a different form. In the smaller bath houses, water may even have been manually lifted into a header tank, but this would have been a cumbersome and expensive business. Far more efficient in the long run was to divert water from an existing aqueduct, or even construct a new aqueduct from scratch.

The first public bath in Rome was constructed by Agrippa (the same Agrippa who built the Pantheon; *see previous page*) between 25 and 19 BC. He created a new aqueduct, the Aqua Virgo, to feed it. The complex consisted of a circular hall with rooms arranged around it and a separate natatio, 'swimming' pool. Still, the building had an *ad hoc* feel to it and there were no other rooms for recreation. The emperors Nero and Titus created more elaborate baths, but it was Trajan who established a ground plan that became the standard. He found a large space left in the ruins of Nero's Domus Aurea, created a vast level platform on it and ordered his favourite architect, Apollodorus of Damascus, to design what was as much a social centre as a bath house. The building went up between AD 104 and 109. The entry fee was small and the citizens of Rome must have felt they were indulging in real luxury as they relaxed in the marble halls. The emperor could only bask in the glory.

Luxurious baths such as Trajan's were known as *thermae* (as opposed to the simpler *balneae*). Not much remains of what Trajan built, but we know that their model was followed on a larger scale a hundred years later in baths given to the city by the emperor Caracalla (ruled 211–17, although they were only completed after his death). These have never been built on, and much of the vast structure is intact. It is the only one of the imperial baths where the extent of the surrounding gardens can still be seen. According to the date stamps on the bricks, the baths were begun in 212, and the same year a branch was diverted from the Aqua Marcia to bring water to service them. This fed into enor-

Luxurious baths complex
Built early 3rd century AD

Facing page: The Baths of Caracalla still astonish by their size but it is hard to imagine how they would have looked crammed with bathers and with their marble and statues intact. The Victorian artist Sir Lawrence Alma-Tadema (1836–1912) specialised in recreating the sensuality of ancient Rome and baths scenes were one of his favourite subjects. His characters still appear more Belle Epoque than Roman.

Left: The Baths of Caracalla today: the bathers are long gone, the marble has vanished from the walls, but the mosaics still remain— and the cavernous dimensions of the great halls.

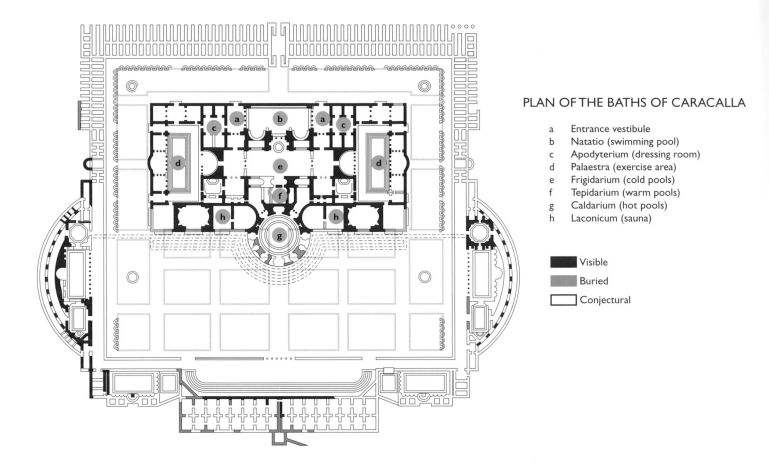

PLAN OF THE BATHS OF CARACALLA

a   Entrance vestibule
b   Natatio (swimming pool)
c   Apodyterium (dressing room)
d   Palaestra (exercise area)
e   Frigidarium (cold pools)
f   Tepidarium (warm pools)
g   Caldarium (hot pools)
h   Laconicum (sauna)

Visible
Buried
Conjectural

mous cisterns, 32 chambers on each of two storeys, which were concealed in the rear wall of the complex behind tiers of seats for open-air performances. They could hold 18 million gallons of water.

Entrance was through a grand vestibule **(a)**. Immediately inside it was a large, unroofed cold swimming pool, the natatio **(b)**; on either side were identical dressing rooms, apodyteria **(c)**. Beyond was huge central hall flanked by palaestrae **(d)**, where gymnastic and other physical exercise could take place before bathing. Traditionally a palaestra was open to the skies and surrounded by a colonnade.

The central rooms were vast. The large main hall, 190 ft by 80 ft in area, doubled as the frigidarium **(e)**, and served to connect the two identical wings of recreational rooms with the tepidarium **(f)** and caldarium. The vaults of the frigidarium rested on eight colossal columns of grey Egyptian granite while the cool pools were placed in niches, entered through more columns so that the centre of this cavernous hall was left open for social gathering. The caldarium **(g)**, the hottest room, was another major building its in own right; its dome was only slightly smaller than that of the Pantheon. In addition to under-floor (hypocaust) heating, it had windows through which the sun warmed its seven pools and the adjoining sauna area **(h)**. By this date meeting halls, libraries and lecture halls had become essential parts of the wider cultural experience of the baths, and all were provided.

The servicing of these baths was, of course, a major undertaking. They would open about noon and stay open until dusk. They could accommodate 1,600 bathers at a time, possibly 8,000 in a single day on one estimate. The water had to be kept running—it is probable that the cold pools were constantly replenished while the hot or warm pools (the tepidarium in these baths had two pools) were only refilled at intervals. Under the public rooms ran two circuits of passageways. One was large enough for carts of wood to be brought in. About ten tons of wood a day were needed to meet the voracious demands of the 50 furnaces, and there was storage space for seven months of supplies. The lower passageways served as drains for used water and sewage. There must have been an army of slaves down below keeping everything in good order.

TREASURES OF THE BATHS

The period when these baths were built is known as the Severan Age after the founding emperor of the dynasty, Septimius Severus (father of Caracalla). It was a period of particular opulence, just before the crisis of the 3rd century—when leadership was unstable and barbarian raids a perpetual threat—shook the empire. The floors of the baths were made in the full range of marbles that were available in the empire's mines and there were many fine mosaics. The most famous are those of athletes and their trainers that were uncovered in the apse of one of the palaestrae in 1824 (they are now in the Vatican Museum). The non-figurative mosaic floor patterns are especially imaginative, but even such flamboyant decoration must have been overshadowed by the large numbers of statues, perhaps 120 in total, which graced the main rooms. In the 1540s Pope Paul III (of the Farnese family) excavated the ruins and collected some of the best examples. Two enormous granite baths from the frigidarium were converted into fountains in the Piazza Farnese in central Rome, where they still stand. Hercules was a favourite protecting god of the Severans and two statues of him, including the so-called *Farnese Hercules*, were among the pope's plunder. Pride of place, however, must go to the *Farnese Bull* (*illustrated*), an extraordinary recreation of the torture of Dirce. All these statues are now in the Archaeological Museum in Naples.

Alessandro Farnese (Pope Paul III; reigned 1534–49) undertook large-scale excavations of the Baths of Caracalla in which he found a mass of statuary. One of the most astonishing pieces is the *Farnese Bull*, sculpted from a single piece of marble. Dirce had mistreated the mother of her stepsons, and in revenge they tied her to the horns of a bull and allowed her to be dragged to her death. The sculpture is probably a 3rd-century AD copy of a Hellenistic original.

THE TERRIBLE LUXURIA OF ROME

'We think ourselves poorly off, living like paupers, if the walls [of our baths] are not ablaze with large and costly circular mirrors, if our Alexandrian marbles are not decorated with panels of Numidian marble, if the whole of their surface has not been given a decorative overlay of elaborate patterns having all the variety of fresco murals, unless the ceiling cannot be seen for glass, unless the pools into which we lower bodies with all the strength drained out of them by lengthy periods in the sweating room are edged with Thasian marble (which was once the rarest of sights even in a temple), unless the water pours from silver taps.'

Seneca, *Letter LXXXVI*. Tr. Robin Campbell

Roman Ostia

Roman port town
Flourished 1st century BC–2nd century AD

It is hard to imagine the city of Rome, eventual centre of a vast empire, as in any way vulnerable, yet it was always open to attack from the sea and early accounts suggest that the mouth (*ostium*) of the River Tiber was settled by a Roman colony in the 5th century to protect it. There was already an ancient route along which salt was carried, and the colony was placed in a fort, *castrum*, whose late 4th-century BC walls still survive. Legend tells of how every village along the course of the river was destroyed to give Rome total security. A century later the small town of Ostia was beginning to benefit from trade with the Greek cities of southern Italy. During the Carthaginian wars it served as a naval base, and the magistrates in charge of the Roman fleet were based here. In the brutal civil wars of the 1st century BC, Ostia suffered from looting and raids by pirates.

It was not until Italy was settled under the emperor Augustus in the late 1st century BC that the town really began to flourish as a commercial centre. Its initial success was short-lived as the river was too shallow to allow boats to unload along the bank, and the emperor Claudius built a major new port, Portus, further north on the coast, with a canal connecting it to the Tiber. However, the administration of Rome's vital grain supply remained in Ostia.

In the early 2nd century there was a major redevelopment by Hadrian. One of the largest baths in the city, the Baths of Neptune, with its fine mosaic floors, was built in this period, just inside the Porta Romana, the gate on the road from Rome. Some of the horrea, the former grain warehouses, became luxurious baths, and private homes replaced many of the tenement blocks. By the middle of the 2nd century the population had reached 50,000. Gradually, however, Mediterranean trade began to decline and by the 4th century Ostia was primarily a residential town—though not without some cachet. Recent excavations show that local aristocratic families began to move in and there was a late phase of opulent new building the scale of which is only just being appreciated. By the 6th and 7th centuries, however, Ostia was in serious decline, and reports tell of the once busy road to Rome being overgrown with grass.

DOMESTIC ARCHITECTURE OF OSTIA

Ostia provides some superb surviving examples of ancient Roman tenement housing, an important feature of city life across the empire, and quite different from the *domus*, found at Pompeii, with its atrium and peristyle (*see p. 174*). On the ground floor of a tenement was a shop, tavern or warehouse, and above were the residential apartments, usually reached by their own staircase. Many must have been rented but there is some evidence that favoured clients of the shopowners or their freedmen lived there. These apartments were normally rectangular with the large rooms at the front overlooking the street, sometimes with a balcony. Bedrooms would be behind. These were quite large apartments of some 2000 square feet, and there was often another storey (the blocks of flats at Ostia were typically three or four storeys tall). The problem was speculators building higher. In Rome Augustus limited the number of storeys to between five and seven and he organised firewatching units in each region of the city.

Facing page: View of the ruins of Ostia showing the remains of brick-built warehouses and apartment blocks among the umbrella pines. The street runs towards the Tiber from the decumanus maximus, the main thoroughfare of town.

Below: Model of a four-storey Ostia apartment block showing the brickwork, the entrance staircases and the first-floor balcony. Though the block in the picture opposite only survives in its lower storeys, these same features are clearly discernible.

The offices in charge of the grain dole to Rome were at Ostia. This mosaic is from the Hall of the Grain Measurers (**E**), and shows the guild's symbol of a hod.

The Forum of the Corporations (**C**) stands just to the south of the original course of the Tiber, and visitors must have walked here from the quayside to do business. A series of offices, many of them with mosaics showing their trade, encircled it and it provides fascinating evidence of the diversity of Ostia's businesses and the ports with which the city traded. There were rope makers and corn merchants, tanners, ship owners and ivory traders, typically represented by an elephant, as shown here. Representatives of Alexandria, the greatest port of the eastern Mediterranean, had their offices next to those from Tunisia, Carthage, Sardinia and Gaul.

The theatre at Ostia (**D**) is large and well preserved, first built at the time of Augustus and enlarged in the 2nd century AD, when Ostia saw a new lease of life as a residential city.

Ostia is typical of a planned town with two main roads crossing each other at the centre. The original walls of the fortified town were dwarfed in the 1st century BC by an extension which enclosed 170 acres and required new gates to be constructed. The road from Rome entered at the Porta Romana (**A**) and became the city's principal thoroughfare, the decumanus. It left the city through the Porta Marina (**B**) and from there headed down to the coast.

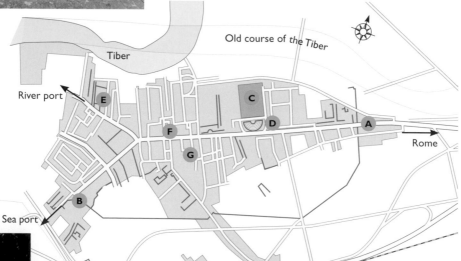

The Forum (**F**) lay at the centre of the original fortified town and had the biggest temple of all, the Capitolium, dedicated to Jupiter, Juno and Minerva, standing opposite a temple to Roma and Augustus.

Each block of the city was a jumble of tenements, bath houses, grain stores and temples. Bars such as the one shown above served hot food. Private houses had shrines for the household gods, often in the form of decorative niches.

Close to the Forum were the *foricae*, the public latrines, extremely well preserved. Adjoining them on the other side of the street were the large public baths (**G**).

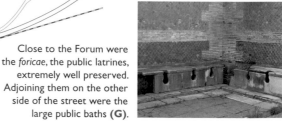

THE CULTS AT OSTIA

Ostia is remarkable for showing how different cults existed alongside each other. There were the ancient Roman cults, of course, but other cults from other parts of the empire also flourished here. There were imported Egyptian religions, those of Serapis and Isis, and that of *Cybele*, the Great Mother, which originated in Asia Minor. The sanctuary to her and her lover Attis was by the southern city gate, the Porta Marina. There was a Jewish community of traders and merchants with its own synagogue and evidence too, during the years of Ostia's decline after the 3rd century AD, of a Christian basilica and other places of worship. Monica, the mother of St Augustine, died here when she and her son were waiting for a ship to Africa.

The cult which most resembled Christianity and which appears to have represented a challenge to it, was that of Mithras, which traces its origins to Persia. Mithras is commonly shown as a male figure, holding back a bull's head and slitting its throat in sacrifice. The spirit of the bull, it was believed, was released by this act, and its blood falling on the ground brought regeneration and renewal. A divine banquet with the sun god, sometimes explicitly shown as Apollo, followed the sacrifice.

Ostia was an important centre of Mithraism, which spread throughout the Roman Empire. Some 500 sanctuaries are known, 35 of them in Rome and 18 in Ostia. They were always underground, in the basements of buildings or in caves. At the eastern end of the sanctuary the god was shown with attendant deities with torches. This represented the light towards which members were moving. Mithraism was especially popular among soldiers. Slaves and ex-slaves were also attracted to the cult although women were excluded from it. One of the cult's attractions was its graded hierarchy. Initiates moved upwards through a series of ranks just as a soldier might do, or a slave who was working towards freedom. The highest grade, a 'Father', was probably reserved for a leader of a congregation, and it was an important enough honour to be recorded on gravestones.

There seems to have been some competition between Mithraism and Christianity over converts, but as Christianity grew more powerful it moved to obliterate Mithraism, and overtook it altogether. By the end of the 4th century, after the edicts of the emperor Theodosius, Christianity was the only mystery religion that survived (*for mystery religions, see p. 220*).

Above: The cult of Mithras was an import from Persia and there are several examples of Mithraea in Ostia. Mithras was normally shown in a Phrygian cap (from Phrygia in Asia Minor), used by the Romans as a symbol of the East. The sacrifice of a bull is crucial to the cult—it is usually seen as a force Mithras must conquer to release the fertility of the earth. Animals join in, a serpent and a dog suck the wound, perhaps to prevent the blood nourishing the earth. A scorpion is often shown attacking the bull's testicles as if to destroy its fertility. The cult draws on ancient Eastern parallels, including Zoroastrianism.

Virtually everything about Mithraism is speculative, however, other than its popularity among Romans. It is not clear how far it retained aspects of other Eastern mystery religions.

Left: Evidence of other cults in Ostia can be seen in this relief of a menorah from the ruins of a synagogue and a floor mosaic of a fish and chalice from a Christian house. Several Christian churches were established in Ostia in the 4th and 5th centuries. The synagogue dates from the 1st century.

Nîmes

A major city of Roman Gaul
Flourished 1st century AD

Facing page: Roman cities could never have developed without a water supply, and this was especially important when the settlement was a planted colony which might need defending. In the Celtic world many colonies were established near springs which had already become spiritual centres. Nîmes is an excellent example. As Roman civilisation developed, the warm springs were fed into baths, and in the days of the *pax romana* (the freedom from civil war that Augustus had brought to the empire) water could be brought in via aqueducts. The picture opposite shows the Jardin de la Fontaine in Nîmes, the public park that now surrounds the ancient spring, and which was once a nymphaeum dedicated to the emperor Augustus.

In what is now southeastern France, the Celts had already developed *oppida*, fortified settlements with public buildings, paved streets and fortifications, by the 2nd century BC. One of these settlements was Nemausus, which took its name from the local deity who was honoured at a spring on the site. An ancient road ran north–south through the *oppidum*, which developed as trade increased with the city of Massilia (the modern Marseilles), founded by the Greeks in c. 600 BC. One impressive Celtic monument was a tower on a hilltop overlooking the spring.

In 121 BC the Romans conquered the area and their new thoroughfare, the Via Domitia (begun in 118 BC), which ran between Italy and Spain, formed a crossroads at Nemausus. The settlement now became important to defend. Julius Caesar awarded it the status of a Latin colony, which gave it privileges, especially in trade. In 31 BC, as part of his policy of disbanding his armies, Augustus settled some of his veterans there. It was Augustus who transformed the Celtic settlement into a Roman town, which quickly prospered from the growing commerce of the region.

The site was developed carefully. One of the first projects was to face the Celtic tower with limestone blocks and recreate it as an octagonal shape with pilasters around its upper storey. The Tour Magne still stands to a height of 100 ft and must have been an impressive landmark in the surrounding countryside (it is now part of an enchanting 18th-century garden, the Jardin de la Fontaine; *illustrated opposite*). The spring below was preserved, with its pool and Celtic temple left untouched, but Augustus surrounded the whole by a portico and nymphaeum and the complex was dedicated to him.

This was a typical Roman policy, to link the imperial cult with local spiritual forces. The so-called Temple of Diana, now largely in ruins, appears to have been built as a library, possibly in its final form in the 2nd century AD. It is reminiscent of the Library of Celsus in Ephesus (*see p. 123*) and it is assumed to have been constructed by craftsmen from the East.

Augustus also paid for the walls and gates of the city, built around 15 BC. They enclosed over 500 acres and ran for four miles. Bastions were built along the walls so the impression of a military settlement survived. Today the most impressive of the gates is the Porte d'Auguste, the gate where traffic from the east would have entered the city on the Via Domitia. There are two large arches for wheeled vehicles and a small entrance on each side for pedestrians.

Nîmes grew, and by the end of the 1st century AD had an estimated population of 30,000. It was now that the largest of its surviving Roman buildings, the amphitheatre, was built. The largest and most famous of the amphitheatres was, of course, the Colosseum in Rome. The amphitheatre at Nîmes was built perhaps 20 years later and had seats for about 20,000 spectators in comparison to the 50,000 of the Colosseum, though the design was very similar.

Every successful city had to face the challenge of finding a good water supply. In Nîmes, the circular settlement tank where the water was cleaned after its arrival via aqueduct still survives. Here, and often in tanks along the route, the sand and other material which had been swept along by the water could be allowed to sink, with the purified flow continuing into the town. At Nîmes there are openings for ten distribution pipes. The aqueduct which brought the water into the town had the Pont du Gard (*see p. 160*) as part of it.

The amphitheatre at Nîmes, once used for gladiatorial games and wild animal fights, and is still used for the latter, as a bullring. The entrance was through arches on the ground floor and then internal stairways led upwards to the higher storeys. The grandees of the city or important visitors would be allocated seats in the front rows. The four lowest rows of seats are marked off from the rest. Just at the same time (late 1st century AD), the neighbouring city of Arles was building its own similar amphitheatre and this suggests competition between the two cities. In fact, a famous speech by the Greek orator Aelius Aristides in AD 150 specifically praises the Romans for diverting the energies of cities into these building projects rather than fighting each other as they used to.

THE MAISON CARRÉE

Augustus had no male heirs, and the question of a successor caused him much anguish. In 17 BC he had adopted two of his grandsons, Gaius and Lucius, sons of his daughter Julia by his trusted general Marcus Agrippa, but Lucius died in AD 2 and Gaius in AD 4. The most prestigious temple in Nîmes, now known as the Maison Carrée, was dedicated to their memory. It is still one of the best preserved Roman temples. Typically for a Roman temple it has a high podium. This originated in the Etruscan custom of the priests ascending a platform from which they could observe the skies and the ways birds flew, so as to tell the *auspices*, who would determine whether or not the omens were propitious. In a manner also typical of a Roman temple as opposed to a Greek, the exterior columns beyond the portico do not stand apart from the cella but are embedded in its walls (*see illustration opposite*). The columns are Corinthian and appear to have been influenced directly by those being built in Rome at the same time, for instance in the Temple to Mars Ultor, dedicated by Augustus in 2 BC.

Right: The Corinthian temple known as the Maison Carrée was built by the emperor Augustus in the 1st century AD in honour of his two young heirs who predeceased him.

THE CORINTHIAN ORDER

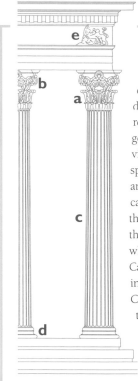

The Corinthian order was born in Greece. The earliest complete example dates from 334 BC (the so-called Lysicrates Monument in Athens). The defining feature of a Corinthian column is the double row of acanthus leaves on the capital **(a)**. There is a good story, reproduced by the Roman architect Vitruvius, that a Greek architect called Callimachus was inspired by a basket he saw left on a grave, through which an acanthus plant had grown. But the Corinthian order can also be seen as an elaboration of the Ionic style in that the volutes are still visible **(b)**. It is not known why the term Corinthian was adopted. It was the Romans who took to the order with enthusiasm and the Maison Carrée at Nîmes is an excellent early example. The Corinthian could be mixed with other orders as it is on the Colosseum, where it appears on the third storey above the Doric on the first and the Ionic on the second, a progression which became standard in the Renaissance. Other characteristics of the Corinthian order are the tall, slender, fluted column shaft **(c)**, which, like the Ionic, stands on a base **(d)**. In the entablature, also like the Ionic order, there is a continuous frieze **(e)**.

While the columns of the portico are free-standing, the lateral columns of the Maison Carrée are embedded in the walls. This is typical of Roman temples, as distinct from Greek, where the columns form a peristyle right around the building.

BECOMING ROMAN

Cities were important ways of establishing and consolidating Roman rule. Gradually in the Western empire the local Celtic elites, who had been known for their general unruliness, became transformed into Romans. The Roman historian Tacitus, writing of Britain under the governorship of his father-in-law Agricola, describes a process that must have been very similar to that effected by Augustus in Nîmes and many other western cities:

'He gave private encouragement and official assistance to the building of temples, public squares and good houses, he praised the energetic and scolded the slack: and competition for honour proved as effective as compulsion. Furthermore he educated the sons of the chiefs in the liberal arts […] The result was that instead of loathing the Latin language they became eager to speak it effectively. In the same way our national dress came into favour and the toga was everywhere to be seen. And so the population was led into the demoralising temptations of arcades, baths and sumptuous banquets...' (From *Agricola*, Tr. S.A. Handford)

There is a record of a Celtic aristocrat, Epotsorovidius, at the time of Julius Caesar. He appears to have been made a Roman citizen by Caesar, and his son is recorded as Gaius Julius Agedomopas, the last still a Celtic name, the others reflecting the patronage of Caesar. A citizen acquired important privileges, the right to be a magistrate in many cities, join the legions and receive special protection under Roman law, including the right of appeal directly to the emperor. By the fourth generation, the family was completely romanised. Its head, Gaius Julius Rufus, was in the Roman army and was a *praefectus fabrorum* in charge of building work. He became a priest of the cult of Augustus and Rome at Lyons and was wealthy enough to donate an amphitheatre to Lyons and a triumphal arch to his home town, the modern Saintes.

The Pont du Gard

Roman aqueduct
Built early 1st century AD

Although aqueducts were known in ancient Persia and Assyria, it was a building form that the Romans made their own. Aqueducts went hand in hand with urbanisation in that they were only needed when local water sources, including rivers and springs, were no longer adequate for a growing city population. The earliest aqueduct in Rome, the Aqua Appia, was constructed in 312 BC and was ten miles long. By 144 BC, the Aqua Marcia ran for 57 miles and brought a staggering 220,000 gallons of water an hour into the city. In the early centuries AD Roman citizens enjoyed a per capita water supply that far exceeds that of modern New York.

The term aqueduct merely means 'water channel', and it was as likely to flow below as above ground (*see diagram on p. 115*). In fact, the underground channels were easier to protect and keep free of pollution. The challenge was to maintain a constant flow. So the Aqua Marcia had a fall of 850 ft overall but this had to be standardised at three feet for every thousand feet in length to keep the flow steady. Often an aqueduct had to go round or through hills and over valleys to maintain the gradient. The aqueduct which supplied Nîmes ran for 30 miles even though the source was only 12 miles away as the crow flies.

Panoramic view of the Pont du Gard. The piers are founded on bedrock and placed so that there is a slight curvature upstream, as the river is subject to flooding. The lowest line of arches varies in width from 80 ft to 50 ft. The second tier of eleven arches is placed on top of the first, with each pier directly above the one below. The whole is given harmony by the highest tier, which carries the aqueduct and which runs along on much smaller arches.

THE PONT DU GARD

The River Gardon runs 20 miles from Nîmes and there was no way that the aqueduct could avoid crossing it. A massive engineering project was put in hand. When completed, the Pont du Gard, the great arched bridge which held the water channel, was 900 ft long and as the valley fell beneath it, it reached a height of 160 ft above the ground. It is one of the most stunning of the many achievements of Roman engineering.

One of the most remarkable features of the Pont du Gard is that all the limestone blocks (which were quarried locally) were put in place without any mortar or clamps. They are held fast solely by the force of gravity. If one looks closely at the inside of the arches, one can see that there are three separate sections which stand independently of each other without the expected cross-bonding between them. There are even masons' marks which show which of the three sections a stone was destined for and where it came in the building order. The quality of the stone-cutting suggest that Greek craftsmen may have been involved. The builders were certainly men of immense confidence, and this confidence was entirely justified. On the second tier the piers were carved into in medieval times so that traffic could pass along the 'road', but the structure has not been obviously weakened as a result.

ARCHES, VAULTS & DOMES

The Greeks knew the principle of the arch. There are examples from the 4th century BC at the entrance to the stadium at Olympia and again at the entrance to the agora at Priene. The Etruscans used arches too, and there is a 3rd-century arched bridge on the Via Amerina, an offshoot of the Via Cassia which ran northwards from Rome. Yet none of this fully foreshadows the enormously important part arches were to play in Roman architecture. In bridges, aqueducts and amphitheatres, the arch played a crucial role.

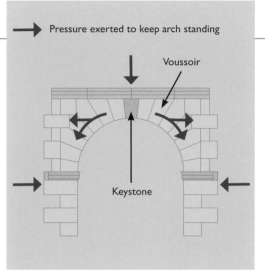

Pressure exerted to keep arch standing

Voussoir

Keystone

The stones that make up the core of an arch are known as voussoirs. They can only be put into place if there is some sort of support, normally a wooden frame, on which they can be balanced during construction, as the arch will not stay up until the last stone, the keystone, is fitted into the centre. The stones narrow from the outside of the arch to the inside so they can be held in place by gravity, and so long as the supporting walls, which receive some pressure outwards from the weight of the voussoirs, are solid, the arch will stand up. If the arch is reasonably thick and is joined to others then it becomes enormously strong: the Pont du Gard provides an excellent example of a series of arches which have stayed up over 2,000 years without any cementing of the stones.

Vaults

An arch that is extended continuously becomes a barrel or tunnel vault. When two barrel vaults intersect at right angles to each other and continue onwards, the roof of the intersection is known as a cross vault or groin vault. Just as they were also perfecting the art of concrete (*see p. 147*), the Romans recognised the potential of vaulting for creating prestige buildings. By the 80s BC vaults were being used in the Tabularium, the state archive building on the Capitoline Hill in Rome.

Domes

As their confidence grew, the Romans also realised the potential of concrete for the construction of domes. There is a limit to the span of a horizontal roof as stone or concrete cannot take a great deal of tension. A dome, however, can support tension much more effectively. An early example is the central domed room in Nero's Domus Aurea in Rome (AD 64), where concrete rises from an octagonal base and evolves into a dome shape as it does so. By the time of the Pantheon (118–126 AD) the technique is perfected, with the dome thickness being reduced as it rises to minimise the weight (*see p. 147*). The skill of the carpenter and the massive amount of timber needed to build the frame on which the dome is placed is easily underestimated.

By the 4th century the Romans were able to put up buildings in which arches, vaults and domes loomed over vast interior spaces. They included basilicas and bath houses as well as palaces, and with the beginnings of imperial patronage, Christianity adopted many of these forms in the early basilicas and great domed churches of the East, the most celebrated of which was Haghia Sophia in Constantinople, where the great dome is raised on pendentives (*see diagram right*).

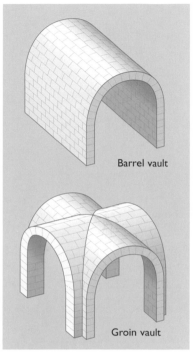

Barrel vault

Groin vault

Above left: The arch, with its voussoirs fanning outwards from the keystone.

Above: A barrel vault, an arch extended lengthways, becomes a groin vault when two intersect each other at right angles.

Below: A dome is raised above a square space by being placed on pendentives, concave triangles which bridge the gap between square and hemisphere.

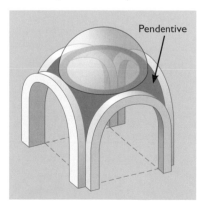

Pendentive

Petra

Petra, in present-day Jordan, is one of the most magical cities of the ancient world. Hidden in a valley, it is approached by a narrow passage which suddenly leads to a lost world that appears to have been carved from the rock (the name Petra derives from the Greek for 'rock'). It is not only the sheer unexpectedness of the ruins that enthralls, it is the harmonious way in which a wide array of Greek and Eastern motifs are combined in an extraordinary set of buildings.

'And this was the city at whose door I now stood. In a few words, this ancient and extraordinary city is situated within a natural amphitheatre of two or three miles in circumference, encompassed on all sides by rugged mountains five or six hundred feet in height. The whole of this area is now a waste of ruins, dwelling-houses, palaces, temples, and triumphal arches, all prostrate together in undistinguishable confusion. The sides of the mountains are cut smooth, in a perpendicular direction, and filled with long and continued ranges of dwelling-houses, temples and tombs, excavated with vast labour out of the solid rock; and while their summits present Nature in her wildest and most savage form, their bases are adorned with all the beauties of architecture and art, with columns and porticoes, and pediments, and ranges of corridors, enduring as the mountains out of which they are hewn and fresh as if the work of a generation scarcely gone by.'
John Lloyd Stephens, *Incidents of Travel in Egypt, Arabia Petraea, and the Holy Land*, 1837

Roman client state
Flourished 1st century
BC–*1st century* AD

Facing page: The colonnaded street marks the central public part of the city, developed in the 1st century AD.

PETRA IN HISTORY

Petra was the capital of the Nabataeans, an Arabic people who had cornered the luxury trade of the Arabian desert. One account associates them with 'frankincense and myrrh and the most valuable kinds of spices'. They were already important and stable enough in the 4th century BC for the Seleucid king Antigonus I to try and subdue them, even though the records of their existence and extent of power remain very sparse until the beginning of the 1st century BC. Nabataean influence appears to have extended over the Sinai desert and the Hejaz, the region along the eastern coast of the Red Sea. They controlled some of the best routes through the desert and must have raised levies on everything that passed or restricted the routes to their own merchants. The demand for incense in Rome was high, and it has been estimated that 50 percent of the selling price in Gaza was pure profit.

The best known of the Nabataean kings was Obodas (c. 96–87 BC). He was a man whose horizons spread beyond his own nation and he was recorded as a lover of Greek culture. He stood up to the kingdom of Judaea and, exploiting its own internal divisions, added the prosperous territories of Galaaditis (the biblical Gilead) and Moab to his kingdom. He then held out against the Seleucids. This gave him great prestige among his people and on his death he was deified.

Despite these successes the Nabataeans always had difficulty in maintaining their kingdom's borders in such a volatile area. It therefore made sense for Obodas' son Aretas III to accept Roman hegemony, and in 61 BC his realm become a client state of Rome. This also gave the Nabataeans the opportunity to develop their capital at Petra, a well-protected hollow in the hills just off the main trade route between Aqaba and Gaza on the Mediterranean coast. Although Petra's buildings have proved difficult to date, most scholars see the heyday of construction as the reign of Aretas IV (9 BC–AD 40). It has been suggested that Aretas was determined to match the great building programme of Herod the Great in neighbouring Judaea (*see p. 210*; interestingly, Aretas' daughter married Herod's son Herod Antipas, ruler of Galilee in Jesus' day, although they later divorced). It was not until AD 106 that the emperor Trajan absorbed the Nabataeans into the Roman province of Arabia. He retained Petra as capital of the province and the city received an imperial visit in 131.

Petra was devastated by an earthquake in 363 but it later became the home of a flourishing Christian community which adapted many of the pagan buildings to their use. Recently a church **(G)** has been found. It is 5th-century in origin and is richly decorated with Byzantine floor mosaics of the 5th and 6th

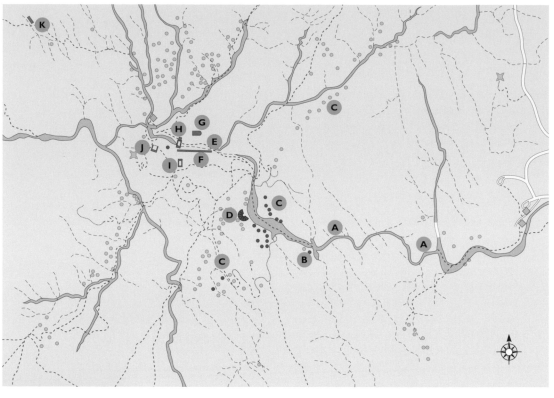

MAP OF PETRA

A Siq
B Khazneh
C Tombs
D Theatre
E Nymphaeum
F Colonnaded street
G Church
H Temple of the Winged Lions
I Great Temple
J Qasr al-Bint
K Deir

centuries. Another devastating earthquake in 551 brought further decline and when Islam spread over the Arabian desert, Petra became a backwater. The first western visitor was Johann Ludwig Burckhardt in 1812. When the first surveys were done in the 19th century, it was found that two thirds of the 800 buildings had some connection with the dead, either as tombs or places where commemorative meals were eaten (in *triclinia*, rooms surrounded by benches on three sides). It was even argued that Petra as a whole had a commemorative function within Nabataean society, though it should also be remembered that the Nabataeans were essentially a nomadic people, and their domestic buildings may therefore have been temporary. Many lived in the natural caves in the rock. As only a small part of the city has been excavated, a much fuller picture of domestic life will eventually emerge. The city is Jordan's leading tourist attraction.

THE TOMBS

The tombs **(C)** can be arranged in a rough chronological order. Before the 1st century BC they were quite plain structures, reflecting the simplicity of a nomadic people unused to frills in their architecture. Gradually more and more Hellenistic influences are seen, with a culmination in the 1st century AD of Roman styles. The tombs become more and more imposing but not necessarily more decorative. The final tomb is that of a Roman governor of Arabia, who chose to be buried here in AD 129. Here the trend is reversed. It is much more modest in size than the Nabataean tombs but more richly ornamented. The combination of the quality of carving in the stunning red rock with the harmony and originality of the designs make these fascinating creations.

PUBLIC BUILDINGS

In the 1st century AD Petra developed its major public buildings. There had long been a street running from east to west and this was now made into a grand paved colonnade **(F)** with an arch at one end, as would be expected in a Graeco-Roman city. Through the arch one entered the sanctuary of what appears to have been the most important temple of the city, the Qasr al-Bint **(J)**. It is the best preserved of all the free-standing buildings in Petra, with its main walls still standing to a height of almost 90 ft and some lovely carved rosettes on the frieze. The final architectural details were created in plaster and this covered the whole exterior. Unfortunately the archway at its entrance and the massive columns, which seem to echo those of the Khazneh (*see below*) in style, fell in earthquakes. The marble hand of a cult statue has been found inside the temple. Many think that the dedication is to Dushara, the Nabataean equivalent of Zeus, but the only inscription refers to Aphrodite and Zeus with his title of *hypsistos*, 'the most high god'.

To the north of the Colonnade another temple was begun in the reign of Aretas IV. It is known as the Temple of the Winged Lions **(H)** from the sculptured figures which graced the columns near the altar. While the altar of the Qasr al-Bint is outside the temple, here the altar is inside. The craftsmen's workshops have been found alongside the temple together with an inscription dating its foundation to AD 27. It seems likely that the dedication was to a goddess, perhaps the Nabataean deity al'Uzza or the Egyptian Isis.

The most baffling of the buildings at Petra is the large enclosure known from the 1890s as the Great Temple **(I)**. It runs to the south of the colonnade and was connected to it by a monumental gateway. The complex went through a number of building phases, during which it was so extensively remodelled that it is likely that its function changed. It may originally have been a royal audience hall but in the 1st century AD the southern end was levelled and made into a colonnaded court. The northern side ended in columned exedrae with two flights of steps leading up to the next level. Was this a new agora (no other has yet been discovered in Petra) or was it the sanctuary of a temple which was now built above it? The building on this upper level was remarkable in that it contained an odeon, a small theatre, which could seat some 600 people. These spaces could be used for speeches, musical contests or sacred ceremonies (one survives in Delos where orgiastic rituals of Syrian gods were held). Yet these odea were also used as the meeting place of councillors and it is possible that this was the odeon's function during the centuries of Roman rule. The archaeological evidence suggests that it was used for the 200 years after the Romans took control. Immediately to the east of this complex was a garden area complete with a pool, and here the Nabataeans initiated the long tradition of ornamental water gardens which became such a feature of Arabian culture.

Left: Mosaic of a man fishing, from the 5th–6th-century Byzantine church at Petra.

Below and facing page: Not least of the attractions of Petra are the rock formations and colourings caused by wind erosion. The tomb shown opposite is known as the Silk Tomb because of its swirls of vivid colours.

It was probably in the reign of Aretas IV that Petra's theatre **(D)** was built. Space within the valley was limited, but such was the desire to be a respected city that a site was chosen in the necropolis, and many tombs were removed to accommodate the seating. As with so many other buildings, the fear of flooding from cascading water was strong and channels were built to divert the water around the seating. The importance of these channels was recognised in 1991 when they had to be unblocked to cope with flooding.

THE KHAZNEH OR TREASURE HOUSE

The Khazneh **(B)** is justly the most famous of the tombs of Petra, as it comes dramatically into view at the end of the Siq. It is usually dated to the reign of Aretas III (87–62 BC), although it is possibly later, from the end of the century. There are two storeys but these give a misleading impression as the ground level was originally 12 ft lower and there was a courtyard, possibly a water garden, in front of the monument.

The lowest storey has a columned and pedimented entrance, originally with statues of the Dioscuri, the sons of Zeus. In Roman mythology these were the twins Castor and Pollux, associated with aid and protection. The second storey has a broken pediment, both sections of which stand on two further columns. There are representations of Medusa, of Amazons, and of winged Victories between the columns. In the space between the columns and pediment sections is a tholos, a small rounded structure. On its façade is a composite goddess bearing a cornucopia of plenty. She combines the iconography of Aphrodite and Tyche, the goddess of fate, while she stands above a relief of a design associated with Isis, the Egyptian goddess of the underworld. Records give Isis a role as the protective goddess of Petra but there is also a specifically Nabataean goddess, al'Uzza, who is linked in some inscriptions to Aphrodite. Many elements of the design, for instance the tholos between a broken pediment, echo similar architecture in Alexandria, and it is possible that Alexandrian sculptors guided the native craftsmen.

The Khazneh is certainly the most dramatic of the Petra buildings because its appearance at the end of the narrow entrance to the site (the Siq) is so unexpected.

There are no signs that anyone was buried in the monument and one suggestion is that it was a 'temple' dedicated to the memory of Obodas, who was reputedly buried at Obada in the Negev desert. The Greek motifs may reflect his reputation as a Philhellene. There remain other legends. The full Arabic name of the monument, the Khaznet Far'oun, the 'Treasury of the Pharaoh', relates to a legend that one of the Egyptian pharaohs left his treasure in the tholos.

THE DEIR OR MONASTERY

A few decades after the Khazneh was built, it was used as the model for the largest of the monuments of Petra, the Deir or Monastery **(K)**, so called because of a tradition that it was used by Christians in the Byzantine era. A long processional route leads up to the monument and there was a colonnaded courtyard in front of it. The façade is more monumental than that of the Khazneh but also much simpler. The frieze on

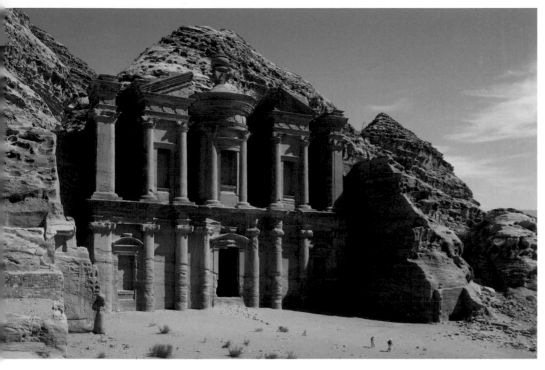

The Deir (illustrated left) is clearly modelled on the Khazneh (illustrated opposite). Inside, one can see the benches of the triclinium (illustrated below), three of them around a central table which was served from the fourth open side. While the idea of the triclinium originates in the Roman house, within tombs it had a ritual purpose as the setting for funerary or commemorative meals.

the upper storey that encircles the tholos and underwrites the broken pediment with its alternate triglyphs and unadorned circular metopes is particularly attractive. An elegant urn surmounts the tholos.

The interior of the Deir has a triclinium, which suggests that it was used for banqueting of some sort. The discovery of inscriptions which talk of 'the associates of the symposium of Obodas the god' would appear to confirm that the building was linked to the cult of the king.

Like most tombs, the Deir was built from the top down. The recess in the rock would be defined and then the craftsmen would be lowered from above to start their work. While the rose-red rock is now a major attraction in its own right, the façades of the tombs were originally covered in plaster and painted in striking colours, notably deep reds and yellows. It was vitally important to protect this plaster from the elements and any water running down from higher cliffs would be diverted by channels.

HYDRAULICS AT PETRA

Petra would never have survived as a community if it had not handled its water supply efficiently. One of the earliest accounts of the Nabataeans talks of their expertise in creating reservoirs in the desert. At Petra they had two major problems. First, the rainfall was irregular: dry for the long summer months but with sudden downpours in the winter. So conservation was essential. Second, the long (half a mile), narrow entrance to the city, the Siq, would become a rushing torrent during storms, and anyone in the defile was likely to be swept away. Much of the water came rushing downwards from the cliffs above, not only through the Siq but in other parts of the city too. The solution was to carve tunnels or channels to divert the water so that much of it would never reach the floor. Ceramic pipes were also used. When the water reached the end of the Siq it was diverted towards a reservoir which was made from constructing a dam across the end of the cliffs. Other cisterns collected water from nearby springs but each house was expected to have its own cistern as well. The accumulation meant that there was ample water for all and the city boasted a fine nymphaeum **(E)** by the main street.

Aphrodisias

Although Aphrodisias is a comparatively remote site, on the borders between what was originally Caria, Lydia and Phrygia in Asia Minor, the region is a fertile one, in a valley fed by the river Meander. There is evidence of an early sanctuary where worship of a goddess, possibly Astarte, the Syrian goddess of love and sexuality, was carried on. With the coming of Rome to Asia Minor in the 2nd century, the city saw the advantage of integrating its goddess with Aphrodite, the Greek goddess who had been given similar attributes. The name Aphrodisias is first recorded on a coin of the 1st century BC and an inscription found in the theatre tells how Julius Caesar presented the city with a gold statue of Eros, offspring of Aphrodite. He was himself making the link with Venus, the Roman equivalent of Aphrodite, whom he claimed as the founding goddess of his family, and he may have visited the city himself while on campaign in the region.

Certainly the connection paid off. Aphrodisias stayed loyal to Caesar's adopted son, Octavian, later the emperor Augustus, and once he was in power Augustus honoured Aphrodisias with a recognition of its independence as a city and exemption from imperial taxation. One of the emperor's freedmen, Zoilus, came from Aphrodisias and was honoured there as a man who engineered favours from Rome for the city.

From the 1st to the 3rd centuries, Aphrodisias enjoyed great prosperity. The shrine of Aphrodite drew in visitors from throughout the Greek world while its excellent local marble (from Baba Dag, the ancient Salbakos Mountains) fostered an important school of sculpture. It reached its height during the reign of Hadrian, when Aphrodisians were working at Hadrian's Villa near Rome (*see p. 180*). The name of one, Antonianus, has been found inscribed on a beautiful relief of Hadrian's favourite Antinous portrayed as the Roman god of the woods. Sixty years later there is evidence that sculptors from Aphrodisias were working on the forum of Septimius Severus' home city of Leptis Magna (*see p. 191*). A number of prominent intellectuals also came from the city. Alexander of Aphrodisias became head of the Lyceum, the school founded by Aristotle in Athens, in the early 3rd century AD and was a major commentator on the works of Aristotle. When Diocletian reorganised the provinces of the empire in the 280s, Aphrodisias was made the capital of the new province of Caria.

As Christianity spread through the empire, the city appears to have kept a school of pagan philosophy intact, but a cult of Aphrodite had no appeal to Christians. When the new religion triumphed, all the inscriptions that mentioned the city's name were erased and replaced with Stavropolis, 'the City of the Cross'. By this time the urban fabric had begun to decay. There was a series of severe earthquakes in the 350s and 360s (they also affected Ephesus). The city was still wealthy enough to repair the damage but the shocks had shifted the water level and the low-lying parts of town were now

Detail of a relief of Prometheus bound to the rock, an example of the marble sculpture for which Aphrodisias was renowned.

often flooded. The original agora had to be abandoned at the end of the 4th century and a new market area created behind the existing theatre. As fresh earthquakes occurred, it proved harder and harder to finance the rebuilding and gradually Aphrodisias fell into ruin. A disastrous earthquake in the early 7th century was the final blow and afterwards the occupation of the site was limited.

Remains of the Temple of Aphrodite at Aphrodisias. The apse of the church built into the temple in the 5th century can be seen behind the columns.

THE APHRODITE OF APHRODISIAS

An interesting merging of themes can be seen in the cult figure of Aphrodite which has been found at Aphrodisias. It is traditional in form, almost archaic in the stiffness of its pose with its arms originally held outwards, and represents the style of this part of the East. Yet she is now Hellenised. The goddess is clothed in a full overgarment and this is divided into panels so that her different attributes can be highlighted in reliefs. The three rows show her as a goddess of heaven, earth and sea. On one panel Aphrodite is shown in a typically Greek pose, half-nude on a sea goat with a dolphin and triton beside her.

The version pictured here is only a bust but the crescent moon between her breasts is clearly visible, denoting the heavenly plane.

The Aphrodisian version of Aphrodite drew on Carian images of goddesses, including that of Astarte, the Syrian goddess of love. Her shape echoes that of the Artemis of Ephesus.

The richness of the sculpture found at Aphrodisias is extraordinary, not least in the way it shows how Roman imperial rule was presented to a Greek city. The example here, which once adorned the Sebasteion, shows the Roman emperor Nero (AD 54–68) being crowned by his mother Agrippina. Agrippina carries a cornucopia, a standard symbol of the fertility of the empire. Agrippina probably murdered the previous emperor Claudius to allow her son to come to power. Ironically, Nero eventually murdered her in turn.

THE SEBASTEION

Many of the cities which had been absorbed into the Roman empire in the 2nd century BC felt impelled to recognise the power of the emperor and his family by offering them cult worship. They had done the same with the Hellenistic kings whom Rome had displaced, so this was essentially a refocusing of loyalties. At Aphrodisias two citizen families offered the imperial family a Sebasteion (*sebastos* was the Greek equivalent of Augustus, 'revered'), and building got under way in the reign of Tiberius (AD 14–37). The remains were discovered in 1979 and are the richest example of a Sebasteion yet found.

The model is taken from Rome, from the fora of Julius Caesar and his adopted son Augustus that had been completed a few decades before (*see p. 138*). A temple formed the backdrop. Leading up to it was a processional way 260 ft long, flanked by two porticoes. In Rome the porticoes were only two storeys high, here they were three. The two patrons divided the work up neatly between them, one built the temple and one of the porticoes, the other the other portico and the propylon (gateway) at the entrance. The whole was completed during the reigns of Claudius (AD 41–54) and Nero (AD 54–68).

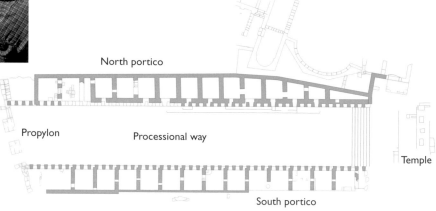

North portico

Propylon   Processional way

Temple

South portico

The glory of the Sebasteion is its sculptures. They do not have the quality of the best of the Classical world but they show how Greek mythology had become integrated with the themes of Roman dominance. They proclaim that this is a Greek city flourishing under the benign rule of Rome. The propylon, for example, boasted statues of the Julio-Claudian family alongside Aphrodite and Aeneas (the legendary founder of the city of Alba Longa, out of which Rome grew), with a dedicatory inscription commending the Sebasteion to Aphrodite, the divine Augusti (at this date both Julius Caesar and Augustus were considered to have become gods) and the people of Aphrodisias. On the second storey of the south portico were scenes from Greek mythology, featuring Dionysus, Hercules and Achilles. On the storey above personifications of Victory are depicted alongside members of the imperial family. Augustus is shown as a heroic nude receiving the fruits of earth and sea. The association of Augustus with fertility and fruitfulness had been a major theme in the way he presented himself, and the local sculptor must have adopted the idea from Roman models. The final section of the portico shows Claudius and Nero, again both heroically nude, with their conquests: Claudius with a personification of Britain, Nero with Armenia. History soon caught up with Nero. After his suicide he was declared perpetually damned and the authorities in Aphrodisias dutifully struck his head off the panel.

The northern portico was badly damaged in an earthquake in the 7th century AD and the panels have not survived well. However, enough fragments remain to show that they had personifications of the provinces conquered or added to the empire by Augustus. Each is shown as a draped female figure.

THE STADIUM

Aphrodisias has the best preserved stadium in the ancient world. The earliest stadia date from in the 6th century BC and were the home of athletic competitions, foot races, wrestling, javelin and discus throwing. A typical stadium consisted of the track itself, which was 600 ft in length so as to accommodate the foot race of that length, and the earth banking where the spectators stood. Often a stadium would be fitted into an existing hillside to minimise the amount of building work. Wealthier cities would make their own seating.

A stadium was only worth building if the city had the right to hold games. The traditional games circuit had consisted of the Olympic, Nemean, Isthmian and Pythian (Delphic) Games, whose status was shown by the symbolic wreaths awarded to the victors (see p. 71). Then the major cities began adding their own to these, although they would always be of lesser prestige. With the coming of the Romans to Asia Minor, cities of higher status such as Pergamon and Ephesus would hold their own four-yearly games and many of these would be associated with emperors (the events bore names such as the Caesarea or Hadrianea). The records at Aphrodisias talk of games held in the Pythian model, so in honour of Apollo.

The stadium at Aphrodisias, which may be as early as the 1st century AD is, in its final form, remarkable not only for its almost complete set of stone seating but for having a bulge in the middle of the long sides which helped spectators see more clearly. It is some 900 ft long and could hold about 30,000. Careful studies of the stone are revealing information about how the seating was stratified according to social class. Normally women were forbidden to watch athletic competitions, but there are women's names carved on some of the seats so the stadium was probably used for other celebrations, such as the processions in honour of the emperor's accession or birthday.

Inscription from a 2nd-century AD funeral monument found at Aphrodisias, a superb description of the expected attributes of a well-educated young man:

The stone sings of Epicrates' son,
Epicrates, who lies under this mound
still a youth. Now the dust (of the gymnasium) is
left behind,
as well as the lyre he strummed and the Homeric
(songs)
and the spears and the round (shield) of willow
with the fine grip
and the horse bridles now covered with cobwebs
and the bows and the javelins. Outstanding in all
these things,
to Hades the fair-famed youth has gone.

Tr. Angelos Chaniotis

Above: The stadium at Aphrodisias. Below: Head of an athlete, a beautiful example of Aphrodisian sculpture.

The wealth of Aphrodisias and the excellent quality of its local marble came together to fill the city with statues, reliefs and every kind of architectural feature. A number of exceptionally fine sarcophagi have also been found. The value to historians lies not just in the number of surviving statues but also in that many still have their original position can be traced. Thus it is possible to see how statues were used to maximum effect in a medium-sized but prosperous city-state.

The earliest fine sculptures are a set of reliefs of the freedman Zoilus being honoured by the people of Aphrodisias as a thanksgiving for his building of the theatre stage. They are among the first of many statues recognising the specific contribution of prominent members of the community to its embellishment. This was a city where the leading families competed with each other to show off their beneficence. When the city awarded someone an honorary statue, the one honoured or his friends had to provide the base at their own expense and one can see how the bases became taller and taller with time.

There is an extraordinary variety of personalities and offices shown, from emperors downwards. Many local grandees wear the distinctive headdress of their priesthoods (a mark of high citizen status). A remarkable number of women were also honoured—wealth and status were certainly not confined to men. One sarcophagus shows both husband and wife as priests of Aphrodite.

Pompeii

Prosperous Roman provincial
town
Destroyed AD 79

'On Sunday we were in Pompeii. So many disasters have happened in the world, but none that have given so much pleasure to posterity. I can think of nothing more interesting.'

Goethe, *Italian Journey*, 13th March, 1787

The eruption that destroyed Pompeii extended the coastline outwards so that today one does not realise that in its heyday the town was a port. Campania, the plain on this western coast of Italy, south of Rome, enjoyed rich, fertile soil (as a result of lava from earlier eruptions), and Pompeii began its life in the 6th century BC as a town which exported produce from the valley of the River Sarno. The origin of its first inhabitants is not known. Greek influence, in the shape of a temple to Apollo and a Doric temple, is obvious and, as was typical also of Sicily to the south, these were prominently placed, on outcrops of lava. There is also evidence of Etruscan settlers.

Even though Pompeii protected itself with a wall, its exposed position on the coast made it vulnerable to mountain raiders and it was overrun in the 5th century by the Samnites. Their language was Oscan, one of the native languages of Italy, and Oscan was still being spoken in the town in the 1st century AD.

When new waves of Samnites entered Campania in the 4th century, there were appeals for Rome to intervene, and by the end of the century the Samnites had been defeated and all the cities of the region had become 'allies' of Rome. Pompeii strengthened its position with the Romans by remaining loyal during the

Left: Bronze bust of Diana. She was originally drawing a bow. It was found in the ruins of the Temple to Apollo next to the forum, one of the oldest sanctuaries in the city, and has now been placed in front of it.

Below: Pompeii has some of the oldest baths in Italy, but when the town became a Roman colony in 80 BC a grand new set of baths was built at public expense in the forum. The photograph here shows the frigidarium, the cold plunge pool. A separate wing for women was added in the Augustan period.

invasion of Hannibal (whose troops reached Campania in 216 BC), and when Hannibal was defeated it entered a great period of prosperity. Its success was not to last. It made the fatal mistake of joining the revolt of the Italian cities in 91 BC, essentially a protest against Rome's high taxation and military conscription. Defeated, it was transformed into a Roman colony and a new elite of Roman settlers was imposed on it.

Between 80 BC and AD 79, the town was refashioned and thoroughly romanised. The city was now dedicated to Venus. It received a new constitution and a hierarchy of magistrates. Latin was to be the written language of all official business. The new settlers were the main beneficiaries, and they were instrumental in creating new administrative buildings and, in the southeastern corner of town, an amphitheatre, the earliest known. The existing baths were enlarged and the ruling elite began building larger houses for themselves. There was no compunction about pulling down existing buildings to make way for new.

As with so many cities, Pompeii gained from the stability that the emperor Augustus brought to the empire. Now that the Mediterranean was secure, trade expanded. Wines were imported from Asia Minor, Judaea and Sicily. Olive oil came from Africa and Spain, pottery from France and Cyprus. In the town itself the forum was remodelled to contain a temple dedicated to Augustus and Good Fortune. The emperor's own favourite deity was recognised by an enlargement of the ancient temple to Apollo and there was an annual festival in Apollo's honour. The wealthy Eumachia, a priestess of the city, donated a grand colonnaded building, the largest in the forum, in recognition of Augustan concord and piety. There was a new aqueduct and the water, gathered in a cistern, the *castellum aquae*, just outside the Vesuvius gate, was distributed through a sophisticated system of pipes to the baths, fountains and wealthier homes.

In AD 62, and probably on one or two occasions afterwards, there were earthquakes which caused considerable damage to Pompeii. With hindsight one can see that these were warning signs of what was to come. Extensive repair work was still going on when Vesuvius erupted in 79, but there had also been the opportunity to create new buildings such as a bath house which incorporated all the latest heating technology from Rome.

Giuseppe Fiorelli became Director of Excavations at Pompeii in the 1860s. It was he who initiated the pouring of plaster into cavities in the ash thereby 'reconstructing' bodies where they had fallen. These are some of the most moving finds in the city.

The traditional date of the eruption of Vesuvius which enveloped Pompeii and Herculaneum is 24th August, AD 79, but there is some coin evidence which suggests it may have been later in the autumn. It began with a minor explosion of steam; then, at midday, there was a massive explosion which sent gases and pumice ten to twenty miles in the air. The drift of the pumice was towards the west. Pompeii would have been in darkness and the pumice gradually fell on the town, probably reaching a depth of some nine feet and causing some buildings to collapse under its weight. Many who stayed indoors were killed as roofs fell in.

It was early the next morning that the pumice and gases began surging down the slopes of Vesuvius. Now it was distance from the volcano which mattered. Herculaneum was overwhelmed by the first two surges. The third surge reached just up to the northern gate of Pompeii and then the next three overwhelmed the town. Many of Pompeii's inhabitants had managed to get away by this time, but those who had not and who were still alive had clambered up onto roofs where a combination of the heat and gas overcame them.

DOMESTIC ARCHITECTURE IN POMPEII

The *domus*, the Roman house, was a combination of public and private spaces (*see plan opposite*). The first indication of its status would be the surface area it occupied, perhaps a whole *insula* (block). The entrance was usually narrow—it was known as the *fauces* **(a)**, from the Latin for 'throat', and in Pompeii was sometimes marked by a mosaic of a guard dog. One assumes that there would have been a porter as well. Through the entry passage, the visitor came to the atrium **(b)**, an open courtyard, partly roofed but with the central space open so that rainwater could run down into the pool, the impluvium **(c)**, and from there via underground pipes into a storage cistern. Around the atrium were the main rooms **(d)**. The grander houses had a further peristyle court **(e)** and this too was surrounded by rooms. What is still largely unknown is how the family worked within this space. How many servants were needed and how far was a family supposed to extend? Recent research suggest that rooms had few fixed functions and were rearranged according to the occasion. If there was no one visiting, everyone came out to sit in the atrium.

The architectural commentator Vitruvius carefully makes the distinction between private and public within the *domus*. The distinction must be understood within the Roman custom of patron and clients. The client attends the patron on a daily basis to offer him a formal greeting (the *salutatio*). The patron receives him in the tablinum **(f)**, a room directly opposite the entrance to the house. It can be a humiliating procedure (one account tells of clients begging for meals from their patrons) but when it worked it could be of mutual benefit. Pliny the Younger specifically names one Julius Naso, who attended him when he had to speak in court or give a reading and showed an interest in the works Pliny had written. In return Pliny helped support Julius in his ambitions to achieve office.

Vitruvius goes on to describe how the status of the owner is expressed by the way he balances private and public spaces. Those with a public role, magistrates, for instance, must have large vestibules, courtyards and peristyles and even basilicas so that matters can be discussed in a large group. Lawyers and professors of rhetoric are also of high status and must have rooms to accommodate their audiences and students. Those who rely on the produce of the land, on the other hand, must find space to store it and so they must be prepared to sacrifice elegance to fit in cellars, barns and storehouses within the house space. The rooms of their house that front the street will be used as shops **(g)** so they can sell their goods. At the lower end of the social scale are those who are never visited and only go to visit others. They simply do not need public rooms at all.

Status would be shown off in different ways. The grander houses in Pompeii had marble columns (marble was an important indicator of wealth), extensive mosaics and, of course, painted walls. In the arid climate of north Africa, having gushing water was especially favoured.

Mythological subjects from the Greek world were popular in Pompeii. This scene from the Temple of Isis shows an episode in the story of Io. Seduced by Zeus, the nymph fled to Egypt, pursued by the wrath of Hera. Here she is shown arriving at the Canopus near Alexandria (the horns on her head allude to the story that Zeus transformed her into a heifer to protect her from his wife's revenge. Hera cunningly sent a horsefly to torment her). The seated goddess Isis, holding a cobra (symbol of Egypt), greets Io's arrival.

PLAN OF A POMPEIAN HOUSE

a Fauces, entrance passage
b Atrium, central courtyard
c Impluvium, pool for rainwater
d Principal family rooms
e Peristyle, colonnaded court or garden
f Tablinum, where the homeowner would greet clients and guests
g Shops
h Service rooms, storerooms, kitchen, latrine

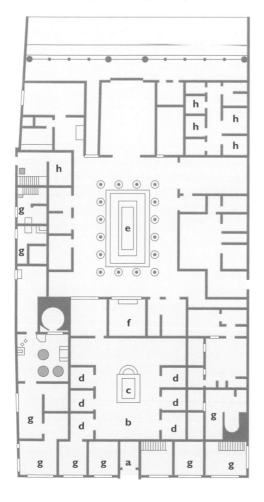

The atrium of the House of Faun, with its impluvium and famous statue. The roof and surrounding walls are all gone, and the faun today (a copy of the original, which is in Naples) stands dancing in the sunlight. It is still possible to appreciate the size of the house: the atrium would have been very spacious indeed.

SOME POMPEIAN HOUSES

The House of the Faun is the largest and most opulent house in Pompeii. It had an atrium and a peristyle but in other ways it is unusual. Its decoration was 200 years old at the time of the eruption and it had been continuously kept in good order. The most extraordinary find was the meticulously composed mosaic of Alexander the Great in battle against Darius III, king of Persia, who is shown in his chariot (*illustrated on p. 109*; it is now in the Naples Museum). There were many other superb mosaics in this house but this reconstruction of a historical event suggests that the owner may have had an ancestor connected with it. In short, the house is being preserved as a museum to the glory of the family, although which family has never been resolved. The house also had well-defined servants' quarters with their own atrium.

The cultural status of a homeowner could also be shown off in other ways. The name of the House of Menander, for example, derives from the wall paintings of the late 4th-century poet Menander, who is shown alongside the 5th-century Athenian tragedian Euripides. One adjoining room might be a library. The paintings date from the last phase of Pompeii and show that an educated interest in Greek drama persists into the 1st century AD.

Real literary figures are joined in many houses by mythological ones. Again the Greek influence is strong, and legends such as the sack of Troy, the exploits of Hercules and the abandonment of Ariadne by Theseus are popular. In the House of the Vettii, a charming set of friezes of cupids engaged in everyday activities adorns the triclinium. There are richly coloured landscape and garden scenes too, as if the lack of space to have real gardens has to be compensated for—although in recent years the extent of garden space within Pompeii has been mapped out and shown to be considerable. In private rooms, erotic scenes with couples making love are common. All these scenes would have been contemplated from couches and this often accounts for the way they are arranged, to be viewed from a reclining angle.

Such opulent homes were of course as rare in Pompeii as they are in any town today. Far more common were the houses which doubled as craft centres or which were fronted by the shops of their owners. One wine shop had 114 amphorae in the house itself, some of which stored flour, fish sauce or olives for the inhabitants, but with most containing wine. Some are labelled and show that not all of the wine was local. Other spaces showed that homes had been converted for the fulling and dyeing of cloth. The Fullery of Stephanus had the full panoply of equipment, a balcony from which to hang cloth, foot basins for treading it and larger basins for rinsing.

THE ECONOMY OF POMPEII

The economy of 1st-century AD Italy was overwhelmingly agricultural, and a town such as Pompeii would have enjoyed a close relationship with its surrounding countryside. Those villas and farms that have been excavated show that wine production was prominent, and even though there is a comment by Pliny the Elder that the wine of this region gave him a hangover, it was probably the main local export. Amphorae from Pompeii have been found throughout the Mediterranean and even as far north as Britain. What is interesting is the extent of cultivation, not just of vines, but of fruit and vegetables on plots within Pompeii's walls. 'Fruit-sellers' are mentioned in several electoral posters.

A famous export of Pompeii was garum, or fish sauce. It was used to flavour other foods and as a cure for dysentery and ulcers. Why Pompeii's recipe was so special is not clear. Traditionally garum came from Spain, and there is evidence of Spanish garum on sale alongside the local variety. In Pompeii, however, one Umbricius Scaurus seems to have cornered the market. The intestines of fish (mackerel is documented in Pompeii, but tuna seems another favourite) were fermented, probably on salt pans outside the town (it was known to be a smelly business) for up to three months and then brought into town be spiced up with the addition of herbs. In Pompeii the finished product was distributed in distinctive pottery containers.

Much of Pompeii's craft and production was local, and the town was full of small workshops producing wool, cloth, bronze tools or pottery for the community. There was obviously an atmosphere of enormous bustle. Shops, taverns and brothels were to be found throughout the town. Pompeii provides a snapshot of a Roman provincial town in AD 79.

POLITICS AND ELECTIONS IN POMPEII

A Roman colony, such as Pompeii became in 80 BC, had a standard constitution, and although Pompeii's has not survived, there is enough evidence to show how the town was governed. The constitution had been established in 80 BC by the *deductor*, who allocated land for new settlers and appointed the first council and magistrates. The city council was made up of some 80 to 100 decurions, wealthy freeborn citizens who were expected to contribute buildings or games for their community. For much

The finds from Pompeii range from the everyday (the dice), to the precious (the blue cameo glass funerary urn with Dionysiac scenes) to the erotic. Pompeian erotica fascinates us today. In the lovemaking scenes there is seldom any sense of engagement between the partners—they are rarely even looking at each other. Are we to conclude that this is the way it was always conducted? At any rate there is a lack of coyness about depicting sexual activity. Phalluses are common at house entrances as a talisman and a warning to intruders. Back rooms are frequently decorated with erotic wall paintings. But we might say the same thing about the prevalence of erotica in our own culture. It does not necessarily mean that what is depicted is a faithful representation of what goes on, nor should we assume that Pompeians were permissive or 'liberated'. It is impossible to define the relationship between the erotic scenes which are depicted and actual sexual activity. Were they designed merely to be looked at, or were they models for sexual behaviour? Certainly here in the *Campania felix*, the 'Happy Land' of the Romans, life does seem to have been enjoyed to the full.

of Roman history the wealth of this class was sufficient for them to consider it an honour to be included. Magistrates automatically became council members at the end of their term of office, and every five years numbers were reviewed and suitable men added.

Younger men with ambition could stand for election as one of the two aediles, the lowest rung on a magisterial career. Voting was open to the whole citizen body, including those who were the sons of freed slaves. A candidate (the word originates in the Latin *candidus*, 'white', the colour of the robe of those seeking election) would gather his own supporters, many of them hoping for patronage from him if elected. In Pompeii there was a large number of groupings of citizens who would proclaim their favoured candidates. Some of these were trade groups—the fruit-sellers, the bakers, the fishermen—or were connected to a temple, so there are those associated with Isis or Venus. The aediles would be responsible for the maintenance of streets and public buildings and the supervision of the town markets. There were also elected officials in each of the *vici*, the city districts.

MYSTERY RELIGIONS AT POMPEII

One of the most popular mystery religions of the Graeco-Roman world centred on the worship of Dionysus (the Roman Bacchus), the god of wine and abandon. There were always public celebrations of Dionysus, the drama festivals among them, but these other cults depended on celebrants coming together in groups and indulging in their own wild frolics. It was said that the god was able to liberate his followers only if they completely abandoned themselves to him. There was no single sanctuary for these ceremonies, but a cave often seems to have been involved in the rituals. The problem was that abandonment could lead to the group turning on others. This was the theme of Euripides' play *The Bacchae*. The initiates, led by Agave, the mother of Pentheus, king of Thebes, start with a joyful celebration of the earth and all its fruits but completely lose themselves in ecstasy. Pentheus spies on their dancing but they spot him and Agave is so frenzied she believes he is a mountain lion and tears off his head. It is only when she returns to Thebes that she realises the horror of what she has done: she has killed her own son.

Here Euripides explored the unsettling nature of wild religious emotion. How can one draw the line between letting go and transcending the conventions of everyday life and the consequences of losing all inhibitions? The Romans too were unsettled by the unconstrained jubilation of the Bacchic mysteries. There was a famous case in Rome in 186 BC when the city authorities suppressed the festivities. They continued in a more restrained form. The famous Villa of the Mysteries in Pompeii contains frescoes of initiation rites (*illustrated right*), which include some form of celebration of the phallus, one symbol of Dionysus, and perhaps a ritual beating (in some folk customs today, a beating is still traditionally held to encourage fertility).

The native mystery religions were joined by the exotic religions of Egypt and the East which flooded into the Mediterranean when Egypt became a Roman province. The cult of the goddess Isis was a particular favourite, and there was an important temple to her at Pompeii. Apuleius' novel *The Golden Ass* (2nd century AD) contains a good account of the initiation rites. The hero, Lucius, is shown special favours by the goddess, who turns him back into a human from the ass he has been. He is then told by the priest of the cult that he must wait until the goddess gives a further sign, at which point he can put himself forward for initiation. When the night finally comes he is dressed in a linen garment and led by the priest into the inner sanctum of Isis' temple. Apuleius does not reveal the full rituals but they last until dawn and are enough to send Lucius into a trance. 'At midnight I saw the sun shining as if it were noon; I entered the presence of the gods of the underworld and the gods of the upperworld, stood near and worshipped them … The solemn rites ended at dawn and I emerged from the sanctuary wearing twelve different stoles … The curtains were pulled aside and I was suddenly exposed to the gaze of the crowd as when a statue is unveiled, dressed like the sun. That day was the happiest of my initiation and I celebrated it as my birthday with a cheerful banquet at which all my friends were present.' (*Tr. Robert Graves*)

The senior magistrates were the two *duumviri*, who could only stand for election once they had already served as aedile. They presided over the entire council and had important powers over finance and justice. Every five years they carried out a census of the town's citizens. Freedmen were keen to get on in the world that had perforce become theirs, but it was only the second generation *libertus* who was eligible for office. There is a good case in Pompeii of a citizen recorded as having financed the restoration of the Temple of Isis after the earthquake of AD 62. He was repaid by being made a council member. However he was only six at the time and it was his father, a freed slave, who had put up the money, having made a fortune but being ineligible himself for membership. Through his son, however, his family could now enter the ruling class. Although it is clear that some families remained important from one generation to the next, this was not a closed society and new wealth was welcomed, especially if it contributed to the glorification of the town.

The frieze in the House of the Mysteries at Pompeii (1st century BC) provides evidence of some form of initiation ritual. The room in which it is displayed could be closed off from the rest of the house suggesting that the rituals may even have taken place here. The frieze shows a woman going through a series of ordeals—possibly a rite of passage between girlhood and maturity—which are related in some way to the god Dionysus. Here we see, from left to right, a child reading the rite to a young bride-to-be, who steps symbolically across a threshold; a seated priestess and female acolytes performing a purification ritual; a satyr playing a harp before a pastoral scene in which a nymph suckles a goat; the initiate fleeing in fright. Later scenes show a phallus, always a symbol of Dionysus, being revealed; and a ritual whipping of the initiate. The final scene shows her being dressed as a bride.

Hadrian's Villa at Tivoli

**Opulent imperial villa complex
Early 2nd century AD**

The Maritime Theatre is a highly original building and one which marks out the villa as a centre of architectural innovation. In the centre was a range of rooms surrounded by a circular pool. A wooden bridge ran across the pool and could be removed by anyone in the centre to create a quiet spot for relaxation. Around the outer edge of the pool was an Ionic colonnade (showed partially re-erected in the photograph) and above this rose a dome. Beyond this was a circular passageway which enclosed the whole. The combination of curves and vaults with their reflections in the water must have been stunning.

Hadrian was one of the 'good' emperors, who ruled during the time of Rome's greatest vigour, in the early 2nd century AD. He was a capricious character, difficult to fathom. 'He was both austere and congenial, serious and fun-loving, deliberate and fast to act, stingy and generous, guarded and open, cruel and forgiving and changeable from one minute to the next', as one exasperated observer put it. The sprawling villa that he created on the plain below Tivoli reflects this personality. It has no organised plan; rather it is a series of building projects which work with the landscape and which reproduce the emperor's own favourite buildings from his dominions in Greece and Egypt. It is impossible to give a truly authoritative description of the complex, especially as recent research is showing that many of the original names given to the structures have no archaeological evidence to support them. Yet the impression given by visiting the site is overpowering, as each domed hall or open square follows another and the majesty of the whole unfolds.

THE VILLA BUILDINGS

A villa dating from Republican times already stood on the plain below Tivoli, and when Hadrian began his own villa in the early years of his reign (he was in Italy between 118 and 121 and 125–28) he used this as his starting point. The villa overlooked a valley on its northeastern side and this was renamed the Vale of Tempe **(1)**, after a famous gorge in Thessaly in Greece. The entrance to the villa appears to have been from this northeastern side (the barracks for the imperial guard and the guest rooms are here) **(2)**. Reception rooms, an official dining hall, a council chamber, often referred to in plans as the Philosophers' Chamber **(3)**, a private library, gymnasium and the domestic quarters make up this core. A group of luxurious heated rooms, each with its private latrine, were probably the emperor and his wife Sabina's adjoining bedrooms **(4)**. On the northern terrace **(5)** buildings once described as libraries are now considered to be summer dining rooms or possibly the main entrance hall. When the emperor needed to withdraw for peace, there was a hall containing an 'island' **(6)**, a smaller complex of rooms that could be isolated by drawing up the connecting bridges (in plans it is referred to as the Maritime Theatre). There was also a circular bath house with a pool in the centre **(7)**. There is no evidence for any hydraulic equipment but there were large windows and this was probably a sauna. An inner garden area flanked by a Doric portico ran alongside the southeastern end of these buildings.

From this core vast new complexes extended as building continued. To the south of the original villa was a large square which was so richly decorated that it became known as the Piazza d'Oro **(8)**. It was a grand area entered through a domed vestibule, with pools in the centre and a nymphaeum at the furthest end. The octagonal space in front of the nymphaeum appears to have been another summer dining area. A rural feel to the whole was given by a frieze of hunting scenes. Hadrian was devoted to hunting, which one account suggests 'he always shared with his friends'. The same account (the late 4th-century *Historia Augusta*) records how 'at his banquets he always furnished, according to the occasion, tragedies, comedies, certain farces, players on stringed instruments, readers or poets', and one can perhaps summon up the convivial atmosphere of a relaxing emperor enjoying an escape from the affairs of state with his sporting or intellectual companions. Much of the finest sculpture of the villa was excavated in this area. Statues of later

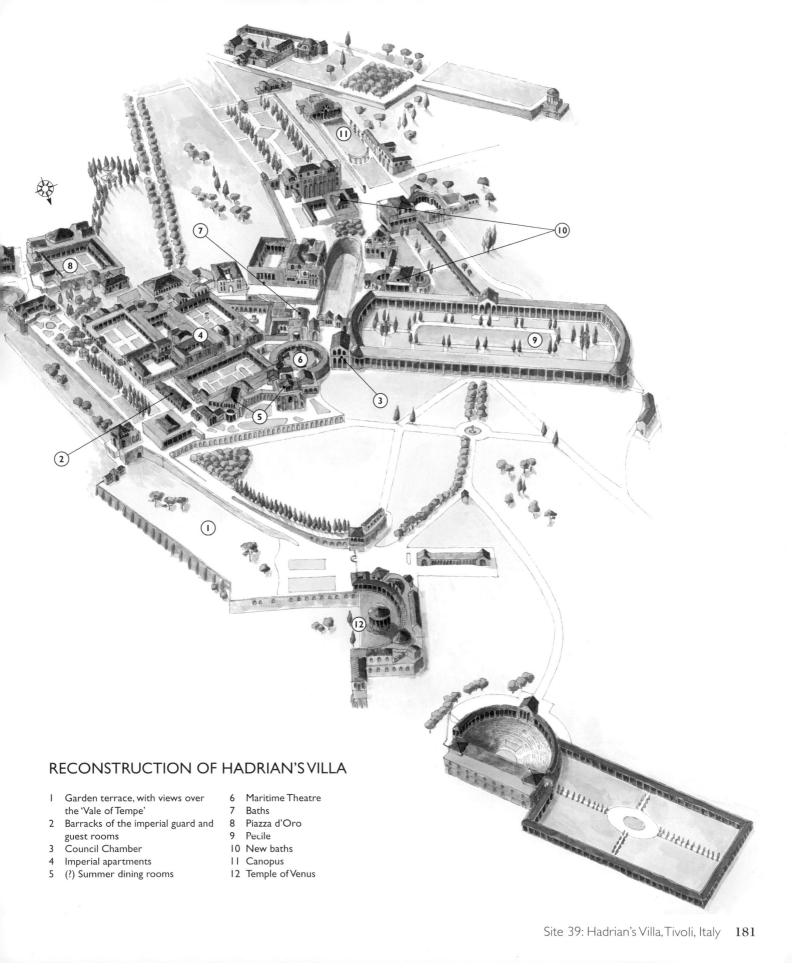

RECONSTRUCTION OF HADRIAN'S VILLA

1 Garden terrace, with views over the 'Vale of Tempe'
2 Barracks of the imperial guard and guest rooms
3 Council Chamber
4 Imperial apartments
5 (?) Summer dining rooms
6 Maritime Theatre
7 Baths
8 Piazza d'Oro
9 Pecile
10 New baths
11 Canopus
12 Temple of Venus

Right: Much use was made of water at Hadrian's Villa. The wide pool shown here was surrounded by a colonnade known as the Pecile, where Hadrian used to take a constitutional stroll. A total circuit along the colonnades, walking up one side, turning round the edge of the wall, and walking back, was 1400 ft and if this was covered seven times, it was the equivalent of one of the measured walks recommended by Roman doctors (just under two miles).

Below right: The Canopus with its Caryatids (four sculptures found on one side of the pool are models of the Caryatids from the Erechtheion in Athens). The area is chiefly thought to represent the Canopus canal in Egypt.

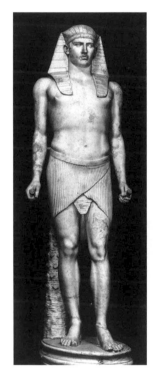

Above left: A statue of Hadrian's favourite Antinous as the Egyptian god Osiris. Antinous died in the Nile in October 130. It may have been an accident, or even suicide as he grew beyond the age at which a boy could be an acceptable lover to an older man. It was claimed that he had then risen again from the Nile, in much the same way that tradition told of Osiris. This statue, however, is much more sensual and Classical than any Egyptian original would have been.

Facing page, top: This copy of the famous mosaic by Sosus of Pergamon (see p. 113) of doves drinking from a bowl was one of many luxury finds from the villa ruins.

emperors, including Marcus Aurelius and Caracalla, confirm that the villa remained in imperial use, although there is no trace of any occupation after the reign of Caracalla (d. 217).

To the west of the main complex is the Pecile **(9)**, a long wall with the remains of a portico on each side. It derives its name from the Stoa Poikile, the Painted Stoa in Athens (*see p. 88*). It is now known that it was used as a space for walking.

Another garden ran to the south of the wall and this rested on top of a whole series of rooms for the service personnel of the villa. Underground passages ran into the villa and most of the supplies and food would have reached their destinations without being seen by the emperor, his guests or officials. The larger the villa grew and the more the emperor used it, the greater would be the numbers of senior staff and visitors on imperial business. To the south of the original villa, a new set of baths **(10)**, one smaller, perhaps for women, and one larger for men, was constructed, probably to meet this demand and prevent the emperor's own quarters from being overwhelmed by outsiders.

The accomplished Apollodorus of Damascus, the favourite architect of Hadrian's predecessor Trajan, was said to have mocked Hadrian for the segmental domes he had designed, likening them to pumpkins. Hadrian certainly had a hand in the design of his villa and he had builders who had perfected the art of concrete. So while the walls are in brick (which would have been covered in marble or mosaic) he was able to create 'pumpkin' and other exotic shapes above them. He revelled in using umbrella domes and curved walls or porticoes (as in the portico of the 'Maritime Theatre'). In the Piazza d'Oro the octagonal courtyard has convex and concave sides alternating with each other. The smaller baths are particularly interesting for the interplay of curves in the various rooms. There is no known equivalent in any other bath complex, so perhaps here the emperor's delight in originality is seen at its best.

Two other buildings in the villa deserve special mention because of how they relate to Hadrian's travels. To the south of the baths is an extension known as the Canopus **(11)**. From the city of Alexandria in Egypt a canal ran to the town of Canopus, where there was a famous temple dedicated to the god Serapis. The *Historia Augusta* refers to a 'Canopus' at the villa, and it has been assumed that the long pool represents the canal while the nymphaeum at the end is some kind of recreation of the temple. Certainly some Egyptian-style sculptures, including a crocodile, have been found there. However, earlier reports show that there were 'Egyptian' statues in other parts of the villa and 'canals' are water features found in other Roman villas, so the link to Egypt is not completely conclusive.

A better case can be made for a small circular temple to the north **(12)**. This seems to be a genuine replica of the famous Temple of Aphrodite from Cnidos, a city at the southwestern tip of Asia Minor. The statue of Aphrodite was a masterwork by the 4th-century sculptor Praxiteles, remarkable as the first life-size nude of the goddess. Its beauty and daring were such that it was a magnet for 'tourists' from throughout the Greek world.

RENAISSANCE REDISCOVERY OF THE VILLA

The monuments of the pagan past held little interest or value for the medieval mind. The need for building material was always more pressing than the claims of antiquaries, and this site was extensively plundered: columns from the villa's halls are to be found in neighbouring churches. It was not until the dawn of the Renaissance in the 15th century that interest in Hadrian's Villa was revived. The first account comes from Pope Pius II, who visited Tivoli in the summer of 1461 and looked down on the villa from higher ground:

'About three miles from Tivoli the Emperor Hadrian built a magnificent villa like a big town. Lofty vaults of great temples still stand and the half-ruined structures of halls and chambers are to be seen. There are also remains of peristyles and huge columned porticoes and swimming pools and baths, into which part of the river Aniene was once turned to cool the summer heat. Time has marred everything. The walls once covered with embroidered tapestries and hangings threaded with gold are now clothed with ivy. Briars and brambles have sprung up where purple-robed tribunes sat and queens' chambers are the lairs of serpents. So fleeting are mortal things.'

The earliest full survey of the site was by Pirro Ligorio in the 16th century, although his motive was primarily to find sculpture for the governor of Tivoli, Cardinal Ippolito d'Este, son of Lucrezia Borgia. By the 18th century, however, every architect of note was showing interest in the site, and Giovanni Battista Piranesi (1720–78) based his belief in the superiority of Roman architecture over Greek on the great vaulted halls here. His drawings provide some of the most evocative pictures of the ruins as they stood in his day. The British Neoclassical architect Robert Adam was another enthusiast. The villa fell prey to intensive looting, and mosaics, sculptures and reliefs are now scattered throughout the world's great Classical collections.

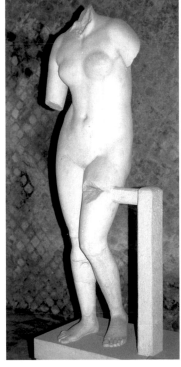

Praxiteles scandalised the Greek world with his nude statue of Aphrodite (the Roman Venus) at Cnidos. However, it became enormously popular and copies were to be found throughout the Greek world. This, from Hadrian's Villa, may be a direct copy of the original, which Hadrian would certainly have seen.

Hadrian's Wall

'Having completely transformed the soldiers, in royal fashion, he made for Britain, where he set right many things and—the first to do so—drew a wall along a length of eighty miles to separate barbarians and Romans.'

Historia Augusta, Hadrian 11.1, late 4th century

By the time the emperor Hadrian came to power (AD 117) it was obvious that the traditional policy of continuous expansion had become self-defeating. Hadrian's predecessor Trajan had conquered Dacia, the modern Romania, and during his reign the empire had reached its greatest extent (over two million square miles). Trajan had hoped to add even more territory to the east, across the Euphrates, but just before his death he had had to turn back. His newly conquered territories were unsettled and there was unrest in northern Britain and Judaea. Seeing the danger of spreading oneself too thin, Hadrian called a halt. From now on, the empire would concentrate on the effective defence of existing, well-defined borders.

> **Roman frontier post**
> Built early 2nd century AD

THE FRONTIERS OF THE EMPIRE

The idea of a permanent frontier did not enter easily into the Roman mind—it went against the grain of a people who were always victorious (ultimately) in war and whose destiny, it was claimed, was to rule others. However, by the 2nd century AD, it was clear that a halt had to be made. The northern border of the empire, from the mouth of the Rhône to that of the Danube, was 1200 miles long, the borders running along the provinces of north Africa twice that.

It was no mean feat to make all these borders impregnable. At the same time, the Romans did not want to seal them off from the vital trade routes which brought so many luxuries into the empire. On the southern borders there were no effective enemies in any case. Ditches and watchtowers manned by auxiliaries were usually all that was needed. To the east, Persia was more of a problem: some ruling dynasties—the Parthians and the Sasanians who succeeded them in the 3rd century AD—were actively expansionist and had major resources and manpower to draw on. When war did come, defeats could be heavy on either side. The mid-3rd century was particularly humiliating for the Romans. The Roman emperor Gordian died in 243 after a major attack on the Sasanians which ended in withdrawal and the payment of a ransom. The Sasanians penetrated Syria in 253 as far as the great city of Antioch, which they sacked. In 260 the emperor Valerian was seized by the Sasanian monarch Shapur I during negotiations, and was used as a footstool from which Shapur mounted his horse. It was only in 297, under the restored empire of Diocletian, that a great victory humbled the Persians and brought peace to the frontier.

The northern borders were subject to low-level raids, which grew in intensity as population pressures among the barbarian tribes grew and forced them into larger groupings. The German borders were protected by the *limes*, a military road with watchtowers. Hadrian strengthened it with palisades. The Roman preference was for pre-emptive attacks into German territory, and this policy was still being successfully employed as late as the reign of Valentinian I (ruled 364–75). After his death fresh pressures came from the Huns, whose expansion from the steppes pushed groupings such as the Goths, Vandals and Franks towards and over the frontiers. By the early 5th century they were breaking through easily and beginning to settle within the empire. The Romans had lost the initiative.

THE WALL

If there is one monument that symbolises the imperial defence strategy it is Hadrian's Wall in the north of England. Following the Roman conquest of southern Britain in AD 43 there had been sporadic attempts to extend Roman control into what is now Scotland. However, the Roman forts established there had proved impossible to hold against the warlike tribes of southern Scotland, the Selgovae and Novantae, especially when these began collaborating with tribes further south, notably the Brigantes. The primary purpose of the wall was to separate the two peoples around a stabilised frontier, although it was never intended to close the frontier altogether. A common Roman tactic was to rush troops into enemy territory to deal with unrest there before it even reached the defences.

When the wall was first planned at the behest of Hadrian, who visited Britain in about AD 122, the defending troops were to be stationed in existing forts and the wall built to the north of these. Attackers from the north would have come first to a ditch some 27 ft wide and nine feet deep before they approached the wall which was to be ten feet thick and probably about 21 ft high. At every Roman mile (1620 yards, slightly under a modern mile), there was to be a milecastle with a gate through the wall. Typically each would have had a garrison of 16 men. At intervals between each milecastle there were to be turrets with temporary living space for those stationed in them. These turrets were about 40 ft high, the same height as the watchtowers on the milecastles, so that continuous watch could be kept for intruders. The garrisons would have been able to fight off small-scale attacks and would have signalled back to the forts for reinforcements if needed.

These buildings were put in hand and the connecting wall between them started, but then a different plan evolved. The evidence suggests that there was considerable local hostility to the wall and it was decided that it would need more vigorous defending. The garrison troops were now to be moved right up to the wall where they would be stationed in forts. Twelve were originally planned and four more added later.

Above: In the northern provinces more attention had to be paid to heating, and the hypocaust developed: air heated from a furnace circulated underground and up through brick vents in the walls. The example illustrated here is from the town of Aquincum, capital of the province of Pannonia Inferior on the Danube border (now on the outskirts of modern Budapest).

Below: Hadrian's Wall snakes across northern England. For the auxiliaries from mainland Europe who were posted here it must have been a bleak life. One of the Vindolanda letters (see overleaf) details the sending not only of sandals but also of undergarments and socks to an officer.

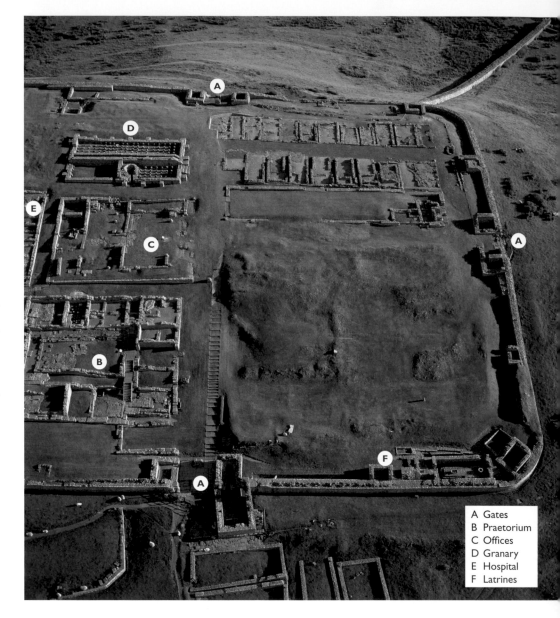

View showing the groundplan of Housesteads fort. A fort would have a standard layout so that a unit could rapidly adapt to a new posting or be able to erect a new fort at short notice if one was needed. Four gates (**A**) opened onto the main streets, which intersected across the inside. There was an impressive house for the commander, the Praetorium (**B**), with the administrative offices behind it (**C**). Usually these offices would have an open courtyard from where officers could address the men. Inside, a room would be set aside for a statue of the emperor and the unit's standards. The community had its own granary (**D**) and hospital (**E**)—with evidence that simple operations could be performed using sterilised instruments. There was a strong emphasis on hygiene and Housesteads has one of the best surviving latrines (**F**), with running water taking the waste well outside the walls. In addition, many forts had their own bath houses, which were placed near running water outside the fort. Outside the south gate at Housesteads are the remains of a civilian settlement, a *vicus*. These *vici* grew up alongside any permanent settlement and there is a good example at Vindolanda, with a rest house for travelling officials with its own bath suite and shops including, probably, a butcher and a brewer.

A Gates
B Praetorium
C Offices
D Granary
E Hospital
F Latrines

With the fighting force strengthened, the wall could be narrowed to eight feet but it was also decided to extend it along to the mouth of the Tyne to what is now, appropriately, called Wallsend. The wall was also extended along the Cumbrian coastline on the Solway Firth in the west. Originally the western part of the wall was built in turf rather than stone (a sign perhaps that this sector needed to be put in place as a matter of urgency) but it was rebuilt in stone later in the century to match the rest. The total length of the wall, from Wallsend on the Tyne to the Solway Firth was 80 Roman miles (74 miles). Its construction appears to have been in the hands of the legions. They had their own building staff, including engineers and surveyors, and the labour to carry out the work.

In front of the wall was a V-shaped ditch, a typical Roman defensive feature. Behind the wall there was originally a monumental earthwork, known as the *vallum*. It consisted of a ditch about ten feet deep with a flat bottom 20 ft wide. On either side of it ran a flat surface and the whole was enclosed by two ridges about six feet high and 20 ft across. Opposite each fort there was an opening in the vallum from which a road led up to its gate. The vallum had no defensive elements and it is hard to know why so much energy was put into constructing it. One view is that it was typical of Hadrian's determination to make an impact wherever he went, another that the frontier of the empire had to be seen to be marked with appropriate formality. It is also probable that the space between the vallum and the wall could be used as a defined military area with limited civilian access. Yet access through the wall was always allowed, even if it would always have been under strict supervision.

Most of the forts along the wall have survived in part, and in some the outline is particularly well preserved. Housesteads (*illustrated opposite*) is one of the most famous because its position overlooking the rugged countryside is so dramatic. Like the others, it is enclosed within a rectangular wall, here some 650 by 400 ft. In the 3rd century it was home to around 1,000 men, most of them auxiliary troops rather than legionaries. The legions were crack troops used only in emergencies and the closest legion to the wall was stationed at York. Recent evidence shows that detachments of legionaries were posted to the forts, but that the vast majority of men in the permanent garrisons were raised from the provinces. At Housesteads the 3rd-century garrison was made up of Tungrians, an infantry unit from what is now Belgium. At Chesters fort the auxiliaries were a cavalry detachment from northern Spain. Excavations of another mounted unit, in the fort at Wallsend, shows that the men lived alongside their horses and did not stable them in a separate block.

Towards the end of the 2nd century, there is evidence that the wall came under attack and local tribes were able to break through it. However, by the 3rd century order had been restored and the wall was well guarded throughout the next two centuries. It was still being restored as late as the 360s, just 50 years before the legions withdrew from Britain. After 400 it fell into decay.

THE VINDOLANDA TABLETS

Vindolanda was one of the Roman forts established well before the building of Hadrian's Wall, probably about AD 85. Nevertheless, when Housesteads fort was built just to the north, Vindolanda was kept in operation. It was rebuilt, but in typical Roman fashion the original building was demolished and its remains sealed underground before rebuilding began. This provided perfect conditions for the preservation of perishable materials.

The most astonishing finds at Vindolanda have been the writing tablets. Normally, in areas where papyrus was not available, these tablets were made of wood with a carved-out centre into which wax was poured. The wax was written on and the impression seldom penetrated the wood itself. Yet at Vindolanda a large number of alder and birch tablets were found where the script had been applied directly onto the wood.

The range of texts which has come to light is astonishing. Many of the tablets refer to the strength of the local unit and its duty register. There are accounts, some linked to supplies for the garrison, others personal, and contracts for the supply of goods. Reports come in from military outposts, soldiers ask for leave and army wives ask their friends to birthday parties. The commander wrote regularly to the governor of the province, often recommending men he knew, includ-

Fragment of a tablet of the late 1st or early 2nd century AD from one Claudia Severa, an army wife, to her sister, wife of the captain of the ninth Batavian cohort, inviting her to a birthday party: 'I shall expect you, sister, farewell sister, my dearest soul.' This is the earliest surviving example of the handwriting of a Roman woman.

ing himself, for promotion. The tablets have been particularly important for the unrivalled—and unexpected—insights they give to the everyday running of auxiliary cohorts. There were daily reports on the level of supplies and the allocation of work to different specialists. These confirm how versatile and self-sufficient a cohort could be. Units could be broken up and were often sent some distance to help with building or defence elsewhere. Yet in all the documents there is virtually no reference to any fighting. All was quiet in this period on the northern front.

Leptis Magna

Leptis Magna, in modern Libya, is the most spectacular of the cities of Roman north Africa. This is due to its original opulence, to its fine state of preservation and to its background against the sea. Leptis was recognised by Augustus as a gateway to the Mediterranean, notable for its olive oil, and he founded a Roman city here. The local citizens were quick to show their loyalty and by the end of Augustus' reign Leptis had its own market, theatre and a monumental portico on the road from the interior. It was recognised as a *municipium* by the end of the 1st century AD and then upgraded to a *colonia* at the beginning of the 2nd. It benefited from the patronage of the emperor Septimius Severus, who was born here.

Roman city in North Africa
Flourished 2nd–3rd centuries AD

THE AFRICAN BACKGROUND

Roman rule in north Africa originated in the defeat of the Carthaginians and the total destruction of Carthage in 146 BC. This did not give Rome full control as there were still important African kingdoms such as Numidia and Mauretania, which alternated between resistance to and acquiescence in Roman rule before being fully incorporated into the empire as provinces. The vast central area of north Africa, where Carthage had been the leading city, re-emerged under Augustus as the province of Africa Proconsularis, which ran eastwards to Cyrenaica. It included much of what had been the kingdom of Numidia (the rest was annexed to Mauretania).

The southern frontiers of these huge expanses were always poorly defined and the Romans were continually involved in low-level guerrilla activity against nomadic raiders. Nevertheless, it is remarkable that only one legion, the Third Augustan, needed to be stationed in Africa. Thirteen thousand strong and aided by another 13,000 local auxiliary troops, it proved sufficient to keep the peace for some 400 years. Its base at Lambaesis has the finest surviving legionary fort anywhere in the empire.

Ancient Carthaginian settlements were supplemented by Roman colonies established by Julius Caesar and Augustus. The important town of Thysdrus (the modern El Djem) was one of Caesar's colonies. In 29 BC, Augustus refounded Carthage and it became capital of the province of Africa Proconsularis. The wealth of the new province was soon obvious. Caesar imposed an annual tribute of three million pounds of olive oil on Tripolitana (incorporated by Augustus into Africa Proconsularis), while the wheat of the province was soon meeting two thirds of the city of Rome's needs. In addition there were ancient trade routes bringing luxuries northwards to the coast from beyond the new frontiers.

The Romans colonised Africa systematically. The division of Africa Proconsularis into agricultural units (four to a square Roman mile) took 160 years and extended into regions of modern Tunisia which are uncultivable today. Settlements were joined by a comprehensive road network. Although much of this has disappeared, 12,000 miles has now been plotted through 2,000 surviving milestones. The major coastal ports were linked to this network and goods, including marble, could be transported easily throughout the Mediterranean.

The prosperity of the provinces was underpinned by their enormous fertility and proximity to Rome, a city that could never feed itself. At this date rains in north Africa were regular during the winter, there was little frost and the summer climate was stable. Inevitably speculators saw their chance and wealthy men soon owned vast *latifundiae* (estates), which were sublet in allotments to peasants. Each province had to provide a tribute of grain, the *annona*, but there seems to have been a surplus for sale in addition. For more than 300 years, the province of Africa sent half a million tons of corn to Rome every year. Where rainfall was lower, as in Tripolitana, olives were cultivated and here again there was a massive surplus for commercial sale.

In no part of the empire did the settlers, native or Roman, take to city life more enthusiastically. In the 30s BC the Romans only recognised seven cities as having full rights: Utica, an ancient Carthaginian foundation which had sided with the Romans during the Punic Wars, and six Roman colonies. As other communities grew they were accorded recognition as *municipia*, a status below that of a *colonia* but one which gave them rights to govern themselves. The numbers grew inexorably. By the 3rd century there are an estimated five or six hundred *municipia*, 200 of them in the rich farmlands of northern Tunisia. There were two very large cit-

Facing page: The face of the Medusa graces many an arcade in Leptis Magna. She was clearly a personal totem for Septimius Severus, the Roman emperor who did so much to promote this city, his birthplace. The head of Medusa is found on his breastplate and also on his coins alongside the word *Providentia*, Providence. Notice the heart shape cut into the Medusa's eye. Such incisions were an innovation of the 2nd century AD and so help to date statues.

ies, Carthage, over 100,000 in population and Leptis Magna, with some 80,000. Then there were a number of coastal cities of between 20,000 and 40,000. The majority of inland cities, some of which were only a few miles apart, had populations of between 5,000 and 20,000, small urban islands in the great estates around them. The wealthier citizens prided themselves on their donations of the typical set of Roman buildings: a forum, theatres and amphitheatres, bath houses, fountains and aqueducts. Thamugadi (the modern Timgad) is an exceptional example of a frontier town which had all the attributes of civilised living including a large library. Especially common in these cities was the triumphal arch, which was used not only as a symbol of loyalty to an empire but as a monumental backdrop to a street or open space. It is because most of these sites were abandoned and never built on again after the collapse of the empire that so many of these buildings remain.

Above: Ruins of the stage buildings of the Roman theatre of Leptis, with the Libyan Sea beyond.

SEPTIMIUS SEVERUS

Septimius Severus' paternal family was north African in origin but its members were thoroughly romanised and Septimius' grandfather had been the leading citizen of Leptis Magna at the time of Trajan. In 191 Septimius was appointed governor of the province of Pannonia Superior, on the northwest Balkan frontier. Two years later he was declared emperor by the legions of the Rhine and Danube border. Four years of civil war followed as he defeated his rivals. He was always popular with the soldiers. He raised army pay for the first time since AD 84 and allowed legionaries to marry officially. By

Far right: The imperial family: Septimius Severus, his wife Julia Domna, and their sons Caracalla and Geta. The portrait of Geta is defaced, a vivid relic of the fraternal infighting that followed Septimius' death.

Right: Bust of Caracalla, after he had become emperor. The famous baths in Rome are his most enduring legacy (see p. 149) but he also gave citizenship to all imperial subjects who were not slaves.

197 he was secure, and in that year he also won a major victory over the Parthians. His triumphal arch in Rome (see p. 142) celebrates this victory, which was central to his propaganda image.

Septimius was determined to create a dynasty. Already in 198 he had granted his elder son, Caracalla, the title of Augustus, while his other son, Geta, was recognised as a Caesar (for the difference between the two, see p. 196). The two boys loathed each other, but Septimius wished them to rule jointly. He took them off to Scotland with him in the hope that by working together to subdue the Scots their animosity might be subdued. The campaign failed but in 210 Septimius elevated Geta to Augustus so that he would succeed equally with his brother. Septimius died at York in February 211, with the famous last words to his sons: 'Don't disagree with each other, give money to the soldiers and ignore everyone else'. It was a vain hope. By the end of the year Caracalla had had his brother murdered and subjected his name to a damnatio memoriae.

THE BUILDINGS OF LEPTIS

The prosperity of Leptis and the breadth of its overseas contacts emerged in the 2nd century when marble was imported from Greece and Asia Minor, notably for the great Hadrianic baths. Then came Septimius Severus. He put in hand a major programme of glorification, both of the city and, by association, of himself. His rebuilding tells us a great deal about his conception of the ideal city.

Septimius added an enormous new forum, but in contrast to the more open colonnaded fora which were typical, his was surrounded by a high wall into which were placed arcaded columns. A large temple to the Severan dynasty on the south-western wall was complemented by an opulent basilica opposite. The space between the basilica and the forum was ingeniously filled with a wedge of shops. The apsed basilica contains two exuberantly carved pilasters, one showing Dionysus, the other Hercules, emerging from foliage in a variety of settings. They are very similar to sculptures in Aphrodisias, which is why it is believed that sculptors from that city (*see p. 168*) were working here.

Alongside the forum a colonnade some 1300 ft long ran towards the sea. As it reached the Hadrianic baths, which are set at an angle, it had to change direction and the shift was brilliantly disguised by placing a magnificent two-storey nymphaeum at the 'join'. The colonnade then continued to a grand new harbour. Unfortunately Septimius' excavations led to its rapid silting up, and it had to be abandoned soon after its completion.

THE TRIUMPHAL ARCH AT LEPTIS

Septimius Severus liked to show off his exploits on triumphal arches. He probably put one up in Byzantium (*see p. 224*), and certainly erected another in the Forum in Rome (where it still stands; *see p. 142*). There is one more in Leptis, dated to around AD 203. It stood at the junction of the city's two main streets and is what is known as a *quadrifrons* arch, made up of four piers with arches between them and a dome linking them above. Each pier is flanked by Corinthian columns surmounted by a broken pediment.

This is impressive enough but it is the sculptural decoration which is most interesting. The rectangular attic at the top of the monument held four friezes of the imperial family. In the first Septimius is shown in triumph in his chariot. It is a static and formal portrayal. Beside him are his two sons Geta and Caracalla and behind the chariot riders gallop, again in a formal, stylised way. The second frieze shows the empress Julia Domna followed in a procession by men on horses and women prisoners carried on litters.

The third and fourth panels tie the imperial family with Rome and the future of their dynasty. On the third panel is the family at sacrifice, that most traditional of Roman rituals, with personifications of Virtue and Rome between them. The final panel is a celebration of imperial unity. Septimius reaches out his right hand to hold that of Caracalla while Geta stands between them. Traditional deities of the city are shown alongside the protecting gods of Septimius. Everything is brought together in harmony.

The rest of the arch was originally covered with symbols of triumph, the siege of a city, personifications of Victory and trophies. The whole is a statement in which the triumph of the emperor is given precedence over a more natural depiction of events or any human portrayal. We are moving into a more formal stage of imperial display.

Above: Septimius Severus' triumphal arch at Leptis.

Top: Winged Victory holding a palm frond and a wreath, from the sculpture on the arch.

Palmyra

Wealthy city on the fringes of the Roman empire
Flourished 1st–3rd centuries AD

For anyone coming across the Syrian desert, either in Roman times or now, the sudden appearance of Palmyra is a magnificent sight. The Jewish historian Josephus, writing in the 1st century AD, gives the first description of a city which—despite what he says about an origin in the days of Solomon—is shown by archaeological evidence to have only just become an urban settlement.

'He [Solomon] advanced into the desert of Upper Syria and, having taken possession of it, founded there a very great city at a distance of two days' journey from Upper Syria and one day's journey from the Euphrates, while from the great Babylon the distance was a journey of six days. Now the reason for founding the city so far from the inhabited parts of Syria was that further down there was no water anywhere on the land and that only in this place were springs and wells to be found. And so, when he had built this city and surrounded it with very strong walls, he named it Thadamora, as it still called by the Syrians, while the Greeks call it Palmyra.'

Palmyra became stupendously rich through the effective exploitation of trade routes with the East. The city had its culture, rooted in the rituals and religions of the ancient Near East; its own language, which was used bilingually with Greek; and distinctive styles of art. Officially part of the Roman empire, it retained an individuality and remoteness which made it a base for a major challenge to the unity of that empire in the 3rd century, under its exotic queen Zenobia.

Left: The mile-long colonnade of the Seleucid city of Apamea may have been what prompted the Palmyrenes to build their own Great Colonnade, pictured on the facing page.

HISTORY OF PALMYRA

The use of the oasis at Palmyra by nomads goes far back in history but it is not until the 1st century BC that archaeology provides evidence of some form of permanent settlement. The first temple to the Syrian god Bel (Baal) was built by this time, while the earliest inscription in the local Semitic language, Palmyrene, dates from 44/43 BC. The Romans regarded the town as part of the province of Syria and in 41 BC Mark Antony's army raided the site. The Palmyrenes took refuge across the Euphrates until he retreated. In the 20s AD further texts show that a number of different tribes had come together as a single settlement and were trading with Babylon. The city's greatest monument, the Temple to Bel, was rebuilt and dedicated in AD 32.

There are signs of increasing Greek and Roman influence in the 1st century AD. Inscriptions show Palmyrene being used alongside Greek and Latin: a text from AD 74 describes the *boule* (Greek for city council) of the *civitas* (Latin for a legally recognised urban settlement) of the Palmyrenes. By this time the more prominent Palmyrenes were gaining Roman citizenship. In 129 Hadrian himself visited the city and awarded it the title of 'Hadrianic Palmyra'.

Now began an impressive rebuilding. The Great Colonnade (*illustrated left*) may have been planned as a response to the mile-long colonnade of the neighbouring city of Apamea (*illustrated above*). Competition among cities in self-glorification was intense in the 2nd century. The temple to Baalshamin, a Syrian supreme deity, equivalent to the Greek Zeus, was rebuilt at this time in a typical Greek form, even though most of the dedicatory inscriptions found there are in Palmyrene.

In the reign of Septimius Severus, Palmyra received the added status of *colonia*, and as such it was ruled by two chief magistrates, the *duumviri* (a similar system to Pompeii; *see p. 179*). Despite this new Roman status, Latin declined in use and the city continued as a bilingual society, with Greek and Palmyrene used alongside each other. The normal requirement was for auxiliary troops to use Latin in their official communications but the Palmyrenes, who are recorded as serving as far west as Hadrian's Wall, were allowed to use their own language.

In the 1st century AD, Palmyra's merchants appear to have acted as intermediaries between the Roman empire and Rome's old enemy Parthia. The city provided an informal way of allowing each empire to prosper despite their differences. A well trodden (by camels) trade route ran across the desert to Hit, the first port where the Euphrates becomes navigable (its line is still visible from the air). The Euphrates was followed as far as the Persian Gulf, where Palmyrene merchants traded with Scythia (now northwest India). Although there are no direct reports of what the trade consisted of, it can be assumed that the Palmyrenes sought the same commodities as other traders: precious stones, silk or cotton. The overland route was dangerous

Above: Palmyrene gods are always shown fully clothed and armed and when a new statue of the goddess Allat was made, Athena, shown in the same way, was used as a model. Deities were often shown as a triad, with the most important god in the centre. In this example, from c. AD 50, the god Baalshamin (centre) is distinguished by his headdress and his beard. On the figure on the left, the crescent cutting through the nimbus identifies him as the moon god Aglibol, while the third figure is the sun god Malakbel. This is a standard trio known from other examples of this period.

The sculpture of Palmyra shows a complex interplay of Persian, Near Eastern and Classical influences, which are often woven into something very original. The funerary reliefs of women are particularly attractive. The elegant example here is typical of the late 2nd century: often one hand is shown raised, the tunic is short-sleeved, and the jewellery is carefully depicted. The grander members of society were provided with their own sarcophagi placed in tomb chambers. After AD 150 the idea of decorating them was imported from the West, but evolved in a distinctive Palmyrene style. Reliefs of banqueting scenes were simply moved onto the top of the sarcophagus so that the deceased was shown reclining on a luxurious couch, as in the example below.

and inscriptions in Palmyra honour men who have protected the caravans on their journeys across open country. The Palmyrenes also stationed their own troops along the route. The enormous prosperity of the city suggests that a combination of commercial skills, military force and diplomatic manoeuvrings kept the trade intact.

In the 250s there is the sudden emergence as ruler of Lucius Septimius Odenathus, a man whose name suggests that his family received Roman citizenship from the emperor Septimius Severus. Odenathus exploited the collapse of Roman power in the East in the crisis of the 3rd century. The aggressive Sasanian dynasty had taken the place of Rome's former *bête noire*, the Parthians, and in 264 the Sasanians reached Antioch and sacked it. On their return home, however, they were ambushed by Odenathus and defeated. The emperor Gallienus accepted Odenathus' position as a subordinate ruler in the East, according him the title of *corrector totius Orientis*, 'He who puts all to rights over the whole of the East', but the evidence suggests that Odenathus had ambitions to become emperor himself (he is recorded in a posthumous inscription of 271 as 'King of Kings', a traditional Persian title). He was about to move towards Asia Minor to campaign against the Goths when he and his son were assassinated by his nephew. His queen, Zenobia, now seized power, as regent to her own son, Vaballathus. Her career is described below.

With the defeat of Zenobia, Palmyra was captured and eventually sacked by the emperor Aurelian. The city was already beginning to lose its prosperity as trade routes shifted further north, but defence of the eastern frontier against any future Sasanian aggression was now paramount for the Romans. The emperor Diocletian converted part of the city into a fort and stagnation set in. Inscriptions no longer proclaimed new buildings but the restoration of the old. With the coming of Christianity in the 4th century, temples were turned into churches. Palmyra was still recognised as an important bastion on the frontier with Persia in the 6th century. In the 7th century, however, it was subsumed by the expansion of Islam.

QUEEN ZENOBIA

Zenobia was Odenathus' second wife. She must have recognised that a position as regent for her son Vaballathus would give her enormous opportunities to maintain a semi-independent kingdom, and there were rumours in hostile Roman circles that she was involved in her husband's murder. The new emperor Claudius II (reigned 268–70) had to accept these developments and he granted Vaballathus the same titles as his father had enjoyed. Zenobia exploited the opportunity to conquer much of Syria and then in 269, in a totally unexpected move, her armies conquered Egypt as well (she may have had Egyptian blood through her mother, but a claim that she was actually a descendent of Cleopatra was probably purely propaganda).

In her brief moment of glory, Zenobia established a court back in Palmyra. Legends talk of her powerful presence, extraordinary beauty (her teeth were like pearls, her eyes black), clemency and learning. She knew several languages, had Greek philosophers to advise her and was proud of her chastity (she claimed she would only let Odenathus sleep with her if she was sure of conceiving).

However, her position depended entirely on the weakness of the Roman empire and when a much tougher emperor, Aurelian, came to power in 270, she was doomed. The Palmyrene armies were strong enough to take on local forces, but not crack legionaries. Egypt was easily brought back under Roman control in 271. Aurelian then entered Syria, defeated Zenobia's forces near Antioch and pursued her back to Palmyra. She desperately proclaimed her son an Augustus in the hope of winning new loyalties from Roman supporters but it was too late. She was captured trying to escape from the city and taken off to be paraded in Aurelian's victory triumph in Rome. Tradition relates that her life was spared and she lived the rest of her days in a villa in Tivoli.

'After three days journeying through arid deserts, on issuing into the plain, I was suddenly struck with a scene of the most stupendous ruins—a countless multitude of superb columns, stretching in avenues beyond the reach of sight. Among them were magnificent edifices, some entire, others in ruins; the earth every-where strewn with fragments of cornices, capitals, shafts, entablatures, pilasters, all of white marble and of the most exquisite workmanship. After a walk of three-quarters of an hour along these ruins, I entered the enclosure of a vast edifice, formerly a temple dedicated to the Sun; and accepting the hospitality of some poor Arabian peasants, who had built their hovels on the area of the temple, I determined to devote some days to contemplate at leisure the beauty of these stupendous ruins… Here, said I, once flourished an opulent city; here was the seat of a powerful empire […]; these piles of marble were regular palaces, these fallen columns adorned the majesty of temples; these ruined galleries surrounded public places. Here industry collected the riches of all climes, and the purple of Tyre was exchanged for the precious thread of Serica; the soft tissues of Cassimere for the sumptuous tapestry of Lydia, the amber of the Baltic for the pearls and perfumes of Arabia; the gold of Ophir for the tin of Thule.'

Comte de Volney, *On visiting Palmyra*, 1796

Diocletian's Villa at Split

Retirement villa of a Roman emperor
Early 4th century AD

This view of Diocletian's Villa shows the arcaded street which leads from its northern entrance towards the emperor's quarters overlooking the sea.

While the later Roman empire is often portrayed as slipping into an inexorable decline, this is not how contemporaries would have seen it. Between 284 and 375 there were three emperors, Diocletian, Constantine and Valentinian I, who, with co-emperors, were able to keep the borders intact. Diocletian divided the empire into four, and organised its rule by two Augusti (senior emperors) and two Caesars (junior emperors). Diocletian's co-Augustus was Maximian, who established his capital at Trier (*see p. 200*).

It was rare for an emperor to abdicate. Yet this is what Diocletian did in AD 305 and he appears to have planned for the event by building a splendid retirement villa near his birthplace, Salonae, the principal city of Roman Dalmatia. The villa was placed on a well-protected inlet: today it is incorporated into the modern town of Split, facing south towards the island of Brač, a fine setting with the mountains rising behind.

Following his abdication, Diocletian spent much of his time in his villa. However, his carefully structured system, which required the two currently junior emperors to take the place of himself and Maximian (whom Diocletian had persuaded to abdicate at the same time), and to appoint two new juniors in turn, was destroyed by the opportunism of those who assumed command: Maximian's son Maxentius, and the son of Maximian's Caesar. Neither man wanted to content himself with a junior role, and power was bitterly contested. Diocletian died in 311; he possibly committed suicide in his despair at what had happened. The following year Maxentius was defeated and killed outside Rome by the son of his father's junior: that man was Constantine the Great.

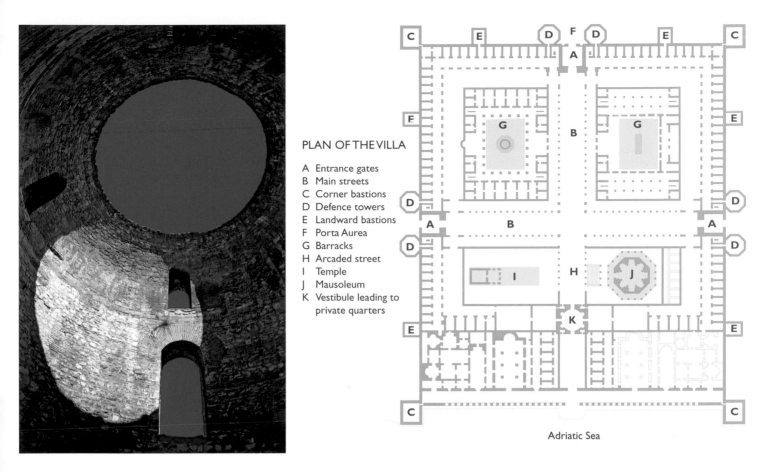

PLAN OF THE VILLA

A Entrance gates
B Main streets
C Corner bastions
D Defence towers
E Landward bastions
F Porta Aurea
G Barracks
H Arcaded street
I Temple
J Mausoleum
K Vestibule leading to
   private quarters

Adriatic Sea

THE VILLA

The entrance to the villa was from the north, the main road from the provincial capital, through the present Porta Aurea **(F)**, although there was access to the sea through a gate in the façade. The military feel of the villa would have been enhanced by the buildings in its northern half, which comprised two blocks of barracks **(G)** reserved for the guards and villa staff. If the visitor continued onwards, across the colonnaded street that ran from east to west, he would have come—and in fact still does—to a peristyle, a short arcaded street **(H)**. The western side of this opens out to a well-preserved temple with a barrel-vaulted ceiling **(I)**. One of Diocletian's strategies had been to link the emperors with the traditional gods of Rome, for it was often said that it was their neglect which had led to the misfortunes of the 3rd-century empire. Diocletian had specifically associated himself with Jupiter, the father of the gods, and it can be guessed that this was the dedication of the temple here.

On the eastern side is Diocletian's private tomb, the mausoleum **(J)**. The word comes from the great tomb built for Mausolus, ruler of Halicarnassus in Asia Minor in the 350s BC. It was one of the Seven Wonders of the Ancient World (*illustrated on p. 119*). While this prototype 'mausoleum' had a square base surmounted by a pyramid, the Romans appear to have adopted a circular shape from the Etruscans. It was not uncommon for emperors (and other grandees) to build their own mausolea: Augustus built one, the base of which survives in Rome; so did Hadrian. His lives on as the Castel Sant'Angelo on the outskirts of the Vatican City. The mausoleum at Split is an octagonal building whose interior contains free-standing columns of Egyptian marble which rise to support a dome. It was once richly decorated with mosaic, but only a frieze with hunting scenes and what are assumed to be the faces of Diocletian and his wife Prisca survive. The emperor's porphyry sarcophagus would have been placed in the centre.

Continuing to the end of the arcade, one entered the residential quarter through a domed vestibule **(K)**. Beyond it lay the private rooms, including a small audience chamber, bedrooms and a dining room.

Above: Diocletian had always been a military man with a rigorous and ordered mind and his villa reflects this. It is typical of a traditional army camp: rectangular, with gates in the centre of each wall **(A)** and the interior divided by crossed streets **(B)**. There were bastions at each corner **(C)** and the three entry gates, all on the landward walls, were flanked by octagonal towers **(D)**. A further six bastions are fitted along the landward walls **(E)**. It is only on the seaward side, where the principal rooms overlook the sea, that there is ornamentation on the outside wall, with arched windows framed by columns on the upper storey (these have been compared to the windows of the Porta Nigra at Trier, which are almost identical in date; *see p. 203*). It is hard to know whether Diocletian genuinely feared attack or whether military architecture was natural to him.

Above left: This domed vestibule stands immediately behind the ceremonial gateway shown on the facing page and would have provided an important space for welcomes and farewells in the inner palace.

Piazza Armerina

**Opulent provincial villa
Early 4th century** AD

Contemporary with Diocletian's villa at Split (4th century AD) is the villa of Piazza Armerina in Sicily. Its good state of preservation is due to the silting up of the area, which caused the villa to 'disappear'. It was not known at all until the 18th century and was only excavated in the 20th.

The ownership of this opulent villa in a comparatively remote part of Sicily has long remained a mystery. Its very size and grandeur, 45 rooms and 37,000 square feet of mosaic, the largest display in any single building of the Classical world, have pointed to an emperor, Diocletian's co-ruler Maximian or Maximian's son Maxentius. More recently a member of the senatorial aristocracy, perhaps even a governor of the province, has been proposed.

The villa provides a contrast with Diocletian's. It was almost certainly the centre of a working agricultural estate, although remains of this are sparse. It did not need to be defended and it was set out in a form which was closer to the sprawl of Hadrian's Villa (*see p. 181*) than the militarised order of a Diocletian building.

The famous mosaic of the 'bikini-clad' girls competing in some form of athletic games is one of the best preserved in the villa at Piazza Armerina. The girls shown here are using hand weights, throwing a discus and running. In a lower register (not shown here) a girl is holding a palm leaf (of victory) and crowning herself with a rose crown. This is a rare example of women engaged in sport—often in the Greek and Roman worlds they were excluded even from being spectators.

The emphasis seems to have been on privacy. Visitors arrived at an entrance courtyard where they would compose themselves before making their way through the formal entrance and into a peristyled garden. A damaged mosaic on the threshold shows figures with candles and branches, probably the welcoming party when the owner arrived to take up residence. If the visitors were to be received formally, they would have progressed to the far side of this to what is an apsidal audience hall. On the northern side of the garden were guest rooms; the owner's private rooms were next to the reception hall on the main corridor. To the south of the villa was a banqueting suite. The villa also had its own bath house and the elaborate heating system can still be seen, with, at the back of the complex, the furnaces and piping which supplied hot water. The bath seems to have been open to a wider public but it had a private entrance from the villa and here a mosaic shows a woman, probably the owner's wife, approaching the bath with her attendants.

The famous mosaics of the villa are believed to have been the work of several teams from north Africa, probably working alongside each other at the same time. One cannot imagine an owner waiting some decades for a smaller team to complete the whole. The subjects are typical of the villas of north Africa but at

Piazza Armerina they have been adapted, probably by the owner himself, to project the image he wishes to portray to others in the public rooms, and to reflect his personal tastes in the more intimate setting of the private apartments. While the quality of the mosaics is not as high as that found elsewhere, the designs stand out for the large numbers of figures used and the sheer variety of themes. A favourite theme is hunting but this is extended, along the 200-ft floor of the Corridor of the Hunt, to include scenes of exotic animals being captured in various parts of the empire. The owner is proclaiming himself to be much more than just a provincial. The scenes of chariot racing in Rome show that he had his links there—he may even have been wealthy enough to finance the games himself. By contrast, the floor showing the Small Hunt is full of scenes of a typical day's hunting on a large estate, complete with breaks for picnicking.

On the whole, mythological scenes in the mosaics are playful, but in the floor of one of the dining areas there is an extraordinary array of bloodthirsty tableaux of the Labours of Hercules. Hercules was always favoured as the enduring hero who overcomes the challenges presented to him and it would not be strange to find that he was a patron of the owner. Part of a colossal statue of Hercules was found in another part of the villa. What is strange is the degree to which, instead of being portrayed in the act of overthrowing his enemies, he is shown exulting in the aftermath. Clearly the owner had some reason to exult in the triumph of his favourite god.

Above: An example of the rich colours used and the imaginative geometric patterns in mosaic that adorn the rooms of the villa.

Below: Detail from the Corridor of the Hunt showing a leopard sinking its fangs into a gazelle, a lion disembowelling another gazelle, and a mounted human hunter joining the havoc. The animals in this 'Great Hunt' are African big game. In the 'Small Hunt' they are more domestic and European (wild boar in the forest, for example). The vegetation in the Small Hunt is European too: there are no palm trees in the background. Another scene from the hunting mosaics, of an ostrich being embarked for the wild animal hunts in the Colosseum in Rome, is shown on p. 145.

Trier

Facing page: This porphyry statue, built
into the outer wall of St Mark's in Venice,
represents the Tetrarchs, the four rulers
of the Roman empire (an Augustus grasps
a Caesar in each pair). The pose is rigid
and the faces without expression, which
suggests that they are an abstract
representation of the four rather
than actual portraits. The group
was seized by the Venetians in
Constantinople during the Fourth
Crusade (1204) and a missing
heel was found back in
Constantinople during
excavations in the 1960s.

Trier was originally a Celtic settlement, of the Treveri peoples, on the River Mosel where there was a river crossing. When Augustus made a tour of Gaul between 13 and 15 BC, he chose it as a good site for a military post in an area which was close to the border and still vulnerable to unrest. The Roman name, Augusta Treverorum, reflected the important role of the emperor in its foundation. Like Nîmes (*see p. 156*), Augusta Treverorum was developed quickly, with a gridiron pattern of streets around a central forum. Again like Nîmes, an amphitheatre was built about AD 100. By this time the city had become a major administrative centre and later it became the capital of the province of Gallia Belgica, the northern part of Gaul.

So long as the border of the empire remained stable, Augusta Treverorum could prosper. A large set of public baths was built in the 2nd century AD, while the new bridge built over the Mosel at the end of that century is the only Roman bridge north of the Alps still in use (it is now a railway bridge). In the 280s the city was transformed by the decision to make it one of the new imperial capitals when the empire was divided into four by Diocletian (*see box below*). The first of these co-emperors was Constantius, who was Caesar (junior emperor) of the West, under the Augustus (senior emperor) Maximian, but given responsibility for the extensive provinces of Britain, Spain and Gaul. In 305 Maximian and Diocletian both abdicated and Constantius became the senior emperor in the West. When he died in York the next year his troops proclaimed his son Constantine his successor. It is Constantine who rebuilt Trier to match his new status.

THE TETRARCHY & ITS CAPITALS

When Diocletian divided the empire into four, establishing what is known as the Tetrarchy, it was a recognition that Rome, or in fact any single city, was no longer an effective base for ruling the vast realm. Diocletian had been proclaimed emperor outside Rome, and although he made benefactions to the city in the form of a restored senate house and monumental baths, he knew that there had to be new capitals dedicated as bases for the defence of the empire. In the East these were at Antioch in Syria and Sirmium in modern Serbia, close to the threatened Danube border. In the West, the capitals were at Milan and Trier. Each city was to have the equivalent of an imperial complex, with a palace, an audience hall for the local emperor, a hippodrome and baths.

These developments went hand in hand with the elaboration of rituals that raised the co-emperors to semi-divine status. When he arrived at a city, especially when it was his designated capital, there would be the ceremony of welcome, the *adventus*. All the dignitaries of the city would assemble: its magistrates and priests of the ancient cults—and, after Constantine's conversion to Christianity, the bishop. Choirs would sings songs of triumph and the city orator would deliver a panegyric in which the emperor would be praised for the fruits of his rule. The emperor would then make a formal entry through the city gate and would process with his retinue through the streets. One of Diocletian's entries into Milan with his co-emperor Maximian is recorded: 'As you drove together through the city, the very roofs, so I am told, were almost set in motion, when children and old people rushed out into the open, into the squares, or else leaned out of the upper windows of buildings. All shouted with joy'. When the imperial procession reached the palace the emperor would show himself to the assembled people in the hippodrome, often with chariot races to complete the day's celebration. Once he was installed he would receive petitions and make appointments in his audience hall, of which the one surviving at Trier is the best preserved.

TRIER UNDER CONSTANTINE

It was essential to have an imperial palace with all the opulent appurtenances such a building required, and in Trier the eastern part of the city was set aside for this. The domestic rooms have vanished, although during rebuilding after the Second World War, the remains of a plaster ceiling with painted panels of what appear to be the women of the imperial family were discovered. They show that the finest craftsmen were being used. Constantine had already refitted the city's 2nd-century baths on a grand scale; now he built an equally fine set for the palace.

The most important survival from the palace is the large imperial audience hall. In effect this is a typical basilica, a monumental brick building built over the smaller basilica of the earlier provincial governors. It is a double square, 100 by 200 Roman feet, with an apse at the end. It is well provided with a double row of windows, but their pattern is broken up so that those in the apse are shorter and lower. The interior is now completely bare, but in one of the niches there are traces of mosaics of blue and green scrolls on a gold background and it can be assumed that the walls were coated with mosaic and marble. The exterior seems rather plain today, but there are marks along the walls to show that there were two wooden galleries that ran round the building at the lower level of each set of windows. The brick was covered in stucco and there were external colonnades around the building as well. It is assumed that the hall was directly connected to the imperial palace, but the city's cathedral was built on the site and the palace has not yet been recovered through excavation.

Above: The missorium of Theodosius I, a silver plate produced to mark the tenth year of his reign (i.e. 388), is an excellent portrayal of the emperor sitting in majesty, just as Constantine would have sat in the audience hall at Trier.

Right: The interior of the audience hall of Constantine's palace. The windows in the apse are visibly shorter and wider than those in the nave. This has the effect of making the emperor, or any official sitting in the apse, look larger than he really is. The method of construction and optical illusions such as this are typical of buildings in Asia Minor and Syria of this period, which suggests that the Western empire was still attracting Greek craftsmen.

Above: The ruins of the imperial baths at Trier, begun by Constantine (but never finished). They are perhaps the most impressive of any provincial Roman bath house to survive.

While building was continuing, Constantine was on the move. In 312 he defeated Maximian's son, Maxentius, at the Battle of the Milvian Bridge outside Rome and became ruler of the entire Western empire. By 324 he had also won over the Eastern empire and was sole emperor of a dominion now reunited. Trier diminished in importance and this may explain why the great gate that Constantine had ordered for the northern entrance to the city was left unfinished, as can be seen from its rough stonework. This gate, the Porta Nigra, so called in medieval times because of the blackness of its stones, is designed to impress rather than to defend. The rows of open windows would have been easy to penetrate. Its survival is credited to an 11th-century hermit, St Simeon, who lived in the abandoned building. On his death it was converted into a church.

Constantine was a great builder of churches, and it is said that his mother Helen, honoured in her own right as Augusta after 325, was the inspiration for a major complex of ecclesiastical buildings in the city. Although the site was much destroyed and rebuilt on, the existing cathedral still has some Roman work in it and is regarded as the oldest cathedral in Germany.

As the empire crumbled, a city so close to the northern borders could not be defended and Trier began to suffer with each successful barbarian raid. By the 360s, the imperial baths were being used as barracks for the garrison that Valentinian I, the last truly effective commander on this border, established here. The city was taken by Maximus Magnus, a usurper from Britain, in his bid to become emperor in the 380s. The ease with which the Roman administration collapsed was ominous and in 395 the capital of Gaul was moved southwards to Arles. Frankish raids followed and by 475 Trier was part of a new Frankish kingdom. While the city may have had a population of 80,000 in the 4th century, by the early 6th century this had shrunk to a mere 5,000.

The early
CHRISTIAN
world

'Let me now obediently sing aloud the new song because after
those terrifying darksome sights and stories, I was now privileged
to see and celebrate such things as in truth many righteous men
and martyrs of God before desired to see on earth and did not see,
and to hear and did not hear … a day bright and radiant, with no
cloud overshadowing it, shone down with shafts of heavenly light
on the churches of Christ throughout the world.'

Eusebius in *The History of the Church* rejoicing at the toleration
of Christianity granted by the emperor Constantine in 313
(Tr. G.A. Williamson)

THE EARLY CHRISTIAN WORLD

	0	100	200	300 miles
0		250		500 km

DACIA

Danube

ILLYRICUM

Milan
Aquileia
Ravenna

Adriatic Sea

Tiber

THRACE

Pontus Euxinus
(Black Sea)

Sinope
Trebizond

MACEDONIA   Philippi

Bosphorus

Constantinople   Nicomedia

Sea of Marmara

Chalcedon

BITHYNIA **PONTUS**

AD 312 ✕ **Rome**

Thessalonica

Nicaea

GALATIA

CAPPADOCIA

Corsica

Halys

EPIRUS

ASIA MINOR

Euphrates

Sardinia

Tyrrhenian Sea

Smyrna

Tralles

CILICIA

Tarsus

Sicily

ACHAIA

Athens

Ephesus

Meander

Antioch

Dura-Europus

Syracuse

Ionian Sea

Miletus

Patmos

Rhodes

Cyprus

PHOENICIA

Damascus

Sea of Galilee

Crete

Mediterranean Sea

Caesarea

SYRIA

SAMARIA

AD 70

AFRICA

Leptis Magna

Jerusalem   Madaba

Bethlehem   *Dead Sea*

JUDAEA

Masada

CYRENAICA

Alexandria

ARABIA

Nile

Sinai

St Catherine's

■ Christian areas by AD 300

□ Christian areas by AD 400

EGYPT

Red Sea

Previous page: Detail of a
6th-century icon (encaustic on wood) of
Christ Pantocrator,
from St Catherine's Monastery, Sinai.

Historical overview

The first archaeological evidence for a religion recognisable as Christianity dates from the 3rd century, evidenced in wall paintings from the catacombs and some sarcophagi. The earliest known church is at Dura-Europus in modern Syria, on what was the far eastern border of the Roman empire, where there is a church and baptistery of about AD 235. The New Testament as we know it today was brought together in its final form some time around the 360s. There are, however, many earlier Christian texts: the gospels and letters of the apostle Paul (or those attributed to him), other New Testament texts from the 1st century AD, and many 2nd-century texts, notably the Gnostic writings, esoteric interpretations of Christianity. In the *Adversus Haereses* ('Against the Heresies') of Irenaeus, bishop of Lyons, of about AD 180, the case is set out for a Church run by bishops who claim authority by succession from Jesus and the apostles. Irenaeus is the first to name the four gospels and to define the concept of heresy for those who oppose the Church's teaching. This was the model of Christianity that was to take root.

The first communities prided themselves on their cohesion and care for their members. However, they also aroused suspicion for their worship of a man who had been executed by the Roman empire but whom they persisted in seeing as the Son of God. Most of the emperors were reluctant to launch witch hunts against Christians, but there is plenty of evidence of local prejudice boiling over into persecution. Martyrs to these persecutions were honoured and remembered, and their bodies preserved if possible. In the later 3rd century Christianity continued to grow. The best archaeological evidence for this is in Rome, where the catacombs, the passageways cut into the rock where Christians were buried and where ceremonies in their memory were held, spread further and further under the ground. The bishops also became more powerful figures, taking on the role of patron for their flocks, organising poor relief and even holding their own courts. This encouraged determined persecution from traditionalist emperors such as Diocletian, who feared that the Christian rejection of the Roman gods was responsible for the troubles of the 3rd century. This was the situation in 310.

Above: While preachers and Christian writers felt free to discuss the Crucifixion ('We preach Christ crucified, a stumbling block to Jews and folly to Gentiles', in the words of Paul), artists remained inhibited. This example from the wooden door of the basilica of Santa Sabina in Rome (c. 420) shows Christ with his arms outstretched but no actual cross. Further inhibition related to the problem of how to show a God suffering or dead on the cross. A solution in the Byzantine world was to illustrate the Resurrection alongside the Crucifixion. In the West by the 10th century there were no longer these inhibitions, and in medieval paintings the sufferings of Christ are shown in grotesque detail.

Far left: Crucifixion was a humiliating punishment and it is clear that Christians were scorned for their worship of a crucified Christ. This extraordinary graffito, found on the Palatine Hill in Rome, mocks one Alexamenos for his belief (the scrawled text reads 'Alexamenos worships his god', the god in question being a crucified donkey).

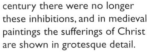

Left: This mosaic of c. 430 from the so-called Mausoleum of Galla Placidia in Ravenna appears to show the four gospels in a cupboard. They are codices rather than papyrus rolls and this is one of the first known depictions of the four together.

Above: Head of the emperor Constantine. The Basilica of Maxentius in the Roman Forum was being constructed when Constantine defeated his rival in battle in 312. Determined to supplant Maxentius in the popular imagination, Constantine installed a massive seated statue of himself there. The head (shown here) and one or two other parts survive. The emperor is shown as transcendent, omnipotent, godly. Gone is the realistic portraiture of earlier imperial Roman sculpture: this is the image first and foremost of a ruler and a conqueror. Portraiture is not entirely absent, however: the prominent eyes and beaky nose do seem to have been true features of Constantine's physiognomy.

Right: The emperor Theodosius at the Council of Constantinople (381), when he enshrined the Nicene Creed in law, thus officially declaring that God and Christ Jesus were of equal majesty, a debate which had been threatening to divide the Church. Theodosius summoned a council of bishops to Constantinople to endorse his decision. The council gave Constantinople an elevated position as second only to Rome in the Church hierarchy, to the fury of older Christian cities such as Alexandria and Antioch. For Theodosius, this was essentially a political coup.

CONSTANTINE THE GREAT: FIRST CHRISTIAN EMPEROR

There has been much discussion of the motives of the emperor Constantine in offering freedom of worship to Christians in his Edict of Toleration, issued at Milan in 313. The year before he had defeated his rival Maxentius just outside Rome, at the Battle of the Milvian Bridge, and his claim that he owed the victory to the support of God may simply have been a means of justifying his absorption of the bishops within the structure of government. Constantine certainly never behaved like a Christian. The bishops were always at his beck and call, not he at theirs; he may have arranged his wife Fausta's death after she falsely accused her stepson Crispus of attempting to rape her, the accusation leading to Crispus' execution; and he is never known to have entered a church. His full commitment, in baptism, only came in the last weeks of his life, in 337.

Yet one should not be too dismissive of his beliefs. Importantly, Constantine valued a single god or divine force in preference to the many Roman gods. He thought it would act as a better focus for order if Christ were seen as God's prefect (the empire's senior administrative official) in heaven, while the emperor was God's prefect on earth. In his own words, 'I am bishop of those outside the Church'. The historian Eusebius, whose *Church History* and *Life of Constantine* glorified the emperor's reign, found precedents from the Old Testament for a forceful warlike emperor who, with God's help, saved the empire from its enemies. Christianity, he believed, should also proclaim itself and its triumph through opulent buildings. Soon large basilicas, dripping with gold leaf and mosaic, were to be found in the larger cities of the empire and on the sacred sites of the Holy Land.

If the Church was to support the state, and receive so many benefits in return, then it had to be a unified body. Before 313 there was little in the way of coherent doctrine, and rival Christianities disagreed with each other about the way their faith should be expressed. A particularly intractable problem was how to define the relationship between God the Father and Jesus the Son. Gospel accounts portray Jesus as subordinate to the Father, whose will he carried out while on earth. The bishop of Alexandria, Alexander, however, argued that God and Jesus Christ were of equal majesty and that Jesus had always been part of the Godhead. He excommunicated one of his priests, Arius, an energetic speaker and networker, who argued the subordinationist view. The Eastern church was split by the issue. The increasing disorder infuriated the pragmatic Constantine, who reluctantly accepted that only a council of bishops could restore peace. The bishops of the East were summoned to his imperial palace at Nicaea.

Constantine's instincts were always in favour of good order and the support of authority. So he put his energy behind a formula in which God and Jesus Christ were declared to be 'one in substance' with each other. This view was expressed in the Nicene Creed, which was approved by the assembled bishops before the council dispersed. In the excitement of the moment there were few dissenters, but once the dust had settled it became clear that Arius and the subordinationists remained strong and still represented the majority of Christians in the empire. There was more embarrassment when no one could find scriptural support for 'one in substance'—and there was intense argument over what the phrase meant anyway. Constantine backtracked, was prepared to admit Arius back into the Church, and allowed one of Arius' supporters to baptise him before his death.

THEODOSIUS AND THE ASSAULT ON PAGANISM

It was not until the emperor Theodosius imposed it by law, in the Eastern empire in 381, and then in the Western empire, that the Nicene Creed achieved the status that it still has today. In the 390s, Theodosius launched another programme, this time to eliminate paganism. His sweeping laws saw the end of the ancient rituals of sacrificing and of all festivals tied to the worship of the gods (the Olympic Games were a famous casualty). Christians also showed themselves ready to assault pagan buildings. The Serapeum in Alexandria, one of the great religious complexes of the Classical world, was destroyed by a Christian mob in 391. The traditional freedom to debate which had underpinned the intellectual vitality of the Greek world withered. A very different spiritual ethos emerged and Classical learning was largely submerged until its revival by the Renaissance humanists in the 14th century. When Theodosius died in 395, the bishop of Milan, the formidable St Ambrose, gave a funeral eulogy applauding his achievements in creating a Christian state and promised that he had reached heaven as a reward.

KEY DATES IN EARLY CHRISTIANITY

c. 4 BC: Jesus of Nazareth born in Bethlehem, during the reign of Augustus

c. AD 30: Jesus is crucified at Jerusalem, during the reign of Tiberius

c. 65: St Paul martyred near Rome during the reign of Nero

c. 67: St Peter martyred in Rome during the reign of Nero

313: Edict of Toleration passed by the emperor Constantine, ending the persecution of Christians

320s: Helen, the mother of Constantine, finds the True Cross in Jerusalem

337: Constantine is baptised

390s: The emperor Theodosius bans all pagan cults

CHRISTIAN PHILOSOPHY: NEOPLATONISM

Plato had always taught that there was a hierarchy of forms, at the summit of which was the Form of 'the Good'. By the 2nd century Platonism had developed so that 'the Good' or 'the One' took on a life of its own as a benevolent entity reaching out to the world below through intermediaries (the lower Forms, often called daemons) and being accessible in return through contemplation and rational thought.

Platonism was brought to a higher level of complexity by the brilliant Plotinus (AD 205–70), whose philosophy is known as Neoplatonism. At the summit of knowledge, he argued is 'the Good' or 'the One', the ground of all existence and the source of all value. At the base of all knowledge is Matter. 'The One' stands as if at the centre of a series of concentric circles of which Matter is the outermost. While 'the One' is by definition a unity, the further one moves from the centre the less unity there is, so Matter as we see it is made up

of a vast range of fragmented objects. The inner circles begin with the World-Mind, the process of lucid thought itself, then there is a World-Soul, which gathers knowledge at a lower level. Each individual human mind can, as Plato had always argued, reach an understanding of these inner circles. In very rare cases it would be possible for a human mind to apprehend 'the One'. Here Plotinus, who seems to have experienced this higher state himself, becomes mystical and his works are among the finest examples of pagan mysticism.

Plotinus makes no comment on Christianity; rather he is working from within Greek thought. However, many Christians grasped that there was much of value in his ideas. It has been said that much of the terminology expressing the relationship between Father and Son put forward by the so-called Cappadocian Fathers when they created a formula for the Trinity derives from Plotinus. St Augustine was also influenced by him.

Jerusalem

Holy city for Christians, Muslims and Jews, site of the Temple of Solomon, the crucifixion and burial of Jesus, and of the ascension of Mohammed into heaven

The two ridges on which Jerusalem is built ensured that it was always a defensible stronghold. The site already had a long history when David, second king of Israel, conquered the city and established the Ark of the Covenant here. In the 10th century his son Solomon built the first temple to house it. However, the Jewish settlement was swept away by the Babylonians, who drove the Israelites into exile in the early 6th century BC. They were only able to return to Jerusalem in the 530s when the Babylonians were overthrown in their turn by the Persians. The exile impelled the Israelites to bring together their sacred writings and they also began the building of a second temple. Nothing of this structure remains, but Judaism was developing as a coherent religion with Jerusalem at its core.

For the next 350 years the Israelites lived under the rule of foreign empires: the Persians until their overthrow by Alexander in the 330s, and then Alexander's Greek successor dynasties, the Ptolemies and the Seleucids. In 168 BC an attempt by the Seleucid king Antiochus IV to ban Jewish rites such as circumcision and to impose Greek festivals led to a revolt by the Jews under the Maccabee brothers. The struggle was fierce but the Seleucid empire was already in decline and in 141 the Maccabees were able to declare an independent Jewish state. It was to last until its overthrow by the Romans.

This was a prosperous period for Jerusalem. The population grew and the city expanded out to the western hillside. Opulent tombs show the wealth of the new rich. Yet squabbles for the succession led to disintegration. In 63 BC, when the Romans were called on for help, the opportunistic general Pompey the Great besieged the city. He outraged Jewish religious sensibilities by entering the Holy of Holies in the temple still in battle dress, and brought the independent Jewish state to an end.

The Romans had no plans to make their new conquest, Judaea, a directly ruled province but an invasion by the Parthians in 40 BC forced them to appoint a strong man to represent their interests. Herod was an Idumaean from southern Judaea (the Idumaeans were recent converts to Judaism) and he persuaded the Romans to give him backing as supreme ruler of the region. He was brutal and vindictive, hated by the Jews for his contempt for their way of life, but an effective overlord. This was what the Romans most cared about. He saw his building programmes as a means of glorifying himself. He created a palace and harbour at Caesarea on the coast, a fortress at Masada and a temple in honour of Augustus in Samaria.

THE TEMPLE MOUNT

Herod's most prestigious project was a massive rebuilding of the temple in Jerusalem, primarily, as he admitted, in his own honour, but possibly also as a concession to the Jews. The new temple was built on a vast platform, as big as any imperial forum in Rome. Herod retained the eastern boundary of the original platform but extended the other three sides. The temple which was then constructed on the platform was built, according to the Jewish historian Josephus, of 'hard, white stones, each of which was about 25 cubits in length, eight in height and twelve in width … the entrance-doors, which with their lintels were equal in height to the Temple itself, he adorned with multi-coloured hangings… And he surrounded the Temple with very large porticoes, all of which he made in proportion, and he surpassed his predecessors in spending money, so that it was thought that no one else had adorned the temple so splendidly.' Building began in 20 BC and the Temple appears to have been quickly completed, although work was continuing on the site well into the 1st century.

The Mount could be entered either by a bridge, which crossed lower ground to reach the centre of the western wall; by steps which ascended by the southwestern corner; or by a wide staircase up the southern wall (rediscovered in the 1960s), at the top of which there were gates which led on up through tunnel ramps to the top. Above these was the grandest building outside the Temple itself, the Royal Portico, which ran along the breadth of the southern wall. It was here that the Sanhedrin, the supreme council of senior priests and court of justice, met.

The Temple itself was the centre of the Jewish world, crammed during the day by those bringing animals for sacrifice and overwhelmed by visitors during the three great annual feasts, Passover, Pentecost and the Feast of the Tabernacles. The Acts of the Apostles well describe the babble of languages that could

Facing page: Orthodox Jew at the Wailing Wall, all that remains of the Temple on the Mount. The lower courses of stone are original, survivals of the massive platform on which stood the temple built by Herod, which in turn stood on the spot occupied by the great Temple of Solomon. The site is still revered by Jews. Their lamentations here mourn the destruction of the Temple.

The Roman general Vespasian was in command of the Roman troops fighting a major revolt in Judaea against Roman rule. When he was elevated to emperor in AD 69, his son Titus took charge and brought the revolt to an end in AD 70 with a bloody destruction of the Temple. Titus was later honoured with a triumphal arch in Rome which shows the booty, including the menorah, the symbol of Moses' Burning Bush, being paraded through the city.

be heard as Jews from communities scattered through the Roman empire came to fulfil their obligations. A Gentile could enter the Mount itself but a six-foot barrier around the Temple prevented any from entering its precinct on pain of death. The entry to the inner Temple sanctuary itself was restricted to the priests, and the simply-furnished Holy of Holies was accessible only to the High Priest, and then only on the Day of Atonement.

Forty years after the death of Christ, by which time Christian communities had spread well outside Jerusalem and entered the Gentile world, Jerusalem suffered the most terrible fate. After four years of conflict with the Roman overlords, the city was taken by Titus, the son of the new emperor Vespasian, and ruthlessly sacked. The Temple was razed to the ground. Any remaining debris was removed by Hadrian after another Jewish revolt, that of the self-proclaimed messiah Bar Kochba, between 132 and 135. Jerusalem was then reconstituted as a Roman *colonia*, Aelia Capitolina, to which no Jew was admitted. There was an attempt to rebuild the Temple by the pagan emperor Julian (the Apostate) in the 4th century, but it was thwarted by a fire.

What remains of the Temple today is the great supporting western wall, known as the Wailing Wall after the lamentations over the destruction of the Temple that have been carried out here over the centuries (the earliest recorded use of the wall for lamentation dates from AD 333).

JESUS & THE ROMAN AUTHORITIES

When Jesus entered Jerusalem for the Passover, probably in AD 30, he was doing no more than an observant Jew would be expected to do. By this date Jerusalem was ruled directly by Rome. Herod had died in 4 BC, about the same time as the birth of Jesus. His son Archelaus had aroused such resentment among the Jews that the Romans removed him from office and established Judaea as a subject province (as opposed to a client kingdom) in AD 6. Pontius Pilate was governor between 26 and 36 but he spent much of his time at his coastal palace at Caesarea and delegated power to the chief priest, Caiaphas. Pilate would come with a troop of auxiliaries to Jerusalem during feasts, when a proper force was needed to keep control. Jesus threatened the power of the priesthood with his teaching and may have upset many conventional Jews by challenging the moneylenders in the Temple. However, to involve Pilate, who alone had the power to order an execution, a political charge, King of the Jews, had to be concocted by the priesthood. Thus it was that Caiaphas brought Jesus before Pilate and the Crucifixion was ordered.

The disciples, and the movement that they gathered around them in memory of Jesus, inhabited a city which was as Herod left it. The Acts of the Apostles record them meeting near the Temple in the Portico of Solomon, probably the portico on the eastern side of the Mount.

THE DOME OF THE ROCK

In 638 the Byzantine empire, the surviving Roman dominions in the East, was faced with the sweeping conquests of Islam, and Jerusalem fell. As the Muslims honoured Abraham and Jesus as prophets, Jerusalem was a sacred city to them, too. The first major Islamic cemetery, the Dome of the Rock, was built on the deserted platform of the Temple Mount between 688 and 691. Unlike most buildings from Jerusalem's chequered history, it stands largely intact. The site chosen was, by Jewish tradition, where Adam had been buried and Abraham had been prepared to sacrifice Isaac. The Holy of Holies stood here and Mohammed had ascended to heaven from here. A sacred site indeed, and the building of the Dome symbolises the bringing to fruition of God's plan as expressed through Mohammed.

The shape of the Dome is borrowed from earlier examples of octagonal domed structures—a link has been made to the mausoleum of Diocletian in Split in particular. The whole is conceived and harmonised in mathematical proportions and this and the glory of its golden dome and mosaics make it one of the great buildings of the world.

The Dome of the Rock, the finest Islamic monument in Jerusalem. 'The outside of the dome is completely covered with gilded glass plates, while the whole of the building proper—floor, walls and drum, inside and out—is decorated with marble and mosaics... At dawn, when the light of the sun first strikes the dome and the drum catches the rays, then this edifice is a marvellous sight to behold, and one such that in all of Islam I have not seen the equal; neither have I heard tell of anything built in pagan times that could rival in grace this Dome of the Rock.' Mukaddasi, *Description of Syria*, 10th century (Tr. G. Le Strange).

CHRISTIAN JERUSALEM

Jerusalem had a Christian bishop as early as the 2nd century but the city took on new life with the recognition of Christianity by Constantine in the early 4th century. His mother Helen set off on a pilgrimage in the 320s to see the city for herself and it was here, according to a legend first recorded in the 390s, that she found the remnants of the True Cross (a *titulus*, the name board, claimed to be that which had been attached to the Cross, is still revered in Santa Croce in Gerusalemme in Rome). Very soon the sites of the Passion were being rediscovered. Unfortunately, most are now known to have been wrongly identified. Pilgrims still visit a Garden of Gethsemane, but the belief that Gethsemane was a garden is not recorded until the 12th cen-

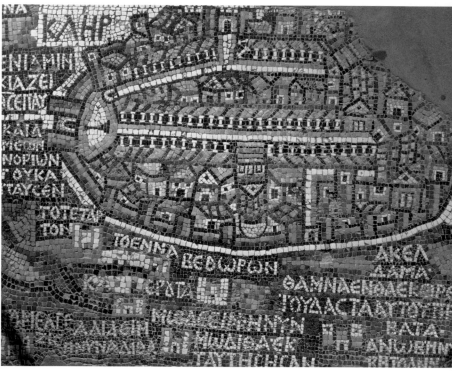

Right: This mosaic of the city of Jerusalem, found at Madaba in Jordan, shows the basilica which Constantine built over the supposed burial place of Christ. It appears as if hanging downwards from the main arcaded street. The steps up to it and its three entrance doors are clearly to be seen.

Above: The Church of the Holy Sepulchre rises above the remains of Constantine's basilica, which in turn may rise above the site of Christ's burial. This possibility makes it one of the holiest sites in the Christian world. The late 19th-century painting here shows the temple that encloses the site of the tomb and a ray of celestial light piercing the building. The effect of the beam of light is no simple artist's fantasy: it is a natural phenomenon.

tury and scholars now believe that the name may refer to a cave. It is certainly more likely that the disciples would have gathered in a cave for shelter, and one is now shown to visitors alongside a church which is believed to hold the tomb of the Virgin Mary, where her body lay before her assumption into heaven (though the Dormition and Assumption are also recorded as taking place at Ephesus).

The site with the greatest claim to authenticity is that of the Church of the Holy Sepulchre, thought to rise over the burial place of Jesus. Yet even this (Catholic and Greek Orthodox) designation is challenged by Protestants, who champion a garden tomb discovered in the 19th century. The case for the Holy Sepulchre rests on archaeological evidence that there was a garden here and tombs cut into the rock on a site that was still outside the city walls in the 30s AD. Hadrian later built a temple to Aphrodite over the site but the tradition that it was the original burial place lingered on so that when Helen enquired about the tomb this was the site she was shown. The Church historian Eusebius describes how digging went on at the site until the tomb was revealed. The rock was then cut out around it so that it stood alone and could be enclosed in a building.

The basilica which Constantine built over the site can be seen on a mosaic map discovered in a 6th-century church at Madaba in Jordan (*illustrated above*). The dome which surmounted the circular rotunda built around the tomb stands out in gold tesserae. In front of the rotunda was an open portico, one corner of which had a stone marking the believed site of the Crucifixion, and then a basilica church with three entranceways from the street. The basilica was extensively damaged by the Fatimid caliph Hakim in the 11th century and much of it was abandoned. The present church is a jumble of different periods with only a few original traces of the Constantinian basilica to be seen (among them two columns of the original rotunda).

Christian Rome

The rock around Rome is volcanic tufa which is easy to carve yet hardens on contact with air. It is ideal for constructing passageways and it was probably the Jews who first built catacombs (the word means 'under the cavities' or 'hollows') alongside the roads outside Rome for the burial of the dead. The custom was adopted by Christians in the 2nd century AD and was popular because it enabled burials and the rituals associated with them to be conducted privately. While there were long periods in Rome when the Christians were tolerated, it still did not pay to make a blatant display of ceremonies that would offend many pagans.

Once a passage had been carved out, the walls could be cut into so that bodies, either in sarcophagi or wrapped in linen, could be placed there and the space covered up. When one level was filled, one could simply tunnel downwards to create another layer of passageways and burial spaces. The larger catacombs have 15 to 20 miles of passages and include rooms for services and, possibly, commemorative meals. The Catacomb of St Calixtus (San Callisto), just off the Via Appia, boasted the bodies of some 16 bishops of Rome and many martyrs, including St Cecilia, a patrician Roman woman martyred c. 180, now the patron saint of music.

After 380, when Christianity was fully tolerated, the ancient taboos against burial within cities became relaxed and the use of the catacombs declined. By the 7th century cartloads of martyrs' bones were arriving at the Pantheon and the catacombs were gradually forgotten. They were rediscovered in the 16th century and there are still new catacombs being found.

Site of much early Christian art and architecture, from the 2nd century AD onwards

Left: In a typical catacomb the deceased would be buried in a loculus, a narrow recess into which the body could be laid, or in a columbarium, a small niche large enough for an urn (it takes its name from the holes in a dovecot; literally a 'pigeonhole'). The example here is a loculus from the Catacombs of St Calixtus, adorned with frescoes of saints and early martyrs (pictured here is an early pope, St Dionysius). On the whole the art is crude, but it provides some understanding of the biblical events early Christians thought important and the saints they worshipped.

Above: Motifs of grapes and vines on the porphyry sarcophagus of Constantia, daughter of Constantine. It is interesting to compare this early Christian iconography with the blue glass funerary urn on p. 177. The idea of crushed grapes as a symbol of the death of the body and release of the spirit is an idea much older than Christianity, though Christianity made the vine its own peculiar symbol.

Above: Detail of an early Christian sarcophagus. The deceased is shown in the centre reading a scroll as if he were a philosopher. His wife is shown next to him as a personification of the traditional Roman virtue of *pietas*, here transferred into Christianity. She holds her hands upwards in a gesture of prayer (*orans*, as it is known). The couple are flanked by two scenes. One shows a Good Shepherd carrying a sheep on his shoulders while next to him a diminutive Christ is being baptised. The other scene shows Jonah lying naked on the shore after he has been vomited up by the whale. Such a mixture of scenes is very common in early Christian art, as if there was a pattern book of acceptable images which could be shown individually or together. It is believed that Jonah is shown naked as a symbol of the baptismal rites for which total immersion was expected—in which case the two ends of the sarcophagus are linked to each other in theme.

Right: The apse mosaic of the church of Santa Pudenziana in Rome (390 or possibly later) is important for its link to the iconography of the pagan emperors. Christ is shown seated on a traditional chair of magisterial authority. His apostles, clad in togas, are grouped either side with hands raised in acclamation. This is also one of the earliest depictions of the apostle Paul at the right hand of Christ, a sign of his elevated status in Rome by this period. Above Christ are what might be symbolic representations of Jerusalem and the Church of the Holy Sepulchre. Symbols of the Evangelists flank a large jewelled cross. The positioning of Christ at the end of the apse echoes the way in which a bishop faces his congregation and a Roman magistrate faced his audience.

THE BIRTH OF CHRISTIAN ART

The catacombs are the home of the first Christian art. This is often rudimentary in quality and awkward in style. One common symbol is the fish: the Greek word for a fish, *ichthys*, can be spelled from the first letters of the Greek words Jesus (*Iesous*), Christ (*Christos*; meaning anointed), God (*Theos*), Son (*Yios*), Saviour (*Soter*). Christ and the apostles were also referred to as 'fishers of men', and the miracles of the loaves and the fishes was another popular theme. The 2nd-century Christian philosopher Clement of Alexandria talks attractively of Christ as 'the fisher of men, of those saved from the sea of evil, luring with sweet life the chaste fish from the hostile tide'. Other motifs that are common in pagan art were chosen by Christians because of their symbolism in the new religion. The words of Jesus, 'I am the vine, you are the branches', in St John's gospel, is probably the reason why the image of grapes and vine leaves was so readily adapted into Christian iconography. A lamb today has strong Christian associations, but there is also a potent link to pagan imagery. Images of Jesus as the Good Shepherd, carrying a sheep on his shoulders (as illustrated in the sarcophagus above), are direct copies of pagan votive statuettes of a youth offering an animal as a sacrifice (*see picture on p. 59*). Other links have no biblical counterpart. Jesus can be seen dressed as Orpheus with his lyre or, in one mosaic from the Vatican cemetery, as the sun god rising to heaven in his chariot. Some images show Christ as a teacher surrounded by pupils as in a typical pagan school of philosophy. Old Testament scenes are also common, the favourite being Jonah thrown up after three days in the whale—taken as a prefiguration of the resurrection of Christ after three days. The story of Noah, as one rescued by God, is often shown in detail, as is the sacrifice of Isaac, another figure rescued at the moment of danger.

While most catacomb art is the work of the poor, it required some wealth to commission a sarcophagus. A few survive from the 3rd century. One, from late in the century, is to be found in the church of Santa Maria Antiqua in Rome (*see illustration opposite*).

The most interesting development in 4th- and 5th-century Christian art, beyond the sheer affluence of church building, is in the adoption of Christ within imperial iconography. Christian art is now public and takes more extravagant forms. The Christ shown as a shepherd in the Mausoleum of Galla Placidia in Ravenna is shown with a golden cross, gold tunic and purple mantle. By 390, in Santa Pudenziana in Rome (*also illustrated opposite*), Christ is shown 'in Majesty', transformed into a Roman magistrate with his apostles offering him an acclamation in a form very similar to that offered to Constantine on his Arch (AD 315) in central Rome. The fully-frontal Christ is, of course, to become an important symbol in Byzantine art, the Pantocrator who gazes down from a central dome, or from the apse in a Western basilica (*see illustration on p. 226*). In the Archiepiscopal Chapel in Ravenna, Christ is even shown as a warrior.

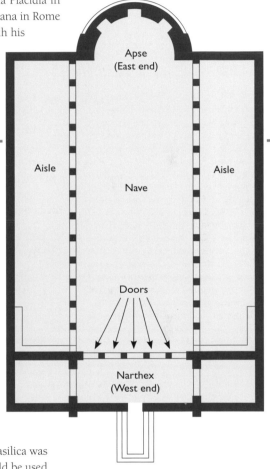

THE CHRISTIAN BASILICA

The basilica, the all-purpose meeting hall, was a common building in Roman cities. It could be used for social gatherings, trials and other legal business or as a display for officials or the emperor himself. New ones were still being built in the early 4th century. In Trier, Constantine had a basilica as his audience chamber (*see p. 202*). In Rome, Maxentius, claimant to the imperial throne, was in the process of constructing a vast basilica, 300 by 200 ft, on the edge of the Forum when Constantine defeated him in 312. It had an enormous central nave, with an apse at the western end and a grand entrance from the east. There were aisles on each side of the nave with coffered ceilings. It was designed as a place where the city prefect would conduct legal business, but it was always also intended as a statement of imperial power. After Constantine had completed the building he placed a colossal statue of himself in the apse, fragments of which have survived (*see illustration on p. 208*).

With such precedents behind him, Constantine saw the advantage of the basilica as the model for Christian churches. Authority, in the shape of the bishop, could preside in the apse. Typically he sat there on his throne with his clergy lined up round the wall on either side. A large congregation could be assembled and the grandeur of the building would show Constantine's own commitment to Christianity. The rectangular form of the basilica was retained. One advantage of a nave and aisles was that the higher parts of the nave walls could be used for windows, yet the aisles gave more space for the congregation. As with the imperial basilicas, the inside could be glorified by marble and mosaic, and the extent of these was breathtaking. The vault of the apse of Christ the Redeemer (later St John Lateran) was covered by 500 lb of gold, of sufficient value, it has been calculated, to feed 20,000 poor for a year. The candelabra and lamps consumed so much oil that specific estates were set aside to provide the income for them.

In Rome the first Christian basilicas, Christ the Redeemer, Santa Croce in Gerusalemme and St Peter's on the Vatican hill, were all built on the outskirts of the city. The Forum and the surrounding area was too rooted in pagan tradition for any church to be built there until much later. St Peter's was the first basilica in Rome to be related to a holy site, that of the burial place of Peter. Constantine's basilicas in Jerusalem and Bethlehem were in the same tradition. One of the largest 4th-century basilicas in Rome, that dedicated to Paul on the road out to Ostia, on the site where he is supposed to have been beheaded, confirms this important development.

The earliest basilicas had an entrance porch, the narthex, and then three or five separate entrance doors. The east–west axis was typical (the east faced the rising sun, the symbol of resurrection), but in cases where other buildings crowded the site, this alignment was not insisted on. As early as the first St Peter's, begun in 317–19, a colonnaded courtyard could be added to the narthex. St Peter's had another important innovation: transepts extended across the aisle at the point where the shrine of St Peter was believed to be. This gave more space for the clergy and for services held close to the tomb.

Ravenna: outpost of Byzantium

Site of the finest mosaics in Western Christendom, made in the 5th and 6th centuries

Ravenna, on the east coast of Italy, became the seat of the Roman emperors in the last troubled years of the Western empire. After the abdication of the last emperor, Romulus Augustulus, in 476, the Ostrogoth Theodoric also made it his capital. It remained under Ostrogoth rule until it was captured by the Byzantine empire in 540.

The church of Sant'Apollinare Nuovo was built by Theodoric as his palace chapel (Theodoric's original dedication was to Christ the Redeemer; St Apollinaris was the first bishop of Ravenna). Theodoric, like all the Goths, was an Arian Christian; in other words he believed that Christ was a later creation of God the Father and subordinate to him, a view which the emperor Theodosius had declared heretical in the 380s.

Because of this belief of the subordination of the Son to the Father, Arian art tends to emphasise the humanity of Jesus. In the magnificent set of mosaics Theodoric commissioned for Sant'Apollinare Nuovo, of the life and miracles of Christ (the first known example of such a sequence), Christ is shown as changing over time (he grows a beard as he grows older, for instance). The later mosaics in the church, which were added after the Byzantine conquest, present him, in contrast, as unchanging, placing the emphasis on the constancy of his divinity. The Byzantine mosaics concentrate on more formal images of Christ, the Virgin and Child and show saints and martyrs in procession

Ravenna is often described as a showcase of Byzantine art, partly because so much art of the same period in Constantinople was destroyed by the iconoclasts of the 8th century. While Western art begins to dwell on the suffering of Christ for mankind, in Byzantine art God the Father is portrayed as a protective figure gazing down on his people while the emperor is regarded as his agent on earth. The use of light on mosaics, the chanting and the incense make the Byzantine liturgical experience altogether other-worldly.

Right: Excavations at Dura-Europus on the Euphrates have uncovered both a Jewish synagogue and the earliest known Christian church. The baptistery of this church is decorated and the healing of the paralysed man is shown as a miracle.

Facing page: The dome mosaics of the two Ravenna baptisteries. While in the Catholic baptistery (bottom) St John pours water from a dish over Christ, in the Arian baptistery he anoints his head directly. Christ is much younger than in the Catholic mosaic and this may be a deliberate attempt to emphasise that he is subordinate to the Father, the core tenet of Arian belief (see box right).

ARIANS & MONOPHYSITES

The theological controversies of the 4th and 5th centuries centred on the relationship of Jesus the Son with God the Father and the way in which Jesus' divine nature fitted with his human one. The first issue was settled by the emperor Theodosius in 381 when he decreed that Father and Son were of equal majesty and convoked a council of like-minded bishops to endorse his ruling (see p. 209). However, the Gothic and other Christian barbarian tribes outside the empire were not subject to these laws and continued with their beliefs that Jesus was subordinate to the Father. This belief (or heresy) was known as Arianism after an Alexandrian priest, Arius, who had preached similar views in the early 4th century.

After intense and often violent theological debate in the 5th century, the declaration of a Church council held at Chalcedon in 451 ruled that Jesus had two natures, one human, one divine, which did not mingle with each other. This was, and still is, accepted by the Western church. However, in Egypt and other parts of the Greek-speaking Christian world, Chalcedon's conclusions were not accepted. These Christians argued that Christ had a single, divine nature to which his humanity was subordinate. They were called the Monophysites and Monophysitism is still the mainstream belief of Coptic Christians in Egypt to this day.

BAPTISM AND BAPTISTERIES

The ritual of baptism was central to early Christianity, the model being, of course, the baptism of Jesus by St John the Baptist. Only a bishop had the right to carry out the sacrament, and the importance attached to the rite is shown by the fact that it took place in a separate building, the baptistery. The earliest known is a converted room next to the church at Dura-Europus (c. 240) where there is a basin in the corner of a room decorated with frescoes. One shows the two Marys approaching the tomb of Jesus, another Jesus and Peter walking on water. There is also a Healing of the Paralytic (*illustrated opposite*).

When Constantine brought toleration, baptisteries could become more public. They needed to be; there was a rush of converts, and each Easter (when baptisms typically took place) there would have been enormous crowds. The shape of the baptistery was derived from circular mausolea, but early baptisteries are often also octagonal or hexagonal. A catechumen (candidate for baptism) would enter by one door, be immersed in the central pool, and then leave on the opposite side.

Two of the finest early baptisteries come from Ravenna and both are admired for their mosaics. The first, the Catholic or Neonian baptistery (named after Neon, an early bishop), was built at the beginning of the 5th century. It is octagonal in design and was converted from an earlier bath house. The font was a pool, 11 ft in diameter and three feet deep. Its mosaics, from later in the century, are stunning. In the centre of the dome above the font (*illustrated below*), John the Baptist is seen baptising Christ who stands in the River Jordan. The river is personified by an elderly man. Encircling this is a magnificent parade of apostles against an indigo background, each sumptuously dressed and holding a jewelled crown. There is yet another ring of mosaics below. These show altars with the gospels open on them alternating with empty thrones. Between these are garden scenes, symbolising paradise, with panels of empty seats awaiting for those admitted to heaven.

By the 490s the Western empire had fallen and Ravenna was occupied by the Ostrogoth king Theodoric, who, though he co-existed easily with his Catholic co-religionists, was determined to create a set of churches for Arians like himself. So he put in hand his own baptistery, close to the Church of the Holy Spirit. It too is octagonal and its central mosaic (*illustrated above*) also shows Christ being baptised. The personification of the river (on the left) is more prominent, and borrows from pagan representations of river gods. In the outer circle, the apostles are shown, here in white robes. Again they have their jewelled crowns although Peter is shown with his keys and Paul with a scroll. They approach a bejewelled throne on which is a wonderful cushion, surmounted by a cross, also encrusted in jewels. Here Christ has been translated into a symbol of treasure.

THE RAVENNA BASILICAS

The basilicas in Ravenna follow the classic model (*see p. 217*), whether they were built by the Arian Theodoric (Sant'Apollinare Nuovo, 490s) or by the Byzantines (Sant'Apollinare in Classe, 6th century). Sant'Apollinare Nuovo has an extraordinary sequence of mosaics including 26 panels showing the miracles and passion of Christ (*example pictured below*). Beneath these are windows with male figures facing frontally between them and then another superb set of processions of saints and martyrs. These end alongside a mosaic of the palace of Theodoric on one side and the town of Classis, the port of Ravenna, on the other. Despite some reordering and replacements of the sequence in the 6th century (mainly to remove any hint of Theodoric and his Arian views), these remain essentially a work of the late 5th century.

The later Sant'Apollinare in Classe is known for its apse mosaic (*illustrated opposite*), the harmonious whole showing how sophisticated the use of symbols and their relationship to a Christian context had now become in Christian art.

After Ravenna, basilicas begin to disappear in the West. They were designed for cities with large populations and immense resources, but Rome's population, for instance, may have dropped to only 60,000. Churches became much smaller while resources were also directed towards abbeys, with the spread of monasticism (*for more on monasticism, see Sinai, p. 227*).

Below: The miracle of the loaves and fishes, from the late 5th-century Arian mosaic cycle in Sant'Apollinare Nuovo. Christ is depicted in Roman purple, but there is an attempt at naturalism in the scene: the figures appear as real people, not as hieratic and numinous manifestations of the godhead.

Facing page: The apse of Sant'Apollinare in Classe, at the port of Ravenna. Here the humanity of the Arian Christ (as seen in the mosaic illustrated right) has been replaced by more symbolic representations. In the apse mosaic (c. 550) the hand of God is shown hovering above a jewelled cross which has a tiny depiction of Christ at its centre. Christ is flanked by Moses and Elijah, so this may be a representation of the Transfiguration, with the three lambs looking up from below symbolising the apostles Peter, James and John, who witnessed the event. The central figure of St Apollinaris is set within a luxuriant landscape and is surrounded by twelve lambs, symbols of his flock. We are a long way from the graphic and detailed miracle stories of Christ in Sant'Apollinare Nuovo and these two churches make the contrast in approach very clear. In the spaces between the windows, four bishops of Ravenna are shown in their vestments. In the 9th century the triumphal arch above the domed apse was also covered in mosaics. There is a central figure of Christ with symbols of the Evangelists on either side: the Eagle (John), a Man (Matthew), the Lion (Mark) and the Bull (Luke). Immediately below this are representations of Jerusalem and Bethlehem. Six lambs process out of each city gate towards the central Christ.

CHRISTIANITY AS A MYSTERY RELIGION

Christianity was not the first 'mystery' religion centred on truths that are inexplicable. There were many, some promising a kind of redemption and renewal (Mithraism; *see p. 155*), some offering hope of an afterlife (the cult of Demeter; *see p. 101*), others requiring a kind of initiation or 'birth' into new life (the worship of Isis; *see p. 178*), still others requiring initiates to give themselves up entirely to the god (the cult of Dionysus; *see p. 178*). Of all these cults, it was Christianity that triumphed; by the 4th century AD it was the only mystery religion that was officially allowed.

The Christians adopted their rite of baptism from Jewish purification ceremonies, but it too became a ceremony of initiation. Catechumens, those seeking conversion, might have to undergo instruction for as much as three years before they were considered ready. Then there was the ceremony itself, normally tied to Easter and thus to the process of rebirth. Baptism was followed by admission to the Eucharist, a ritual meal in its own right with the consumption of bread and wine in memory of the Last Supper. Some accounts suggest that Christians believed that the symbolic consumption of the body and blood of Christ gave them a transformed body. The secrecy of Christian worship added to the mystery. One opponent, writing about AD 200, described Christians as 'a crowd that lurks in hiding places, shunning the light; they are speechless in public but gabble away in corners'. There were even rumours of cannibalism and free love.

Constantinople

Capital of the Byzantine empire, declared such by Constantine in AD 330

The ancient city of Byzantium was founded as a Greek colony in the 7th century BC. It was an excellent site, overlooking the Bosphorus, the only entry to the grain-rich shores of the Black Sea, while being defensible on its promontory on the 'European' side of the straits. Once incorporated into the Roman Empire, it became a lynchpin for the East. The Via Egnatia came in across Greece, the sea crossing was short, and then roads led eastwards into Asia. When the borders of the realm stabilised along the Danube and the Euphrates, it became an obvious base for the defence of the Eastern empire.

When Septimius Severus launched his bid for the empire in 193, he knew he had to control Byzantium and he besieged the city for two years (193–95) before it fell. There was much destruction, but Septimius put in hand a reconstruction of the city on the eastern tip of the promontory just at the same time as he was restoring his native city of Leptis Magna (*see p. 189*).

Some 140 years later, in 324, Constantine chose Byzantium as his new eastern capital and named it Constantinople after himself. The security of the site must have been its main attraction, although it has also been argued that Constantine wished to emphasise his independence from the Church by choosing a site that had no Christian heritage. Certainly it was not a Christian city at first. Constantine treated it as his own creation, and though he preserved the lines of Septimius' city, he expanded westwards by constructing a new set of walls and adding his own forum. The extension increased the area of Septimius' city fourfold. Constantine traced the outline according to traditional Greek foundation rituals and then commissioned a conventionally Roman set of buildings. He enlarged the hippodrome, modelling it on the Circus Maximus in Rome, and built an imperial palace and a large set of baths, the Zeuxippus. A senate house was built and a new square, the Augusteum, was placed close to the Milion (*see box overleaf*), which became the official starting place for roads from the city. He imported a vast array of pagan statuary. His Christian biographer, Eusebius, was deeply shocked by this and argued that the statues had been set up so that they could be mocked. In fact, it is known that the population revered and respected them and for centuries they remained intact along the main ceremonial route of the city, the Mese.

When Constantine built a church for the small Christian community, he gave it a neutral name, Haghia Eirene, Holy Peace. When he began another larger church alongside it, it was dedicated to Haghia Sophia, Holy Wisdom. Constantine acknowledged that this was still a largely pagan city and the use of an overtly Christian dedication might provoke a hostile reaction. Before his death in 337, however, the Church of the Holy Apostles was completed, and became his mausoleum.

Whether he intended Constantinople to become a mainly Christian city or not, Constantine knew that it had to be planned as a large capital. There was a quarter set aside for mansions for its administrators, and a new harbour was built along the southern edge of the promontory, for the grain ships from Egypt to dock twice a year. In the 5th century, vast underground cisterns were built to store water that flowed in through aqueducts. The city grew rapidly. One estimate is that the population had reached 90,000 by Constantine's death. No wonder that one 4th-century orator complained that the sweat of the cities of the East was being transferred into the fat of the 'second Rome'.

HAGHIA SOPHIA

The first Haghia Sophia was completed in 360 in a city that by then was rapidly becoming Christianised (a visitor in 381 noted how even the bath attendants discussed theology). In 532, the church burned down in a riot and the emperor Justinian decided to rebuild it in an even grander form. The final result was the last great building of antiquity. The new Haghia Sophia, rededicated in 562, was the largest single-roofed building of the Roman empire, not to be equalled in the Christian West until the construction of Seville and Cologne cathedrals in the 13th century.

By now most new churches were reusing the columns and marbles of disused pagan buildings. In Haghia Sophia almost everything was new. Justinian clearly expected his architects, Anthemius of Tralles and Isidore of Miletus, to come up with something special, although it is disputed whether their inspiration came from Rome (the Pantheon and the Basilica of Maxentius) or Persia. The most important innovation

Facing page: The dome of Haghia Sophia has aroused the amazement of all those who have seen it, from the 6th century onwards. The mosaics of this great church were illuminated by thousands of candles so that this dome glowed in the night and acted as a beacon for returning sailors. Although it was converted into a mosque by the Ottomans, in the pendentives which support the dome can be seen traces of the original Christian decoration, in the form of a six-winged seraph.

Above: The great dome of Haghia Sophia soars above a vast open space, 180 ft high in total. The need to roof this space ushered in a method of basing a dome that became common in Byzantine architecture. The dome rests on pendentives, which convert the circular space above to the angled space below (*see diagram on p. 161*), transmitting the weight of the dome to the supporting corner piers. The example pictured here is from another church in Constantinople, the Pammakaristos (Church of the Joyous Mother of God), now the Fethiye mosque.

Above right: Christ flanked by the Virgin and St John the Baptist. One of the surviving Christian mosaics from Haghia Sophia.

was the dome, 100 ft across, balanced on four arches, each 120 ft high. There were half-domes added on the eastern and western sides, with a further smaller half-dome forming the apse. Through the western arch was a vast entrance which led out onto a cloister. The northern and southern arches incorporated columned arches at two levels. Surviving until the conquest of Constantinople by the Ottoman Turks in 1453 and then converted into a mosque, it continues to astound.

Two famous contemporary descriptions survive, one by the historian Procopius and one by a court official during the reign of Justinian, Paul the Silentiary. Both comment on the quality of its lighting: 'The church is singularly full of light and sunshine; you would declare that the place is not lighted by the sun from without, but that the rays are produced within itself, such an abundance of light is poured into this church.... A spherical-shaped dome standing upon this circle makes it exceedingly beautiful; from the lightness of the building, it does not appear to rest upon a solid foundation, but to cover the place beneath as though it were suspended from heaven by the fabled golden chain.' (from Procopius, *De Aedificiis*, Tr. W. Lethaby and H. Swainson). Paul the Silentiary describes the lighting of the dome as being so intense that sailors out at sea would see it glowing in the night.

THE MILION ARCH

At the end of the Via Egnatia, the Roman road which leads into Constantinople, the emperor Septimius Severus built a triumphal arch, the Milion. One 8th-century description tells of how it was surmounted by 'a chariot of Zeus Helios [Zeus as the sun god] with four fiery horses driven headlong beside two statues'. Recent dating techniques of the famous four horses of St Mark's, Venice (*illustrated here*), looted from Constantinople by the Venetians during the Fourth Crusade of 1204, have resolved the question of their dating. The horses are not bronze, as is commonly assumed, but gilded copper. It is now understood that the method of gilding, which involved mixing gold and mercury in a paste and heating off the mercury, blemished bronze, which is why any statue that required gilding had to be cast in copper. This gilding technique appears only in the 2nd century AD, ruling out an earlier date for the horses. It is therefore possible that the horses of St Mark's were a commission of Septimius Severus and are the very group described as still being

on the Milion in the 8th century (their elongated legs confirm that they were designed to be seen from below). The two statues would then have been Septimius' sons Caracalla and Geta, in line with the iconography of the imperial family found at Leptis (*see p. 191*). This attribution must be taken with caution but may, after many centuries of speculation, be the closest we can get to the origin of one of the finest works of art surviving from antiquity.

MARTYRIA AND MAUSOLEA

The Church of the Holy Apostles in Constantinople was designed in the conventional circular form of the mausoleum: symbolic 'tombs' of the Twelve Apostles were grouped around a central space, where Constantine, the thirteenth apostle as he saw himself, was buried.

The circular mausoleum was pagan in origin. Two fine examples remain in Rome, the mausoleum of Augustus and that of Hadrian, and there is Diocletian's in Split. So there was nothing unusual about an emperor—or indeed anyone who deserved special honour—being buried in this way. An important difference was that traditionally Romans had been cremated whereas Christians were buried. This had been the Jewish custom, as is seen in the burial of Christ after the Crucifixion. It was a Christian belief that the body would be raised after death. Martyrs were believed to have become transformed through their martyrdom—often it was said that a martyr's body could be recognised by its failure to decay, and with the rising tide of belief in relics, there was every incentive to preserve a body or what remained of it.

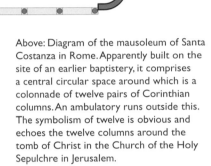

The Church of the Holy Apostles no longer exists; over its foundations rises the great Fatih Çamii, resting place of Sultan Mehmet, conqueror of Constantinople in 1453. There is an excellent example of an imperial Christian mausoleum in Rome, however, Santa Costanza (*diagram right*), designed in the 350s by Constantine's daughters Constantia and Helena as their burial place (a copy of Constantia's porphyry sarcophagus still remains *in situ*; the original has been moved to the Vatican; *see picture on p. 215*).

The largest of the centrally-planned churches in Rome is that dedicated to St Stephen, whose martyrdom is recorded in the Acts of the Apostles. As the great age of relics got under way in the 4th and 5th centuries, St Stephen's body was 'discovered' (near Jerusalem in 415). There was a major translation of his bones into Constantinople in 428; St Augustine had access to others; while others still may have arrived in Rome (though the evidence is disputed). Santo Stefano Rotondo was built to honour the saint by pope Simplicius (468–83). The building had three consecutive rings. The central one is a colonnade, then there is a further colonnaded circle, still extant, giving the building a diameter of 130 ft. There was yet another circle, now demolished, extending the whole to a diameter of over 200 ft. Double- or triple-shelled churches with their focus on the martyr or imperial tomb were elegant ways of creating a space in which, unlike a basilica, all could participate equally in the worship of the one honoured.

Above: Diagram of the mausoleum of Santa Costanza in Rome. Apparently built on the site of an earlier baptistery, it comprises a central circular space around which is a colonnade of twelve pairs of Corinthian columns. An ambulatory runs outside this. The symbolism of twelve is obvious and echoes the twelve columns around the tomb of Christ in the Church of the Holy Sepulchre in Jerusalem.

Left: The church of Santo Stefano Rotondo in Rome, dedicated to Stephen, the first Christian martyr, is one of the oldest circular churches. The closest model is the circular core of the Church of the Holy Sepulchre in Jerusalem and this is an understandable inspiration for a saint who died in the city but is commemorated elsewhere. The photograph here clearly shows how the church was structured and where worshippers would have processed around the centrally-placed tomb.

The mosaics over the ambulatory in Santa Costanza surprise because they are of bucolic scenes: the gathering of the harvest, the trampling of grapes, with a mass of bird and animal life (*illustrated above*). If they had not been in this setting they would be considered pagan, but vines of course are a potent Christian symbol and in a Christian context they can be read to show the rebirth of God's creation. In apses off the ambulatory there are two remarkable mosaics of Christ. One shows him as the lawgiver, handing out a scroll of the Law to Peter, with Paul in attendance on Christ's right hand. The bringing together of Peter and Paul, whose row over eating with the Gentiles is recorded in Acts, is an important feature of 4th-century iconography and they are increasingly shown in harmonious poses (and given the same feast day, 29th June). The other mosaic (*pictured left*) is the earliest representation of Christ as Pantocrator, 'ruler of the world'. He sits on a globe and presents the keys to Peter.

PLAN OF SAN VITALE

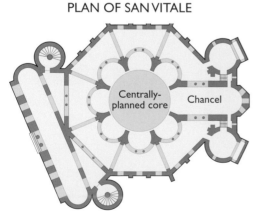

By far the most sophisticated of these centrally-planned buildings was San Vitale in Ravenna (c. 530–47). It was built by a wealthy banker, Julianus Argentarius, but its famous mosaics of Justinian and his empress Theodora are so prominent he may have been the front man for an act of imperial propaganda to celebrate the retaking of Ravenna from the Goths in 540. San Vitale is an octagonal building with each angle of the central core marked by a tall pillar joined to its fellow by an arch. Through seven of the arches is an exedra (a recessed space). The eighth arch breaks up the symmetry in that it leads into a chancel. Although the church was apparently designed as a martyrium for San Vitale, its chancel transformed it into something else and soon after its completion it was actually referred to as a basilica. The martyrium and the basilica were becoming confused, as Eastern and Western architecture moved in different directions. While the centralised domed building became the dominant form of church architecture in the Byzantine empire—witness Haghia Sophia under construction at the same time as San Vitale—in the West the martyrs' bones tended to be moved under the high altar, leaving the nave free for the congregation.

St Catherine's Monastery, Sinai

'On this Mt Sina live monks whose life is a kind of careful rehearsal of death, and they enjoy without fear the solitude which is very precious to them. Since these monks have nothing to crave—for they are superior to all human desires and have no interest in possessing anything or in caring for their bodies, nor do they seek pleasure in any other thing whatever—the Emperor Justinian built them a church which they have dedicated to the Mother of God, so that they might be enabled to pass their lives therein praying and holding services.'

Procopius, *De Aedificiis* (Tr. H.B. Dewing)

The oldest continuously inhabited monastery in the world. Founded in the 4th century

The 4th-century bishop of Alexandria, Athanasius, wrote a popular life of St Anthony, a hermit who lived in the Egyptian desert. According to Athanasius, Anthony was beset by the devil in all kinds of disguises, and the story became a popular subject in Christian art. Here the saint is shown surrounded by demons and naked ladies in an early 16th-century painting by the Netherlandish artist Herri met de Bles.

The word monastery is derived from the Greek *monos*, which means single or alone. In the Christian world monasticism began in the 4th century AD, when there was a rise in asceticism, possibly as a direct reaction to the new wealth of the Church. The idea that the mind could conquer the body, which was swayed by sensual desire and greed, went back to Plato in the 4th century BC, so ascetic living was not hitherto unknown as a disciplined response to materialism. Yet Christian asceticism took more extreme forms. Many early ascetics talked of the need to remind themselves that Christ had suffered and that he required the suffering of others in his memory. This meant that they had to withdraw from normal life, and here the desert provided a setting in which the heat and drought reached extremes. The most prestigious destination for the ascetic was the Egyptian desert. The contrast with the lush valley of the Nile was obvious, and from time immemorial the Egyptians had believed that demons haunted the sandy wastes. Some ascetics talked of going out to the desert to battle with the devil and famous ascetic lives, such as that of the hermit Anthony by bishop Athanasius of Alexandria, described the hero as being thrown to the ground by a crowd of evil monsters or lured by images of naked women.

While there were always those who preferred to live alone, the drawbacks soon became obvious. Perceptive ascetics realised that living on one's own seldom brought spiritual peace. It was almost as if the silence of the desert opened the way to morbid obsessions. Was it possible to combine asceticism with communal living and support? It seems that some ascetics had already begun to do this by the 320s, when an ex-army officer, Pachomius, inspired and led the first disciplined communities. They were immensely popular and by the time of Pachomius' death in 348 there may have been as many as 7,000 monks and nuns in the Egyptian desert. Much must have depended on Pachomius' personality but gradually 'Rules' began to evolve which laid down guidelines for communal living.

ST CATHERINE'S

The oldest continuously inhabited monastery, still active today, is St Catherine's in the Sinai desert. Mount Sinai always had a resonance for Christian (and, of course, for Jewish) pilgrims as the site of the Burning Bush and the place where Moses received the Ten Commandments from the hand of God. St Catherine's was reached in 383 by a determined Spanish Christian, Egeria, whose diary ticks off a sequence of holy sites. She records that there was already a church here, allegedly founded by St Helen, and that the Burning Bush was preserved in a garden.

It was the emperor Justinian who created a more formal structure for the community. He provided a new church, in which an inscription records its construction in memory of his empress, Theodora (d. 548), and its dedication to the Virgin Mary. It was later believed that the remains of St Catherine of Alexandria had been translated to the monastery, and she became the patron saint of the community after her bones were miraculously found in c. 800. The Burning Bush was preserved within the new structure and the whole enclosed within a fortified wall, marked by crosses. This was an isolated and dangerous area; the early monks were frequently harassed by local nomadic tribes, and the bringing of artists, stonecutters and mosaicists as well as all the material they needed to the site was a major undertaking.

St Catherine's monastery, Sinai, a remote oasis huddled within its protective walls, with its garden at the back. The land around it is a desolate waste. The tenacity of those who have lived here, without interruption, for 17 centuries, is extraordinary.

Icon from Sinai illustrating the *Heavenly Ladder*, a popular spiritual work by St John Climakos, which describes the road to salvation up a ladder with 30 rungs, inhabited severally by vices and virtues. Here the saint himself (robed in white) is seen leading a band up the ladder to heaven, where Christ waits to greet them.

Despite this, there was considerable intellectual vitality at Mount Sinai. *The Heavenly Ladder*, by one of the 6th-century abbots, St John Climakos, was a highly influential spiritual work The themes of the mosaics inside the church are also varied and imaginative. The topmost mosaics over the apse in the new church, *Moses at the Burning Bush* and *Moses Receiving the Tablets of the Law*, relate to the events which inspired the founding of the community. Below these is an arch which is interesting as an early portrayal of Mary and John the Baptist as mediators between the human world and the divine, here represented as the Lamb of God. The central mosaic within the apse shows Christ transformed by the Transfiguration. Moses and Elijah,

the two prophets who visited Mt Sinai, are on either side of him and the three apostles Peter, John and James are amazed at the sight. Below these are medallions of the apostles, many of the Old Testament prophets, and two monks who associated themselves with the work. Here the Old and New Testaments are brought together in a dazzling array of colour that must have provided a startling contrast to the austerity of the monks' daily life. A common theme in the spiritual literature of the period is that the vast expense of these decorations was justifiable because the decorations provided a glimpse of what heaven would be like.

Monasticism spread to the West in the 5th century. A key figure was Cassian (c. 360–435), who had experienced monastic life in Bethlehem and Egypt but came to the West when he was sent from Constantinople to plead a cause with the pope. In 415 he founded a complex of monasteries for both men and women at Marseilles. He wrote widely on the issues of monastic life and his writings became part of every monastic library. One of those influenced by him was Benedict of Nursia (480–547), whose own Rule incorporated Cassian's sensible precepts of community living which preserved frugal habits within a framework of moderation.

Right: Haghia Eirene, the first church begun in Constantinople by Constantine, preserves one of the most famous examples of iconoclastic decoration, dating from the period in the 8th century when all human representations of divine subjects were condemned. A cross, rather than a figure of Christ, is in the apse now.

Above: 6th-century icon from Mt Sinai which survived the destructions of the iconoclastic period. It shows the Virgin enthroned, an example of the elevation of Mary in Christian art after the Council of Ephesus of 431 declared her to be the mother of God.

TEXTS & ICONS AT ST CATHERINE'S

The isolation of St Catherine's had an important effect on the style and quality of its icons. Today the monastery is increasingly recognised as one of the most important centres of icon painting. There are many precious examples still remaining here, some from as early as the 5th century. The reason for their survival is because the monastery avoided the iconoclasm of the 8th century, which swept through Constantinople and other major cities of the Byzantine empire causing wholesale destruction of earlier images. There is also an extraordinarily rich library of early texts at St Catherine's. They are a reminder that the languages of the early Church were not only Greek and Latin but included Coptic (Egyptian written in Greek script), Syriac and Armenian. The *Codex Sinaiticus*, one of the earliest complete, hand-written Bibles, including the first complete New Testament, was composed about AD 350 and was originally part of this library but the largest section was moved (fraudulently according to St Catherine's) to Russia in the 19th century and was bought by the British Museum (now the British Library) in 1933.

Bibliography

EGYPT

Kathryn Bard, *An Introduction to the Archaeology of Ancient Egypt*, Blackwell Publishing, 2007.

Mark Collier and Bill Manley, *How to Read Egyptian Hieroglyphics*, British Museum Press 1998.

Gay Robins, *The Art of Ancient Egypt*, Harvard University Press, 2008.

John Romer, *The Great Pyramid: Ancient Egypt Revisited*, Cambridge University Press, 2007.

Ian Shaw, *The Oxford History of Ancient Egypt*, Oxford University Press, 2003. Scholarly and thorough introduction.

Ian Shaw and Paul Nicholson, *The British Museum Dictionary of Ancient Egypt*, British Museum Press, London (Harry N. Abrams, USA), 1995.

Eugen Strouhal, *Life in Ancient Egypt*, Cambridge University Press, 1992.

The Thames & Hudson series 'The Complete Book of …' is especially helpful for Egypt. They are published in both the US and UK. The relevant titles are:

Mark Lehner, *The Complete Pyramids*, 2008.

Nicholas Reeves, *The Complete Tutankhamun*, 2007.

Nicholas Reeves and Richard Wilkinson, *The Complete Valley of the Kings*, 2000.

Richard Wilkinson, *The Complete Temples of Ancient Egypt*, 2000.

Richard Wilkinson, *The Complete Gods and Goddesses of Ancient Egypt*, 2003.

Joyce Tyldesley offers excellent introductions:
Daughters of Isis, Women of Ancient Egypt, 1995.
Hatchsepsut: The Female Pharaoh, 1996.
Tales from Ancient Egypt, 2004.
And on the rediscovery of ancient Egypt, *Egypt: How a Lost Civilization was Rediscovered*, BBC Books, 1996.

On the legacy of ancient Egypt, Charles Freeman, *The Legacy of Ancient Egypt*, Checkmark Books, 1997.

On Ptolemaic and Roman Egypt, Alan Bowman, *Egypt after the Pharaohs, 332 BC–AD 642*, British Museum Books, 1986.

Peter Parsons, *City of the Sharp-Nosed Fish*, Weidenfeld & Nicolson, 2007, tells the story of the Oxyrhynchus papyri.

GREECE

General

Charles Freeman, *The Greek Achievement*, Penguin, 1999. Attempts an overview of the whole course of Greek history from the Mycenaeans through to the Roman period.

Charlotte Higgins, *It's All Greek to Me*, Short Books, 2008. Lively introduction to why the Greeks matter.

Christopher Mee and Antony Spawforth, *Greece*, Oxford Archaeological Guides, Oxford University Press, 2001. Good surveys, background history and plans of the sites of the Greek mainland.

Antony Spawforth, *The Complete Greek Temples*, Thames & Hudson, 2006. Includes all the Sicilian temples.

Minoans and Mycenaeans

J. Alexander MacGillivray, *Minotaur, Sir Arthur Evans and the Archaeology of the Minoan Myth*, Pimlico, 2000.

J. Lesley Fitton, *Minoans*, British Museum Press, 2002.

Donald Preziosi and Louise Hitchcock, *Aegean Art and Architecture*, Oxford History of Art, Oxford University Press, 1999.

Louise Schofield, *The Mycenaeans*, British Museum Press, 2007.

Mary Renault is still very appealing—wonderful to read in Greece itself on an island with the sun setting on the sea. Try, for instance, *The Bull from the Sea*.

Greece 800–300 BC

The *Iliad* and the *Odyssey* remain gripping reads—perhaps even better to listen to. The translations by Robert Fagles are especially good.

Herodotus, *The Histories* (of the Persian Wars) makes absorbing reading. Thucydides, on the later Peloponnesian War, is a more austere account by a master of narrative. More recent accounts of the wars include Tom Holland, *Persian Fire*, Little, Brown, 2005 and Donald Kagan, *The Peloponnesian War*, HarperCollins (Viking, USA), 2003, slimmed down from his classic four-volume history.

Mary Beard, *The Parthenon*, Wonders of the World Series, Profile Books, 2002. Exuberant Classicist tackles the finest building of the period.

John Camp provides by far the best accounts in *The Athenian Agora*. His accounts are updated as new material emerges, so look out for the latest edition.

Paul Cartledge has written widely on the Spartans, see also his *Thermopylae*, Macmillan, London (Overlook, USA) 2006.

James Davidson, *Courtesans and Fishcakes, The Consuming Passions of Classical Athens*, HarperCollins, 1997. Well-written insight into life in Classical Athens.

Jeffrey Hurwit, *The Athenian Acropolis*, Cambridge University Press, 2000, is the most thorough study of the site.

Donald Kagan, *Pericles of Athens and the Birth of Democracy*, Touchstone, 1991, an excellent and thoughtful book the nature of democracy as much as on Pericles alone.

Robin Osborne, *Archaic and Classical Greek Art*, Oxford History of

Art, 1998 (compare the older and more conventional Martin Robertson, *A Shorter History of Greek Art*, Cambridge, 1981).

Judith Swaddling, *The Ancient Olympic Games*, British Museum Press, 1980.

HELLENISTIC

Lucilla Burn, *Hellenistic Art*, British Museum, 2004.

Paul Cartledge, *Alexander the Great*, Macmillan, London (Overlook, USA), 2004. Short but clear introduction to the life of the great conqueror.

Peter Green, *Alexander to Actium: The Hellenistic Age*, Thames & Hudson, 1990. Vast, sprawling account but excellent on personalities and events.

R.R.R. Smith, *Hellenistic Sculpture*, Thames & Hudson, 1991. Good introduction by the excavator of Aphrodisias.

James Steele, *Hellenistic Architecture in Asia Minor*, Academy Editions, London (St Martin's Press, USA), 1992. Mainly a photographic survey of the major cities but gives an excellent picture of what is still standing.

F.W. Walbank, *The Hellenistic World*, HarperCollins, 1992. Perhaps rather dated but still a very useful introduction.

ROME

There is a wealth of books on the Roman empire and its many leaders. A good starting point is Christopher Kelly, *The Roman Empire: A Very Short Introduction*, Oxford University Press, 2006. Simon Baker, *Ancient Rome: The Rise and Fall of an Empire*, BBC Books, 2007, is a readable account which concentrates on six turning points in the history of the empire. Readers can follow it up with many of the fine biographies available, for instance Adrian Goldsworthy on Julius Caesar, Weidenfeld & Nicolson (Yale, USA), 2006; Anthony Everitt, *The First Emperor, Caesar Augustus and the Triumph of Rome*, John Murray, 2007; or Anthony Birley, *Hadrian, the Restless Emperor*, Routledge, 1997 (the Routledge imperial biographies, of which this is one, are very reliable).

On the impact of the Roman empire on its subjects there is Janet Huskisson (Ed.), *Experiencing Rome: Culture, Identity and Power in the Roman Empire*, Routledge, 1999.

For translations of original sources on social history, see Jo-Ann Shelton, *As the Romans Did*, Oxford University Press, 1988.

Rome

Amanda Claridge, *Rome*, Oxford Archaeological Guides, Oxford University Press, 1998, and Filippo Coarelli, *Rome and Environs: An Archaeological Guide*, University of California Press, 2007, have the essential archaeological background. Coarelli includes Ostia and Hadrian's Villa. See also Mary Beard and Keith Hopkins, *The Colosseum*, Profile Books, 2005, as a lively introduction. For a witty alternative, Philip Matyszak, *Ancient Rome on Five Denarii a Day: A Guide to Sightseeing, Shopping and Survival in the City of the Caesars*, Thames & Hudson, 2007, is fun.

Roman Italy, general

T. Potter, *Roman Italy*, British Museum Press, 2007.

Hadrian's Villa

William MacDonald and John Pinto, *Hadrian's Villa and Its Legacy*, Yale University Press, 1995, has the full story from the building of the villa to its rediscovery and the dispersal of many of its treasures.

Pompeii

Mary Beard, *Pompeii, Life in a Roman Town*, Profile Books, 2008, gets below the surface of the ruins to show daily life. Joanne Berry, *The Complete Pompeii*, Thames & Hudson, 2007, has detailed background to the archaeological studies.

Africa

Susan Raven, *Rome in Africa*, 3rd edition, Routledge, 1993.

France

Henry Cleere, *Southern France: An Oxford Archaeological Guide*, Oxford University Press, 2005.

Petra

Jane Taylor, *Petra and the Lost Kingdom of the Nabataeans*, Harvard University Press, 2002.

Asia Minor

James Steele, *Hellenistic Architecture in Asia Minor*, Academy Editions, 1992, is also good for the 'Roman' cities of Asia Minor such as Ephesus.

Roman builders

Jean-Pierre Adam, *Roman Building: Materials and Techniques*, Routledge, 1999, is excellent on how the buildings were actually put up.

A. Trevor Hodge, *Roman Aqueducts and Water Supply*, 2nd edition, Duckworth, 2002.

Rabun Taylor, *Roman Builders*, Cambridge University Press, 2003.

John Ward-Perkins, *Roman Imperial Architecture*, Harmondsworth, 1981, is still very useful.

EARLY CHRISTIAN

General

Philip Esler (Ed.), *The Early Christian World*, two volumes, Routledge, 2000. Covers most themes in early Christian history.

Charles Freeman, *A New History of Early Christianity*, Yale University Press, 2009. One-volume survey of emerging Christianity up to AD 600.

Holy Land/Jerusalem

Karen Armstrong, *History of Jerusalem*, HarperCollins, 2005.

Jerome Murphy O'Connor, *The Holy Land*, Oxford Archaeological Guides, 4th edition, 1998.

Hershel Shanks, *Jerusalem: An Archaeological Biography*, Random House, 1995.

Art and Architecture

Robin Cormack, *Byzantine Art*, Oxford University Press, 2000. Includes St Catherine's Monastery.

Jaś Elsner, *Imperial Rome and Christian Triumph*, Oxford University Press, 1998. Good study of the transition from Roman to Christian art.

Robin Margaret Jensen, *Understanding Early Christian Art*, Routledge, 2000.

Richard Krautheimer, *Three Christian Capitals*, University of California Press, 1987. Deals with Rome, Milan and Constantinople.

Jeffrey Spier et al, *Picturing the Bible: the Earliest Christian Art*, Yale University Press, 2007. Well illustrated with good introductory essays.

Roger Stalley, *Early Medieval Architecture*, Oxford University Press, 1999, starts with the emergence of the Christian basilica and includes Ravenna.

GENERAL

Katherine Dunbabin, *Mosaics of the Greek and Roman World*, Cambridge University Press, 2001. The best introduction not only to what survives, but also to how mosaics were made.

Susan Alcock and Robin Osborne (Eds.), *Classical Archaeology*, Blackwell (Oxford and Malden, Massachusetts, USA), 2007. Scholarly but important for showing the main themes in this field.

Brian Fagan, *From Stonehenge to Samarkand: An Anthology of Archaeological Travel Writing*, Oxford University Press USA, 2006.

Glossary

Abaton Inner chamber at a healing sanctuary where the sick would sleep and hope to receive instructions about their cure in a dream

Agora Originally the market place of a Greek city. Many also became the site of ceremonial and administrative buildings

Ambulatory An area, often within a church where a procession can take place e.g. around the tomb of a martyr

Amphora (pl. amphorae) Large clay vessel for the storage or transportation of wine or oil

Antigonids Macedonian dynasty of the Hellenistic age, founded after the death of Alexander the Great by one of his generals, Antigonus

Apse Semicircular recessed end of a basilica (*see diagram on p. 217*), where a magistrate would officiate. In the Christian west, this became the site of the bishop's throne

Attalids Dynasty of the Hellenistic age in Asia Minor (*see p. 112*)

Attic Either pertaining to the land of Attica, the southeastern peninsula of mainland Greece, or denoting the topmost storey of a building

Augustus Title meaning 'revered' awarded to Octavian by the senate in 27 BC and by which he became known as the first Roman emperor. When the Roman empire was divided by Diocletian in the 3rd century (*see p. 196*), it became the title for the two senior co-emperors (*see also Caesar*)

Architrave Lowest horizontal part of an entablature, coming below the cornice and the frieze, and directly above a window or door aperture; effectively a lintel

Basilica Large rectangular meeting hall in ancient Rome, which became the prototype for early churches in the Christian west

Bouleuterion Council chamber of an ancient Greek or Hellenistic city

Caesar The cognomen of Gaius Julius, most famous of all the Roman political and military leaders. It became the term used during the 3rd century, when the Roman empire had four rulers (*see p. 196*), for the two junior co-emperors

Caldarium The 'hot room' in a Roman baths complex

Canopic jar Pottery container with a lid shaped like an animal or human head, in which the entrails of the dead were placed in ancient Egyptian burials

Cella The inner sanctum of an ancient Roman temple (*see also Naos*)

Centrally-planned Denoting a temple, church or other sacred building designed around a central point, so not planned with a linear orientation

Chancel In the Christian west, the part of a church beyond the nave, where the clergy officiate

Chryselephantine Made of gold and ivory

Client kingdom Under the Roman empire, a state that aligned itself with Rome, enjoyed Roman protection and lent Rome support in return, but which was self-governed

Codex Leaves of papyrus or parchment bound into a book form. It superseded the papyrus roll from the 3rd century AD onwards

Colonia A colony of Roman settlers, usually veterans, placed in a strategically important area within the empire. *Coloniae* were at the top of the hierarchy of Roman towns

Corinthian Classical order of architecture that arose in the 4th century BC (*see p. 159*)

Cyclopean walls Walls made of masonry blocks so large that it was believed they must have been constructed by giants (the Cyclopes)

Doric The earliest of the Classical orders of architecture, originating in Greece before the 6th century BC (*see p. 98*)

Exedra In a Classical building, a semicircular bay or recessed area, often, like an apse (*qv*) covered with a half-dome

Forum Originally the market place of a Greek city but many fora became the site of ceremonial and administrative buildings

Frigidarium The 'cold room' in a Roman baths complex

Hippodrome Circuit around which chariots race, the largest and most spectacular sports area of a Graeco-Roman city

Hittites Civilisation based on a capital at Hattusas in Anatolia which flourished between 1650 and 1200 BC. Adversaries of the Egyptian New Kingdom

Iconoclasm A movement that swept the Byzantine empire in the 8th century, destroying icons and other pictures on the grounds that it was sacrilegious to depict god and the saints in human form

Ionian Coming from Ionia, the shores of what is now western Turkey

Ionic Pertaining to the order of architecture that emerged in Asia Minor in the 6th century BC (*see p. 120*)

Ka In ancient Egypt, the spirit double or immortal life force

Lapiths Legendary people of Thessaly, Greece, known for a battle with the centaurs, a favourite theme of ancient temple sculpture

Maenad Female participant in the orgiastic rites of Dionysus

Magna Graecia Name for southern Italy and sometimes also Sicily, during the time of Greek colonisation from the 8th century BC until conquest by Rome

Martyrium (pl. martyria) Temple or shrine, typically centrally-planned (*qv*), built above the burial place of a saint or martyr

Mastaba Ancient Egyptian tomb consisting of a rectangular, flat-roofed building raised above a subterranean burial chamber

Mausoleum Memorial building usually over the actual burial place of a king or emperor. Derived from the tomb of Mausolus, a local ruler of the area around Halicarnassus in southern Turkey

Metope Panel carved with a decorative relief between triglyphs (*qv*) on the frieze of a Doric temple (*see p. 98*)

Mortuary temple Temple in which the body of a pharaoh would rest before being buried in the pyramid or tomb chamber being prepared for him. In the New Kingdom, a temple where the dead pharaoh's union with the presiding deity was celebrated

Municipium A town within the Roman empire which was given special privileges of trading and self-government, ranking below a *colonia* (*qv*)

Nabataeans A nomadic people who established a major settlement inside the rock formations at Petra (modern Jordan) during the 1st century BC

Naos The inner sanctum of an ancient Greek temple

Nymphaeum A monument which centres on the effective display or provision of water, usually in a central pool. Often embellished by statues of local heroes or water gods and nymphs

Parthians A people of the ancient Near East, from what is now northwest Iran. They came into frequent conflict with Rome during the later empire

Pantocrator Fully-frontal representation of Christ as the ruler of the world; the Almighty

Peloponnese The southernmost peninsula of mainland Greece

Peristyle Colonnade surrounding a courtyard or building. By extension, the colonnaded area itself

Pithos (pl. pithoi) Very large ancient Greek storage jar

Propylon (pl. propylaia) In ancient Greece, a monumental entranceway, flanked by pylons (*pyla*). The plural form was used when there was more than one entrance door

Province Administrative unit of the Roman empire. A region governed by a Roman official, not by a local chief (*cf Client kingdom*)

Prytaneion The building in a Greek city which housed the executive officials. At Olympia it was also used for the ceremonial banquet of victors

Ptolemaic Pertaining to the dynasty of the Ptolemies (*qv*)

Ptolemies Hellenistic dynasty founded by one of Alexander the Great's generals, Ptolemy. They became rulers of Egypt

Pylon Monumental entranceway to an ancient palace or temple, particularly in ancient Egypt

Quadriga Two-wheeled chariot drawn by four horses. A Roman emperor would ride in triumph (*qv*) in such a chariot after a victory

Sasanians A people of the ancient Near East, whose empire stretched over present-day Iran after defeat of the Parthians (*qv*) and threatened the borders of Rome

Seleucids Hellenistic dynasty founded after the death of Alexander the Great by one of his generals, Seleucus. He became ruler of Babylonia

Serapeum Shrine or temple to the god Serapis, a deity who emerged in Hellenistic Egypt as a fusion of Greek and Egyptian gods of fertility and the afterlife. His most famous temple was at Alexandria

Sidelock Braid of hair falling over one side of the head, worn until the onset of puberty by young boys in ancient Egypt. The rest of the head was shaven

Sistrum (pl. sistra) Ceremonial rattle particularly associated with the cult of the Egyptian goddess Hathor

Skene The stage buildings or backdrop of a Greek theatre, behind the performance area. In a Roman theatre, this is known as the scena

Stadium A running track used for local and Panhellenic games e.g. at Olympia. The more sophisticated examples, for example those at Delphi or Aphrodisias, were provided with stone seats

Stela (pl. stelae) Inscribed commemorative panel, often in the form of a free-standing slab

Stoa Covered, colonnaded, free-standing hall (often housing a row of shops) in an ancient Greek town

Tepidarium The 'warm room' in a Roman baths complex

Tholos A circular building, commonly found in shrines in the Greek world of the 4th century BC, as at Olympia and Epidaurus

Transepts In a Christian basilica or church, the 'arms' stretching left and right from the top of the nave

Triclinium In a Roman house, loosely a dining room; a room in a house or tomb with dining couches arranged around three of the walls

Triglyphs Small panel of a Doric frieze carved with three vertical channels (*see p. 98*)

Triumph Victory procession of a Roman emperor (*see p. 142*)

Uraeus Cobra deity, a protector of kings in ancient Egypt. A cobra often appears on royal headdresses

Window of Appearance Ceremonial window from which an Egyptian pharaoh and his family would traditionally dispense patronage and honours

Gods and goddesses of ancient Egypt

The ancient Egyptians had hundreds of gods. The list below features the most important, and those encountered in this book.

Amun: The principal god of Thebes and patron of the Theban rulers of the Middle and New Kingdoms. He is generally represented as a man with two plumes on his head and carrying the crook and the flail. His consort was Mut (*qv*). His sacred animals were the ram and goose.

Amun-Ra: A hybrid deity combining aspects of Amun (*qv*) and Ra, the solar deity of Heliopolis. He was the chief imperial deity of the New Kingdom, worshipped throughout Egypt. He is represented as a man wearing a double-plumed headdress with a sun disc.

Anubis: A god of the cemetery and a protector of the dead, he was said to have invented mummification and was the patron god of embalmers. He is represented as a jackal, or as a man with the head of a jackal; funerary priests are shown wearing jackal masks to enact the role of Anubis during funeral rites.

Apis: The sacred bull of Memphis, the Apis was regarded as the soul of the god Ptah. After death, Apis bulls were buried in the Serapeum at Saqqara.

Aten: An ancient solar deity elevated to sole state god under Akhenaten (*see p. 34*). Representing the universal creative energy of the sun, Aten was shown as a sun disc emanating rays terminating in hands, sometimes holding small ankh symbols, which convey blessings on the royal family.

Bes: An Asiatic domestic god, the protector of children and women in childbirth, he was also associated with music and dancing. He is shown head-on, as a dwarf with a lion's mane and ears.

Geb: The earth god, brother and consort of the sky goddess Nut and father of Isis, Osiris, Seth and Nephthys. He is always represented as a man, sometimes with green skin indicating his role as a god of vegetation; his symbol, a goose, is sometimes shown on his head.

Hapy: God of the Nile inundation. Shown as a hermaphrodite figure with a crest of papyrus on his head, and bearing produce such as fish, fruit and flowers. One of his principal cult centres was at Aswan, where he was believed to live in a cavern under the Nile Cataract.

Harpocrates: 'Horus-as-a-Child', son of Osiris and Isis. Represented as a naked child wearing the sidelock of youth and with a finger to his mouth, often seated in his mother's lap. On the magical stelae

known as 'Cippi of Horus', which protected children against poisonous creatures and dangerous animals, he is shown standing on crocodiles and grasping snakes and scorpions.

Hathor: An ancient fertility goddess represented as a cow or as a woman, sometimes with cow's ears or a horned sun-disc headdress. The consort of Horus and mother of Ihy, she was a goddess of love, sex and motherhood, identified by the Greeks with Aphrodite. Also associated with music, Hathor's symbol was the sistrum, a ritual rattle with an image of the goddess on the handle. Her principal cult centre was at Dendera. In her funerary aspect as Imentet ('Lady of the West') she welcomed the dead to the afterlife, and her image in this manifestation sometimes appears on the inner base of coffins and sarcophagi.

Horakhty: The solar aspect of Horus (*qv*), represented as a falcon-headed man with a sun disc on his head.

Horus: An ancient falcon god, associated with the king from Early Dynastic times and later identified as the son of Osiris and Isis. Horus was worshipped in various forms at several cult centres, including Edfu in Upper Egypt. Since Horus had succeeded Osiris as ruler of Egypt, every ruling king was regarded as a living incarnation of Horus.

Imhotep: The deified chief of works of King Djoser and architect of the Stepped Pyramid (*see p. 17*). Venerated as a sage, he was later identified with Asclepius and worshipped as a god of medicine. He is shown as a seated man with a papyrus scroll on his lap. His principal cult centre was at Saqqara, where he also became identified with the gods Thoth and Ptah.

Isis: The wife of Osiris and mother of Horus, Isis was one of the great mother goddesses of Egypt, the goddess of magic, one of the four protectors of the dead and a guardian of the Canopic jars. Normally shown as a woman with a throne on her head, in funerary contexts she is sometimes represented as a kite. She is also shown wearing a horned sun disc with plumes. Centres of her cult included Philae and Dendera, and her cult became popular throughout the Roman empire.

Khepri: A creator god depicted as a scarab beetle or a man with a scarab for a head, Khepri represented the rising sun, and was thus a god of renewal, rebirth and resurrection. The association between the scarab and the reborn sun seems to be connected with the scarab's practice of wrapping its eggs in a ball of dung to provide warmth, protection and food for its young. Observing the young emerging from the ball, the Egyptians imagined that the beetles were capable of spontaneous generation; furthermore, the spherical form of the ball suggested a connection with the sun. It is believed that most temples contained a colossal stone scarab representing the temple as the primeval mound from which the first god emerged.

Khnum: A creator god, represented as a man with a ram's head, thought to have created man on the potter's wheel. His cult centre was at Elephantine.

Khons: A moon god, one of the triad of Thebes. He is represented mummiform, either falcon-headed or as a youth with a sidelock, wearing a lunar disc and crescent on his head. There is a temple to Khons in the southwestern corner of the main complex at Karnak.

Ma'at: The goddess of truth, justice and divine order. Shown as a woman with an ostrich feather on her head, she most commonly appears in offering scenes and at the judgement of the dead.

Montu: The war god of Thebes, and guardian of the king in battle, represented as a falcon-headed man. There was a temple complex dedicated to Montu to the north of the main complex at Karnak.

Mut: A goddess of Thebes, the consort of Amun. She is normally represented as a woman with a vulture headdress surmounted by the White Crown or Double Crown. Her main cult centre was her temple to the south of the main complex at Karnak.

Nephthys: The sister of Isis, Osiris and Seth. One of the four protector goddesses of the dead, and a guardian of the Canopic jars. Her name means 'Lady of the House' and she is identified by these hieroglyphs, usually above her head; in a funerary context she is sometimes shown as a kite. She was often regarded as the wife of Seth, and sometimes as the mother of Anubis.

Nut: The sky goddess, wife of Geb and mother of Isis, Osiris, Seth and Nephthys. She is normally shown as a woman, sometimes with her body arched over the earth, her fingers and toes touching the cardinal points, and often with her body spangled with stars. The ceilings of some royal tombs in the Valley of the Kings are painted with scenes of Nut swallowing the sun as it sets and giving birth to it at dawn the next day. Nut also appears as a protector of the dead on the underside of coffin and sarcophagus lids.

Osiris: Ruler of the underworld and principal god of the dead, Osiris was also a god of agriculture and fertility. He is represented as a mummiform king, carrying the crook and flail. Because of his association with vegetation and the earth, his skin is often shown green in colour. Osiris was the son of Geb and Nut and brother of Seth, Nephthys and Isis, who was also his wife and mother of his son Horus. Just as the living king was identified with Horus, so the deceased king was regarded as Osiris, a status later accorded to all the righteous dead.

Ptah: The creator god of Memphis, and the patron of craftsmen, identified by the Greeks with Hephaistos. He is normally represented mummiform, wearing a close-fitting blue cap, and holding a distinctive sceptre comprising the symbols of life, stability and power.

Ra: The sun god of Heliopolis. During the Old Kingdom, his cult attained supremacy, and from the Fourth Dynasty onwards, all Egyptian kings bore the title 'Son of Ra'. As one of the principal state gods, Ra was often worshipped with other major deities in hybrid forms including Amun-Ra (*qv*) and Ra-Horakhty (*qv*). He is usually represented as a man with a falcon's head, or, in funerary contexts (*as illustrated on p. 31*), with a ram's head.

Ra-Horakhty: God embodying the attributes of both Ra (*qv*) and Horus (*qv*), represented as a falcon-headed man with a solar disc on his head.

Serapis: A composite deity combining aspects of the Egyptian god Osorapis with attributes of a number of Hellenistic gods including Zeus, Helios, Hades, Dionysus and Asclepius. Serapis was associated with fertility, healing and the funerary cult. Shown as a bearded man with a grain measure on his head, he was introduced during Ptolemaic times as a focus for national religious unity. Along with that of Isis, the cult of Serapis became popular throughout the Hellenistic world, and later the Roman empire. His cult centre was the Serapeum at Alexandria.

Seth: The brother and murderer of Osiris, Seth was the personification of chaos and disorder, the bringer of storms and war, and thus the counterbalance to Ma'at (*qv*). Many of these qualities were regarded as desirable in a ruler, and several kings of the late New Kingdom, such as Seti, incorporated his name into their own. He is usually represented by a canine creature with a long snout and erect tail.

Taweret: A female deity, the protector of women in childbirth. Represented with the head of a hippopotamus, the foreparts of a lion and the back and tail of a crocodile, her full belly and large breasts identify her as a fertility goddess. She often holds a *sa* (protection) symbol (*as shown on p. 33*).

Thoth: A lunar deity, the scribe of the gods, and a god of healing, later identified with Hermes and Asclepius. He is usually shown as an ibis-headed man with a moon disc and crescent on his head.

PRINCIPAL GODS & GODDESSES OF ANCIENT GREECE & ROME

GREEK NAME	ROLE	ROMAN NAME
Aphrodite	Goddess of love, beauty and sexuality. A protectress of sailors	Venus
Apollo	God of light and reason, son of Zeus and twin brother of Artemis	Apollo
Ares	God of war, son of Zeus, lover of Aphrodite	Mars
Artemis	Virgin goddess of woodlands and the hunt, twin sister of Apollo	Diana
Asclepius	God of healing and medicine, son of Apollo	Aesculapius
Athena	Goddess of wisdom and patron goddess of Athens	Minerva
Demeter	Goddess of the harvest, associated with renewal, rebirth and the afterlife	Ceres
Dionysus	God of wine and fertility, son of Zeus and half-brother of Apollo	Bacchus
Eros	God of physical love, offspring of Ares and Aphrodite	Cupid
Hades	God of the underworld, brother of Zeus	Pluto/Dis
Hephaistos	God of the forge, husband of Aphrodite	Vulcan
Hera	Queen of the gods, goddess of married women and childbirth	Juno
Hermes	Messenger of the gods, protector of wayfarers, guide of souls to the underworld	Mercury
Poseidon	God of the oceans, brother of Zeus	Neptune
Zeus	King of the gods, lord of the heavens and of thunder	Jupiter

EASTERN CULTS ADOPTED IN GREECE & ROME

Astarte Near Eastern goddess of nature, fertility, sexuality and conflict, integrated in some cities with Aphrodite/Venus

Atargatis Syrian goddess of the sea and fertility. She also shares some aspects of Aphrodite

Attis Phrygian god of nature, lover of Cybele

Cybele Phrygian goddess of the earth, similar to the Greek Gaia. She was worshipped by the Romans as the Magna Mater, 'Great Mother'

Isis Egyptian goddess associated with the afterlife (*see pp. 178 and 236*)

Mithras Persian sun god who must slay the primal bull to release its fertility and save the earth and mankind (*see p. 155*)

Serapis Hybrid Egyptian god of fertility (*see p. 237*)

GOVERNMENT OF ANCIENT ROME

- **Kingdom of Rome (753–509 BC)**

- **Roman Republic (509–27 BC)**

First Triumvirate (Julius Caesar, Crassus, Pompey)	60–53 BC	Second Triumvirate (Mark Antony, Lepidus, Octavian)	43–27 BC
Pompey (dictator)	52–47 BC		
Julius Caesar (dictator)	45–44 BC		

- **Roman Empire (27 BC–AD 395)**

Augustus (formerly Octavian) 27 BC–AD 14		Balbinus (co-emperor)	238
Tiberius	14–37	Gordian III	238–244
Caligula	37–41	Philip I	244–247
Claudius	41–54	Philip II	247–249
Nero	54–68	Decius	249–251
Galba	68–69	Gallus and Volusian	251–253
Otho	69	Aemilianus	253
Vitellius	69	Valerian	253–260
		Gallienus	260–268
Flavians		Claudius II	268–270
Vespasian	69–79	Quintillus	270
Titus	79–81	Aurelian	270–275
Domitian	81–96	Tacitus	275–276
Nerva	96–98	Florian	276
Trajan	98–117	Probus	276–282
		Carus	282–283
		Carinus	282–285
Antonines		Numerian (co-emperor)	283–284
Hadrian	117–138	Diocletian	285–305
Antoninus Pius	138–161	Maximian (co-emperor)	286–305
Marcus Aurelius	161–180	Constantius Chlorus	305–306
Lucius Verus		Galerius	305–310
(co-emperor)	161–169	Licinius	308–324
Commodus	180–192	Flavius Severus	306–307
Pertinax	193	Maxentius	306–312
Didius Julianus	193	Constantine the Great	306–337
		Constantine II	337–340
Severans		Constans (co-emperor)	337–350
Septimius Severus	193–211	Constantius II (co-emperor)	337–361
Caracalla	211–217	Magnentius (co-emperor)	350–353
Geta (co-emperor)	211–212	Julian the Apostate	361–363
Macrinus	217–218	Jovian	363–364
Elagabalus	218–222	Valentinian I (in West)	364–375
Alexander Severus	222–235	Valens (in East)	364–378
Maximinus Thrax	235–238	Gratian	367–383
Gordian I	238	Valentinian II (usurper)	375–392
Gordian II	238	Theodosius I	378–395
Pupienus	238		

- **Western Empire (395–476)**

- **Eastern (Byzantine) Empire (395–1453)**

Index

Entries rendered in bold upper case are to the 50 sites. Page numbers where more detailed or explanatory information can be found (where there are several references to choose from) are given in bold. Numbers in italics refer either to an illustration or to information found in caption text.

Picture Credits

The photographs used in this book have been drawn from a number of sources and are credited below. The greatest number from a single photographer, including the cover, come from Bill Hocker of Berkeley, California. Mr Hocker travelled as a Peace Corps volunteer in the 1970s, is a former architect, and as well as being a photographer is proprietor of Wm Hocker Toy Soldiers. More information on billhocker.com.

Every effort has been made to contact the copyright owners of material reproduced in this guide. We would be pleased to hear from any copyright owners we have been unable to reach.

Cover and title pages
Front cover: View of the temples at Paestum. Photo: Bill Hocker.
p. 1: View of the temples at Paestum. Photo: Bill Hocker.
p. 2: View of the ruins of Palmyra, Syria. Photo: Bill Hocker
p. 4: Interior of the inner coffin of Sutimes. The Art Archive/Musée du Louvre Paris / Gianni dagli Orti

Ancient Egypt section
p. 9: Head of Akhenaten, Luxor Museum, Egypt. Red Dot/ © Richard T. Nowitz/Corbis
p. 10: Red Dot/ © Tibor Bognar/Corbis
p. 12: Above: Statue of a scribe, Cairo museum, Egypt. Red Dot/ © Sandro Vannini/Corbis. Below: Coffin-shaped Canopic jar, Egyptian Museum, Cairo. Red Dot/ © 1996–98 AccuSoft Inc. All rights/Robert Harding World Imagery/Corbis
p. 13: Collar of Khnemet, a princess of the Middle Kingdom, Egyptian Museum, Cairo. Red Dot/ © Gianni dagli Orti/Corbis
p. 14: Watercolour of Hatshepsut by Howard Carter. Private Collection. © 2008. Photo Scala, Florence/HIP
p. 15: Detail from the temple reliefs at Deir el-Bahri, Egypt. Red Dot/ © Gianni dagli Orti/Corbis
p. 16: Left: Red Dot/ © Eddie Gerald/Alamy. Right: © javarman/www. stockexpert.com
p. 17: Photo by Bill Hocker
p. 18: Red Dot/ ©Kazuyoshi Nomachi/Corbis
p. 19: © Mahmoudmahdy/Dreamstime.com
p. 20: Detail of a statue of Khafra, Cairo Museum, Egypt. Red Dot/ © The Art Archive/Corbis
p. 21: Red Dot/ © Larry Lee Photography/Corbis
p. 22: Painting from the tomb of Nefertari, wife of Ramesses II, Western Thebes. The Bridgeman Art Library
p. 23: Top: Detail from a Book of the Dead from Thebes (c. 1275 BC), © The Trustees of the British Museum (London). All rights reserved. Bottom: Scarab pectoral from the tomb of Tutankhamun. The Art Archive/ Egyptian Museum Cairo/Alfredo dagli Orti
p. 24: Photo: Shutterstock
p. 25: Photo: Shutterstock
p. 26: Relief from the Festival Temple at Karnak. The Art Archive/Gianni dagli Orti
p. 27: Above: Procession of ram-headed sphinxes at Karnak. © iStockphoto.com/Richmatts. Below: Interior of the Hypostyle Hall at Karnak. Red Dot/ © Wolfgang Flamisch/Corbis
p. 29: Red Dot/ © Kelly-Mooney Photography/Corbis
p. 30: Belzoni's graffito signature in the Ramesseum at Thebes, west bank. Red Dot/ © Jean-Dominique Dallet/Alamy
p. 31: Above: One of the two Colossi of Memnon. Red Dot/ © Frank

Chmura/Alamy. Below: Funeral barque, detail from the tomb of Seti I. Giraudon/The Bridgeman Art Library
p. 32: Left: Contemporary photograph of the discovery of the tomb of Tutankhamun, Stapleton Collection, London. © 2008. Photo Scala, Florence/HIP. Centre: Canopic jar with gilt stopper. Red Dot/ © Sandro Vannini/Corbis. Right: Inner coffin of Sutimes. The Art Archive/Musée du Louvre Paris / Gianni dagli Orti
p. 33: Above: The ruins of Deir el-Medina. © Dreef/Dreamstime.com. Below: paints and pigments from a tomb at Deir el-Medina. Red Dot/ © Gianni dagli Orti/Corbis
p. 34: Limestone plaque, found at Amarna, now in the Egyptian Museum, Cairo. © 1997. Photo Scala, Florence
p. 35: Detail from a bust of Akhenaten. Egyptian National Museum, Cairo/ The Bridgeman Art Library
p. 36: Clockwise from the left: Head of Meritaten, Egyptian Museum, Cairo. Red Dot/ © The Art Archive/Corbis; Nefertiti, limestone bust in the Ägyptisches Museum, Berlin. The Bridgeman Art Library/ Alinari Archives, Florence; unfinished limestone statue of Akhenaten and one of his daughters, Egyptian Museum, Cairo. © Werner Forman/TopFoto/Alinari Archives, Florence; detail of a wooden bust of Tutankhamun, possibly a dummy on which to hang clothes and jewellery, found in his tomb. Egyptian Museum, Cairo. Red Dot/ © Robert Harding World Imagery/Corbis
p. 37: Above: The Art Archive/Gianni dagli Orti; Below: The Art Archive/ H.M. Herget/NGS Image Collection
p. 38: Photo: Wikimedia Commons
p. 39: Gold collar, Egyptian Museum, Cairo. © Werner Forman/TopFoto/ Alinari Archives, Florence
p. 40: Red Dot/ © Rolf Richardson/Alamy
p. 41: The Stapleton Collection/The Bridgeman Art Library
p. 42: Above: Red Dot/ © José Fuste Raga/Corbis. Below: Red Dot/ © Chris Salomon/Alamy
p. 43: © Jsanchez_bcn/Dreamstime.com
p. 44: Alinari Archives, Florence
p. 45: © 2005. Photo Spectrum/HIP/Scala, Florence
p. 46: Red Dot/ © Yann Arthus-Bertrand/Corbis
p. 47: Red Dot/ © Christine Osborne Pictures/Alamy
p. 48: Above: Photo, Shutterstock; Below: Dendera Zodiac © 2008 Photo Scala, Florence/HIP
p. 49: Above: Figurine of Harpocrates (3rd century BC), Pushkin Museum of Fine Arts, Moscow. RIA Novosti/TopFoto/Alinari Archives Florence; Below: The Stapleton Collection, © 2008. Photo Scala, Florence/HIP
p. 50: Photo: Bill Hocker
p. 51: © The Trustees of the British Museum. All rights reserved

Ancient Greece section
pp. 52–53: The Art Archive/National Archaeological Museum, Athens/ Gianni dagli Orti
p. 56: Blue Monkey, restored fresco at the palace of Knossos, photo by Gábor Bodó; detail of the Warrior Vase, found at Mycenae, watercolour by Edit Nagy
p. 57: Restored fragment of a processional frieze, Knossos. Photo: Gábor Bodó
p. 58: Young Spartans Exercising (c. 1860), Edgar Degas. The Art Archive/ National Gallery London/John Webb
p. 59: Statues, clockwise from top: Museo Nazionale Archeologico di Reggio Calabria; Alinari Archives, Florence, reproduced with the permission

of the Ministero per i Beni e le Attività Culturali; Acropolis Museum, Athens. Alinari Archives, Florence. Watercolours of pots by Edit Nagy

p. 60: View of the palace of Knossos. Red Dot/ © Roger Wood/Corbis; giant pithos at Knossos, photo by Annabel Barber; Kamares war jug, watercolour by Edit Nagy

p. 61: Ashmolean Museum, University of Oxford

p. 62: Photo: Phil Robinson

p. 63: Horns of consecration, from the palace of Knossos, photo: Annabel Barber; Theseus and the Minotaur from a Greek red-figure vessel, watercolour by Edit Nagy; restored bull-leaping fresco from the palace of Knossos, photo: Phil Robinson

p. 64: Giraudon/The Bridgeman Art Library

p. 65: Red Dot/ © Rolf Richardson/Alamy

p. 66: Gold 'Mask of Agamemnon', in the National Archaeological Museum of Athens. Photo: Wikimedia Commons; Mycenae Lion Gate, photo: Roger Barber

p. 67: DEA Picture Library/Getty Images

p. 68: bpk/Herbert Kraft

p. 69: Red Dot/ © Vanni Archive/Corbis

p. 70: Red Dot/ © IML Image Group Ltd/Alamy

p. 71: Left: Alinari/The Bridgeman Art Library; Right: Alinari Archives, Florence

p. 73: Engraving from *Entwurf einer historischen Architektur*, by J.B. Fischer von Erlach (1721), engraved by J.A. Delsenbach. Later colouration. The Stapleton Collection/Bridgeman Art Library

p. 74: Omphalos, Delphi Museum. Red Dot/ © Peter Horree/Alamy; View of Delphi: Red Dot/ © terry harris just greece photo library/Alamy

p. 75: Stadium: Red Dot/ © Bettmann/Corbis; Charioteer, Delphi Museum. Giuliano Valsecchi/Alinari Archives, Florence

pp. 76–77: Photos: Arion

p. 78: German engraving of the Delphic Oracle (19th century). The Granger Collection/TopFoto/Alinari Archives

p. 79: Dodona theatre. Photo: Roger Barber; Temple of Zeus. Red Dot/ © Wolfgang Kaehler/Corbis

p. 80: The Art Archive/Gianni dagli Orti

p. 81: Bronze statue of Asclepius, Capitoline Museums, Rome. Red Dot/ © Araldo de Luca/Corbis

p. 83: © 2008 DeAgostini Picture Library/Scala, Florence

p. 84: SXC

p. 85: Red Dot/ © Yann Arthus-Bertrand/Corbis

p. 86: © The Trustees of the British Museum. All rights reserved

p. 87: The Art Archive/Acropolis Museum Athens/Gianni dagli Orti

p. 89: Top: Photo by Arion. Bottom: Red Dot/ © Petr Svarc/Alamy

p. 91: Alinari Archives, Florence. Reproduced with the permission of the Ministero per i Beni e le Attività Culturali

p. 92: Red Dot/ © Gianni dagli Orti/Corbis

p. 93: © 2008 Photo Scala, Florence

p. 94: Above: Photo: Shutterstock. Below: The Bridgeman Art Library

p. 95: Red Dot/ © Roger Wood/Corbis

p. 96: The Art Archive/National Archaeological Museum, Athens/Gianni dagli Orti

pp. 96–97: Watercolours by Edit Nagy

p. 98: Photo: Bill Hocker

p. 99: Red Dot/ © Roger Wood/Corbis

p. 100: Photo: Bill Hocker

p. 101: Above: Photo by Giacomo Mazza. Below: The Art Archive/Jean Vinchon Numismatist, Paris/Gianni dagli Orti

p. 102: Above: Photo by Bill Hocker. Below: Red Dot/ © Mimmo Jodice/Corbis

p. 103: Photo: Bill Hocker

p. 104: © 2007. DeAgostini Picture Library/Scala, Florence

p. 105: Red Dot/ © Vanni Archive/Corbis

Hellenistic section

p. 107: The Art Archive/Archaeological Museum, Venice/Gianni dagli Orti

p. 109: Red Dot/ © David Lees/Corbis

p. 110: bpk/Red Dot/ © Adam Eastland/Alamy

p. 112: Red Dot/ © Images&Stories/Alamy

p. 113: Above: Copy of a famous Hellenistic mosaic, Vatican Museums, Rome. © 1990. Photo Scala, Florence. Below: *Dying Gaul*, statue in the Capitoline Museums, Rome. Alinari Archives, Florence

p. 114: Top: Early 19th-century illustration of the Altar of Zeus. Red Dot/ © Bettmann/Corbis. Centre: © 2003. Photo Scala, Florence/Fotografica Foglia. Courtesy of the Ministero per i Beni e Attività Culturali. Bottom: Photo by Róbert Szabó Benke

p. 115: Red Dot/ © Yann Arthus-Bertrand/Corbis

p. 116: Photo by Michal Manas

p. 117: Both images TopFoto/Alinari Archives, Florence

p. 119: Photo: Shutterstock. Inset: The Bridgeman Art Library

p. 120: Top: © The Trustees of the British Museum. All rights reserved. Bottom: dasar/www.stockexpert.com

p. 121: Red Dot/ © Hanan Isachar/Corbis

p. 123: Joanna McCarthy/Riser/Getty Images

p. 124: Above: Roman version of the Artemis of Ephesus, Vatican Museums, Rome. Alinari Archives, Florence. Below: Red Dot/ © The Art Archive/Corbis

p. 125: SXC

Ancient Rome section

p. 127: Photo: Bill Hocker

p. 131: Clockwise from the left: Watercolour by Edit Nagy; The Art Archive/Museo di Villa Giulia, Rome/Alfredo dagli Orti; The Art Archive/Gianni dagli Orti

p. 132: Top: The Art Archive/Musei Capitolini, Rome/Gianni dagli Orti; Bottom left: The Art Archive/Musei Capitolini, Rome/Gianni dagli Orti; Bottom right: The Art Archive/Museo della Civiltà Romana, Rome/ Gianni dagli Orti

p. 133: Busts of emperors: Alinari Archives, Florence. Bottom photo by Annabel Barber

p. 134: The Art Archive/Museo Nazionale Romano (Palazzo Massimo alle Terme), Rome/ Gianni dagli Orti

p. 135: Alinari Archives, Florence. Reproduced with the permission of the Ministero per i Beni e le Attività Culturali

p. 136: Above: The Art Archive/Musei Capitolini, Rome/Gianni dagli Orti; Below: Photo by Annabel Barber

p. 137: Alinari Archives, Florence

p. 138: Red Dot/ © Stapleton Collection/Corbis

p. 140: Above: Watercolour by Edit Nagy. Below: The Art Archive/National Museum, Bucharest/Gianni dagli Orti

p. 141: Base of the lost Column of Antoninus Pius, Vatican Museums, Rome. © 1990 Photo Scala, Florence

p. 142: Above: Photo by Thomas Howells; Below: Photo by Annabel Barber

p. 143: Photo: Thomas Howells

p. 144: The Granger Collection/TopFoto/Alinari Archives

p. 145: Top: Mosaic in the Museo e Galleria Borghese, Rome. Alinari Archives, Florence. Reproduced with the permission of the Ministero per i Beni e le Attività Culturali; Bottom left: Photo by Giacomo Mazza; Bottom right: Red Dot/ © Roger Wood/Corbis

p. 146: Photo: Thomas Howells

p. 147: Photo: Annabel Barber

p. 148: Sir Lawrence Alma-Tadema: *The Baths of Caracalla* (1899), detail. The Art Archive/Private Collection/Eileen Tweedy

p. 149: Photo: Bill Hocker

p. 151: Red Dot/ © Mimmo Jodice/Corbis

p. 152: Red Dot/ © Araldo de Luca/Corbis

p. 153: Photo: Thomas Howells

p. 154: All photos by Thomas Howells and Annabel Barber, except the elephant mosaic, Alinari Archives, Florence. Reproduced with the permission of the Ministero per i Beni e le Attività Culturali

p. 155: Top: Roman fresco, 2nd century AD. The Granger Collection/ TopFoto/Alinari Archives; Centre and bottom: photos by Annabel Barber

p. 157: Red Dot/ © Art Kowalsky/Alamy

p. 158: Above: Red Dot/ © Kalpana Kartik/Alamy; Below: Photo: Shutterstock

p. 159: Photo: Shutterstock

p. 160: Reinbaw/www.stockexpert.com

p. 162: Photo: Bill Hocker

p. 164: Photo: Gábor Bodó

p. 165: Above: Red Dot/ © Annie Griffiths Belt/Corbis; Below: Photo: Bill Hocker

p. 166: Red Dot/ © Sergio Pitamitz/Corbis

p. 167: Above: Photo by Bill Hocker; Below: Photo by Gábor Bodó

p. 168: Red Dot/ © Jonathan Blair/Corbis

p. 169: Above: © iStockphoto.com/earleliason; Below: The Art Archive/ Aphrodisias Museum/Gianni dagli Orti

p. 170: Red Dot/ © Jonathan Blair/Corbis

p. 171: Above: Red Dot/ © José Fuste Raga/Corbis; Below: Red Dot/ © Jonathan Blair/Corbis

p. 172: © iStockphoto.com/Dhuss

p. 173: Above: © iStockphoto.com/Annette05; Below: © iStockphoto.com/ Dhuss

p. 174: Red Dot/ © Roger Ressmeyer/Corbis

p. 175: © iStockphoto.com/risamay

p. 176: Red Dot/ © Mimmo Jodice/Corbis

p. 177: Above left and bottom: Red Dot/ © Mimmo Jodice/Corbis; Above right: Red Dot/ © Richard T. Nowitz/Corbis

pp. 178–79: Alinari Archives, Florence. Reproduced with the permission of the Ministero per i Beni e le Attività Culturali

p. 180: Valeria 73/www.stockexpert.com

p. 181: Watercolour by Imre Bába

p. 182: Clockwise from left: Antinous as Osiris, Vatican Museums, Rome. Alinari Archives, Florence; Wikimedia Commons; © iStockphoto.com/ ROMAOSLO

p. 183: Above: Wikimedia Commons. Below: Alinari Archives, Florence. Reproduced with the permission of the Ministero per i Beni e Attività Culturali

p. 185: Above: photo by Annabel Barber. Below: Red Dot/ © Adam Woolfitt/Corbis

p. 186: Red Dot/ © Skyscan/Corbis

p. 187: Courtesy of the Centre for the Study of Ancient Documents and the Trustees of the British Museum

p. 188: Red Dot/ © Robert Preston/Alamy

p. 190: Clockwise from the top: Shutterstock; The Granger Collection/ TopFoto/Alinari Archives; Photo by Thomas Howells

p. 191: Above: Red Dot/ © Roger Wood/Corbis; Below: © Witr/ Dreamstime.com

p. 192: Photo: Bill Hocker

p. 193: Above: Photo by Gábor Bodó; Below: Relief of Palmyrene gods, 2nd–1st centuries BC, Musée du Louvre, Paris. CM Dixon/HIP/ TopFoto/Alinari Archives, Florence

p. 194: Above: Red Dot/ © Araldo de Luca/Corbis; Below: Photo by Bill Hocker

p. 195: Photo: Bill Hocker

p. 196: © 2008. DeAgostini Picture Library/Scala, Florence

p. 197: © Plotnikov/Dreamstime.com

pp. 198 and 199 bottom: © 1990. Photo Scala, Florence. Courtesy of the Ministero per i Beni e le Attività Culturali

p. 199: Above: Shutterstock

p. 201: Photo: Phil Robinson

p. 202: Above: The Missorium of Theodosius, silver, 4th century. Real Academia de Bellas Artes de San Fernando, Madrid. The Bridgeman Art Library/Alinari Archives, Florence; Below: Shutterstock

p. 203: © iStockphoto.com/ToGo

Early Christianity section

pp. 204: The Bridgeman Art Library/Alinari Archives, Florence

p. 207: Top: Alinari Archives, Florence; Bottom left: Drawing by Edit Nagy; Bottom right: © 1990. Photo Scala, Florence

p. 208: Top: Photo by Thomas Howells; Bottom: DEA Picture Library, licensed by Alinari

p. 211: © iStockphoto.com/Richmatts

p. 212: Photo: Thomas Howells

p. 213: Red Dot/ © PhotoStock-Israel/Alamy

p. 214: Left: Eugène-Alexis Girardet, *The Sacred Fire of Jerusalem* (c. 1898). Red Dot/ © Christie's Images/Corbis; Right: The Art Archive/Gianni dagli Orti

p. 215: Left: © 1990. Photo Scala, Florence; Right: Photo by Thomas Howells

p. 216: Top: Alinari Archives, Florence; Bottom: Alinari Archives, Florence. Reproduced with the permission of the Ministero per i Beni e le Attività Culturali

p. 218: Courtesy of the Gill/Gillerman slide collection, Yale University

p. 219: Top: The Art Archive/ Alfredo dagli Orti; Bottom: The Art Archive/ Baptistery of Orthodox Ravenna/Alfredo dagli Orti

p. 220: © 1990 Photo Scala, Florence. Courtesy of the Ministero per i Beni e Attività Culturali

p. 221: The Art Archive/Alfredo dagli Orti

p. 223: Red Dot/ © Adam Woolfitt/Corbis

p. 224: Clockwise from top left: Photo by Roger Barber; photo by Hadley Kincade; Red Dot/ © Goodlook Pictures/Corbis

p. 225: Red Dot/ © Bildarchiv Monheim GmbH/Alamy

p. 226: Both photos Scala, Florence. Above: © 1990; Centre: © 2008

p. 227: Herri met de Bles, The Temptation of St Anthony (16th century), Museo Correr, Venice. Alinari Archives Florence

p. 228: Red Dot/ © Edward North/Alamy

p. 229: TopFoto/Alinari Archives, Florence

p. 230: Above: TopFoto/Alinari Archives, Florence; Below: Wikimedia Commons